A Student's Guide to AS Music

for the **Edexcel** Specification
2001–2004

by

Paul Terry and David Bowman

Edited by
Lucien Jenkins and Monica Leiher

R·

Rhinegold Publishing Ltd
241 Shaftesbury Avenue
London WC2H 8TF
Telephone: 020 7333 1721
www.rhinegold.co.uk

Rhinegold Study Guides
(series editor: Paul Terry)

A Student's Guide to AS Music for the AQA Specification
A Student's Guide to AS Music for the Edexcel Specification
A Student's Guide to AS Music for the OCR Specification

A Student's Guide to A2 Music for the AQA Specification *
A Student's Guide to A2 Music for the Edexcel Specification *
A Student's Guide to A2 Music for the OCR Specification *

* To be published summer 2001

Rhinegold Publishing also publishes Music Teacher, Classical Music, Opera Now, Piano,
Early Music Today, The Singer, British and International Music Yearbook, Music Education Yearbook,
British Performing Arts Yearbook, Rhinegold Dictionary of Music in Sound.

First published 2001 in Great Britain by
Rhinegold Publishing Limited
241 Shaftesbury Avenue
London WC2H 8TF
Tel: 020 7333 1721

You should always check the current requirements of the examination, since these may change.
Copies of the Edexcel Specification may be obtained from Edexcel Examinations at
Edexcel Publications, Adamsway, Mansfield, Notts. NG18 4FN
Telephone 01623 467467, Facsimile 01623 450481, Email publications@linneydirect.com
See also the Edexcel website at http://www.edexcel.org.uk/

A Student's Guide to AS Music for the Edexcel Specification (2001–2004)
British Library Cataloguing in Publication Data.
A catalogue record for this book is available from the British Library.

ISBN 0-946890-90-0

Printed in Great Britain by Perfectaprint (UK) Ltd

No composer believes that there are any short cuts to the better appreciation of music. The only thing that one can do for the listener is to point out what actually exists in the music itself and reasonably to explain the wherefore and the why of the matter. The listener must do the rest.

Aaron Copland

Contents

The authors

Paul Terry was director of music at the City of London Freemen's School for 15 years and subsequently taught music technology at Kingston Polytechnic (now Kingston University). He currently works as a music editor, engraver and publisher. He has been a music examiner for more than 20 years and has worked as a consultant to various examination boards. Paul has served as a member of the Secondary Examinations Council and its successor the Schools Examinations and Assessment Council. He was chief examiner for the Oxford and Cambridge Schools Examinations Board (now part of OCR) and he was a chief examiner for London Examinations (now part of Edexcel).

Paul Terry's publications include two books on aural for A-level music, written in collaboration with David Bowman (see below). He is also co-author with William Lloyd of *Music in Sequence, a complete guide to MIDI sequencing* (1991), and its companion volumes *Classics in Sequence* (1992) and *Rock in Sequence* (1996), and also *Rehearse, Direct and Play: A Student's Guide to Group Music-Making* (1993), all published by Musonix/Music Sales.

David Bowman was for 20 years director of music at Ampleforth College where he still teaches. He was a chief examiner for the University of London Schools Examination Board (now Edexcel) from 1982 to 1998. He now spends more time with his family, horses and dogs.

David Bowman's publications include the *London Anthology of Music* (University of London Schools Examinations Board, 1986), *Sound Matters* (co-authored with Bruce Cole, Schott, 1989), *Aural Matters* (co-authored with Paul Terry, Schott, 1993), *Aural Matters in Practice* (co-authored with Paul Terry, Schott, 1994), *Analysis Matters* (Rhinegold, Volume 1 1997, Volume 2 1998) and numerous analytical articles for *Music Teacher*. He is a contributor to the *Collins Classical Music Encyclopedia* (2000) edited by Stanley Sadie and author of the *Rhinegold Dictionary of Music in Sound*.

The editors

Lucien Jenkins is editor of the *Music Teacher* magazine. He was a contributor to and consultant for the *Collins Classical Music Encyclopedia*, and is the editor of the *Rhinegold Dictionary of Music in Sound*.

Monica Leiher is head of woodwind at Christ's Hospital School in Horsham, West Sussex.

Acknowledgements

The authors would like to thank Dr Hugh Benham, chief examiner in music to Edexcel, for his expert advice so freely offered throughout the preparation of this book, and Dr Julia Winterson of Edexcel for her suggestions and corrections to the text. Nevertheless if any errors have been made it is only right to state that these are the responsibility of the authors.

Introduction

This book is intended to assist students preparing for the Edexcel examination in AS Music. Like other *Rhinegold Study Guides* it is intended to supplement, but not supplant, the work of teachers.

We have included many suggestions and tips which we hope will help you do well in performing and composing, but the main emphasis is on preparation for the *Listening and Understanding* unit. This is because it is our experience that even candidates who are talented performers and imaginative composers can be very unsure of the responses that are required in written work. It is therefore our aim to help you focus on what is important in this part of the exam, and to help you relate your work in listening and understanding to the music that you perform and compose.

In the chapters dealing with the areas of study we have outlined essential information for each piece. The questions during the course of these chapters will help you check your understanding of the context, style and technical features of the music – they are not intended to be representative of actual exam questions. If you have difficulty with these, you will generally find the right answers by rereading the preceding pages. The sample questions at the ends of these chapters are more demanding and should be worked under exam conditions. For examples of the questions that are likely to be encountered in the exam, you should be guided by the specimen papers and (when available) past papers produced by Edexcel.

We have included a glossary of the main technical terms you are likely to encounter in the set works. If you need further help with these, or with other terminology you encounter during the course, we recommend you consult the *Rhinegold Dictionary of Music in Sound* by David Bowman. This comprehensive resource not only gives detailed explanations of a wide range of musical concepts, but it also illustrates them using a large number of specially recorded examples on a set of accompanying compact discs, thus enabling you to hear directly how theoretical concepts are realised in the actual sounds of music.

The *Rhinegold Dictionary of Music in Sound* is published by Rhinegold Publishing Ltd, ISBN: 0-946890-87-0.

Planning is the secret of success especially if, as is common, you are taking AS as a one-year course. Initial ideas for composing are best formulated during the early weeks of the first term, and plans and practice for performing need to get under way as soon as possible. Preparation for the *Listening and Understanding* unit needs to be completed in time to allow for revision and the working of mock exams in the weeks before the actual examination.

For success in work at this level, it will help enormously if you can perceive the many varied connections between the music you hear, the music you play and the music you compose. Understanding the context and structure of music will not only enhance your enjoyment when listening, but will also inform your performing and illuminate your composing. Composing, performing, listening and understanding are all related aspects of the study of music, and this integration of activities is fundamental to the course on which you are embarking.

AS Music

You will be studying three units: *Performing*, *Developing Musical Ideas* and *Listening and Understanding*. The first two of these each account for 30% of the total AS mark, while the third is weighted at 40%.

Performing

There are two parts to the *Performing* unit:

- ✦ you will have to give a five- to six-minute solo performance
- ✦ you will also be assessed on your performing during the course; for this you will need to keep a log of the pieces you have performed and then choose the best four for assessment (one of which must be of one of your own compositions).

Your solo performance will be recorded and marked by an Edexcel examiner. Performing during the course will be assessed by your teacher and the mark moderated by Edexcel (for moderation purposes a recording of one solo piece from the log is required).

Developing Musical Ideas

There are two coursework tasks in this unit, both assessed by an Edexcel examiner:

- ✦ you will have to write one composition lasting at least three minutes, based on a given choice of topics
- ✦ you will also be assessed on two exercises in compositional techniques chosen from set tasks provided by Edexcel.

Listening and Understanding

For the *Listening and Understanding* unit there are two separate assessments, both marked by an Edexcel examiner:

- ✦ a 45-minute listening test consisting of four questions on music that will be played to you on CD; you will be required to identify various aspects of the music, including a comparison of two performances of the same piece
- ✦ a 1½-hour written paper based on questions about two areas of study you have prepared from the *New Anthology of Music*, an unmarked copy of which you must use for reference in the exam.

The details of the specification are correct at the time of going to press, but you and your teachers should always check current requirements for the examination with Edexcel as these may change.

Key Skills

Key Skills are becoming increasingly important for success at work, entry into higher education and for making the most of everyday life. AS Music offers a number of opportunities for you to develop your knowledge and understanding in five of the six Key Skills: Communication, Information Technology, Working with Others, Improving own Learning and Performance, and Problem Solving. You are therefore recommended to discuss with your teachers the ways in which the work you undertake for AS Music might also be used as evidence for your acquisition and development of skills for these Key Skills units at Level 3.

Performing

1. Performing during the course

This section accounts for 50% of the marks for performing. It provides an excellent opportunity for you to receive credit for the performing you do during the course, but it needs careful planning and log-keeping.

In particular you need to plan for the following requirements:

- ✦ you must submit four *different* pieces for assessment; these must not include any items that you are offering in the solo performing sections of this unit or, if you are taking A2, in Units 4 or 5
- ✦ at least one of the four pieces must be a solo
- ✦ at least one of the four pieces must be an ensemble item
- ✦ one of the four must be a piece you have composed
- ✦ the last date for performances is 14th May in the exam year
- ✦ one solo item must be recorded for moderation purposes
- ✦ your teacher must have been present for at least three of the four performances.

To be sure of meeting all these requirements it is going to be essential to make your plans at the start of the course and to discuss with your teacher the practicalities of the last two points above. Remember that there may be little time to arrange performances at the start of the summer term in the exam year.

You can include a performance in which you were the director or conductor of an ensemble, but you may submit only one such piece. The composition you perform can be the one you submit for Unit 2 or it can be any other composition you have written. You can perform it as a soloist, or as a member of an ensemble, or as a director of an ensemble. The quality of the composition is not assessed in this unit, but the piece needs to be one in which you can demonstrate technical and expressive skills of interpretation.

The combined length of the four pieces you submit must be at least 5–6 minutes, but there is no maximum time limit. The difficulty of the music is taken into account in assessment and is expected to equate with grade 5 standard (your teacher will help explain what this means if you do not take graded exams). The mark scheme allows credit if the music is of a higher standard. Although the highest marks are not available if the pieces are below grade 5 in level of difficulty, you will probably get a much better mark if you choose music that is well within your capabilities rather than pieces that are so hard that they will cause you to struggle and perhaps even break down in performance.

The performances can be given in class to your fellow students, or they may include events such as lunchtime concerts, rock gigs, music festivals or concert tours – but remember that your teacher must be present for at least three of the performances you submit. You may include playing on any instrument or singing, but marks are awarded for quality and not variety, so there is no advantage in including music on instruments that you don't play well.

There must be an audience at the performances, even if it is only a couple of people, and for that reason you are not allowed to include performances given at music exams or auditions in which there is no audience in the normal sense of the word. However you can include exam and audition pieces if you perform them on some more public occasion.

Ensemble performances can be of many different kinds – piano duets, wind trios, string quartets, jazz bands, rock groups, choirs or orchestras. However a piece in which you are the one dominant performer throughout does not count as an ensemble. Thus in a piece for flute with piano accompaniment the flautist cannot submit the work as an ensemble item, although the accompanying pianist can. When choosing ensemble performances to include on your list, remember that the work will need to be assessed – this may be difficult if it is a piece in which you have played a very minor role in a large ensemble.

Some advice on solo performing is given in the next section of this guide. A useful handbook which will give you many ideas for getting the best out of ensemble performing of all kinds is:

Rehearse, Direct and Play by William Lloyd and Paul Terry.
Musonix Publishing, 1993. ISBN: 0-9517214-3-7.
Available from Music Sales Ltd. (Order No. MX 30053, £4.95)

Music Sales Ltd, Newmarket Road,
Bury St Edmunds, Suffolk IP33 3YB.
Telephone: 01284 702600;
fax: 01284 768301
http://www.musicroom.com/

Keeping a performance diary

You will need to keep your own diary of performances, which should include the following information:

- the precise title of the work you performed and the movement(s) performed if it was not complete
- the name of its composer
- a note of whether it was a solo or ensemble item
- the nature of the occasion (such as lunchtime recital, rock concert, arts festival, etc)
- the role in which you participated (such as flute in wind trio, second trumpet in county youth orchestra of 80 players, bass guitar in rock group, one of 12 altos in choir of 60, etc)
- the date and whether it was an internal event at your centre or an external event that occurred elsewhere.

Remember that you will need a recording of one of the solo items which you submit.

By early May in your exam year you will have to select the four best pieces from your diary, in accordance with the requirements listed on the previous page, and transfer the details to a log form provided by Edexcel. When you do this be careful not to include the same piece more than once, and do not include any pieces that you intend to offer in the solo performing section of this unit or, if you are also taking A2 music, Units 4 or 5.

2. Solo performing

Solo performing accounts for 50% of the marks for Unit 1. You are required to perform one or more solo pieces, lasting between five and six minutes in total. There must be an audience of at least two people (your teacher and one other person) but you can have more present if you wish, such as a group of friends and fellow students. The performance could even be part of a large-scale public concert.

Choice of music

Choosing the right music is of paramount importance. The piece(s) should allow you to show technical and expressive control as a performer as well as an understanding of the music you present. Remember that some types of music, such as technical studies, easy arrangements and some styles of pop music, may focus on only a limited range of techniques and not give you much of a chance to show what you can do as a performer. Music that offers some contrasts in mood and the opportunity to show different types of technical skill is likely to serve you best. Remember that the music you choose must not be the same as any of the pieces you are offering for *Performing* during the course.

The technical difficulty of the music you choose also needs careful consideration. Easy pieces played musically are much more likely to be successful than difficult pieces marred by hesitations and breakdowns. In order to be able to achieve the highest marks the pieces need to be of grade 5 standard or higher. However there is no need to struggle to reach this standard (and risk a potential disaster if it proves too difficult) since you will be given credit for what you can do with the music you offer.

Whatever your technical standard it is better to choose music that you can perform with confidence than to attempt a difficult work which stretches your technique to its limit. A work that is too demanding will leave no leeway for the inevitable nervousness that *will* arise under the conditions of a live assessment. The anxiety and tension it generates will be communicated to the listener, and will inevitably impede your musical interpretation.

Choose music that you enjoy playing, but just be a little careful about well-worn 'party pieces' which have proved successful over the years. Most examiners have heard performances of such works trotted out with considerable dexterity but sometimes with little thought or feeling or even musicality. A *little* adrenalin arising from a work which is a challenge, but not an insuperable obstacle, usually enhances the work of even the greatest performers.

Accompaniment

If the music is intended to have an accompaniment (as will be the case in most music apart from that for piano and other chordal instruments) then it is important that it should be played with the accompaniment otherwise it will sound very incomplete.

Try to work with an accompanist who can rehearse with you regularly, or at least on several occasions before the day. Even the most accomplished accompanist will not be able to let you sound your best if the first time you perform together is at the performance.

You are allowed to use other types of accompaniment, such as a small group of performers or a backing tape, providing your own part can be clearly distinguished.

You can observe standard performing conventions by omitting repeats or curtailing long sections of accompaniment, but it is not really acceptable to cut passages because they happen to be too difficult or to stop a piece in the middle because it is too long. If such possibilities arise it is better to choose a different work.

Preparation

Having chosen and studied the programme with your teacher, and practised the pieces to a standard that you feel is acceptable, it is essential that you try out the music under performance conditions – not to your instrumental teacher, parents or anyone else who has heard you working on the music week by week, but to someone who is able to hear the performance fresh. This could be a visiting relative, your fellow students, or another teacher at your school or college.

A small slip or two in this trial performance should not concern you greatly, but if you find you are often hesitating in difficult passages or that the piece completely if unexpectedly breaks down then it is a sign that you may have chosen something which is too difficult. This means that you will need to decide if the work is viable or whether it would be better to make a more realistic choice.

In planning this run-up to the performance allow much more time than you think you need. Illness may curtail practice time and other commitments may prevent adequate rehearsal with accompanists.

Try to have a run-through of the music in the venue in which you will be performing. If it is a large hall you will probably find that you need to project the sound and exaggerate the contrasts much more than when practising at home. Conversely if you are playing a loud instrument (brass or electric guitar, for example) in a small room, you will almost certainly need to limit louder dynamics.

Decide where you are going to sit or stand and check that the lighting is adequate but not dazzling. If you have an accompanist make sure that you have good eye contact without having to turn away from your listeners. If the piano is an upright one it may take some experimentation to find the best position. If you play an instrument that needs tuning before you start, plan how you are going to do this and remember that tuning is not necessarily something that all accompanists are able to help with.

Whether the piece is accompanied or not, spend some time trying out the opening in various ways. For pieces with a tricky start it can be easier to set the right speed by thinking of a more straightforward phrase from later in the piece and establishing a mental image of the right tempo from that.

If the performance is to be given to an audience of any size you should also spend a few minutes practising walking on and off stage, and deciding how you will react to applause. The audience will be disappointed if you shamble on at the start and rush off at the end. Audiences need plenty of time to show their appreciation:

a hurried nod in their direction as you exit will appear clumsy, if not downright rude. If there is no printed programme, it makes a friendly start if you announce the piece(s) you are going to perform.

The performance

On the day make sure you leave time for a warm-up. Check that you have to hand any extra equipment you might need (mutes, guitar foot-stools, spare strings and so on). If you require a music stand, check that you know how it is adjusted and secured – collapsing music stands are good for comedy acts but they can seriously undermine your nerve in a performance.

You will also need a photocopy of your music (just your own part) for your teacher, who is required to send it to the moderator with the tape recording of the performance. In the case of jazz, rock and popular music any suitable notation, such as a chord chart and a detailed description of what is being attempted in improvised passages, is acceptable in place of a fully notated score.

Expect to be a little nervous but remember that the more experience you can get of performing to others during the course, the more natural and enjoyable it will become. Blind panic will only normally set in if the music is under-rehearsed or too difficult and this, as we have explained, can be avoided by selection of the most suitable music for your needs and a sensible period of careful preparation.

What is assessed?

Out of a total of 25 marks for solo performance, 15 are allocated for *accuracy* and 10 for *interpretation*. A small number of marks are added if the difficulty level of the music is greater than grade 5 standard, or deducted if the music is below this standard but, as mentioned earlier, the final mark is always likely to be better for a fluent performance of an easier work than a faltering struggle through a work that is too difficult.

A good mark for *accuracy* requires technically secure performing, although the occasional well-covered slip that can happen in even the best-regulated performances should not be a matter of great concern. If the performing lacks fluency and coordination, perhaps being marred by stumbles, poor intonation or inability to maintain the correct speed, it is unlikely to reach a satisfactory mark in this category.

A high mark for *interpretation* requires good tone, effective and appropriate contrasts, and a sense of the style of the music. It will help if you have a clear image of what you are trying to convey in the performance, such as rhythmic energy, a dreamy atmosphere, elegant phrasing, dramatic contrasts or subtle blends.

Focus on the detail throughout the music. Rather than thinking of a passage as merely 'happy' try to decide if you mean boisterous, contented, frivolous, celebratory, cheeky or just cheerful. If it is 'sad', do you mean tragic, doom-laden, nostalgic, angry or solemn? Then try to convey the moods you intend in your interpretation of the piece, whether it be it the glittering ballroom of a minuet, the moonlit night of a nocturne or the smoky languor of a blues club. Never be content with merely 'getting the notes right'.

Developing musical ideas

There are two parts to this unit: (i) composition, which accounts for 50% of the available marks for the unit, and (ii) two exercises in compositional techniques, which account for the other 50%.

1. Composition topics

You have to write one composition lasting not more than three minutes, chosen from the following topics:

- Variations
- Romantic miniatures
- Neo-classicism
- Post-modernism
- The popular song
- Club dance and hip hop
- Fusions
- Film and television
- Music theatre

Examples of a number of these types of music can be found in the *New Anthology of Music*, used in Unit 3. In addition, the Edexcel specification makes many suggestions for other types of music and composers that can be studied as models. For instance variations by Mozart, romantic miniatures by Mendelssohn, 32-bar popular songs by Gershwin, and so on.

It is important to study as many models as you can for the topic you choose, as this will provide you with a variety of ideas on how to go about structuring and developing your own piece. However it is important to realise that you are **not** expected to write in the style of any specific composers. In fact attempting to do so is likely to make the job much more difficult since it would require a very thorough understanding of the style to sound convincing. Just seizing on a couple of superficial features, such as a tune in constant four-bar phrases accompanied by broken chords, is not going to produce an imaginative re-creation of a set of classical piano variations. It might be useful to consider how easy you would find writing a short story in the style of Charles Dickens, or producing a painting in the style of Monet. Your conclusion might very well be that working in your own style is likely to be more productive and will give you greater scope to develop your own creative ideas within the topic you choose.

Remember that you are required to perform one of your compositions as part of *Performing during the course* for Unit 1. This does not have to be the piece you write for Unit 2, but there are opportunities to integrate the work for both units if you wish. For instance you could write an impressive set of variations to show off your technique as a performer, or you might write a pop song, a piece of dance music or a song for a musical that would fit well with the other types of music you offer for coursework performing.

The score of your composition will need to be completed, and the piece recorded, in time to reach the examiner by 15th May in the examination year.

Planning the work

You will first need to decide on the resources you are going to use. If other performers are to be involved it can often be best to write for people who will be available to work with you during the whole composing process, so other students in your group or with whom you regularly rehearse and perform would be a good choice. Start by discussing the instruments and/or voices concerned, and how their characteristics may best be exploited. Try to identify the skills (and weaknesses) of each performer so that you can use their individual strengths in your composing. Discuss what sorts of things are easy and what are difficult for each instrument or voice and try some improvising both separately and together.

Compositions may be in any style you wish, providing it is appropriate to the topic you choose, but you will want to show the best you can do, so it is probably best to choose a format that will allow you to use a variety of textures and techniques. If you adopt a style that is exceptionally repetitive or very slow-moving you may well have to write a piece rather longer than the three-minute minimum in order to show that you can achieve some variety and a sense of development in your composing.

Composing takes time and most people find that initial ideas have to be worked over repeatedly before a satisfactory shape starts to emerge. Considerable rewriting – perhaps even starting again – should be expected as ideas are tried out in performance. It is therefore advisable to start your compositions as early in the course as possible, so that you have time both to reject the ideas that don't work and to refine the ideas that do.

Some people find that developing compositions at a MIDI workstation can be a good way of working, even if the piece is destined for eventual performance by live musicians. Sequencer systems can also be useful to produce an approximation of a performance for recording purposes if live instrumentalists are unavailable.

This method needs a few words of caution, though. Firstly, MIDI software is not very good at warning you that what you write may be unplayable by live musicians – you can easily find that the string chords which sound so good on a synthesizer are simply impossible on a violin, or that your 80 bars of flute music without a breathing point will cause your flautists to faint, or that your untransposed trumpet part descending into the depths of the bass clef leaves your trumpeter totally bewildered. If you are using a sequencer to develop a piece for live players it will therefore be wise to try out ideas with the performers at every opportunity.

Secondly, you will need to clarify whether your work is conceived as an electronic studio piece or as a composition for live musicians. There is a great deal of difference between the two, and your intentions will seem confused if you submit a score and recording that seem to fit neither type of resource very effectively.

Your score may be fully notated, or it may be a lead-sheet, chord chart, track diagram, or in graphic form. Whatever format is chosen it must be sufficiently clear and unambiguous for the examiner to make an assessment of the piece.

A well-chosen title can help to make your intentions clear but features such as computer-typeset title pages, colourful artwork and elaborate bindings will gain you no extra marks. Aim for a clear, simple layout with numbered pages clipped together in the right order. Bar numbers, either at the start of each system or every ten bars, are a helpful addition to any score.

If you use a fully notated score and the piece includes a number of different instruments, make sure the staves are labelled with an instrument or voice name at the start of every system, although abbreviations can be used for this after the start of the piece. When writing more than one system on a page it will help the layout if you leave a blank stave or two between systems. Remember that you can use conventional repeat signs in the score to avoid copying out identical sections of music.

Computer-generated scores

Computer-generated notation is allowed and can produce very neat results, but there can be many pitfalls, especially if you generate a score from sequencing software. Sequencers are designed to record note-lengths very precisely, just as they are played. If those note-lengths are then displayed as a musical score, the result can become a performer's nightmare, with a simple crotchet perhaps appearing as triple-dotted quaver followed by a hemi-demi-semiquaver rest or as a long succession of very short notes tied together. It is not that the software is wrong – it is simply attempting to display note-lengths in far too much detail for a performer easily to interpret.

Most sequencer software has facilities, such as score quantization, to help achieve more acceptable results, but you will still need to check the output carefully for eccentric note-lengths, and unnecessary rests and ties.

Software usually handles pitch better than rhythm, but again you must be on your guard for incorrect accidentals (eg A♯ in F major, when the note should be a B♭). Check carefully for anachronisms such as printing low clarinet notes in the bass clef. Excessive leger lines should be avoided, either by using a different clef if appropriate, or by using an *8va* sign. In particular, be sure to check that the software is correctly handling parts for instruments whose music should be written an octave higher than it sounds.

Remember that you will probably need to edit in the phrasing and articulation that you require, and to make sure that the staves are labelled with the instruments you intend, and not just track numbers. Most software should be able to produce correct stem directions and accurate beaming (grouping of notes), but again you should check that you have the right settings for the music concerned.

You will also need to know how your software handles repeats. It may well print the music out again in full, when what is really required is a repeat sign or a *da capo* direction, perhaps with first- and second-time bars in order to differentiate different endings.

Most of these problems can be overcome by careful study of the software manual, but remember that it is most unlikely that you will be able merely to press the 'Print' button in order to achieve an acceptably accurate score. If you are lucky enough to have access to high-quality software optimised for music notation the task will be somewhat easier, but will still need very careful checking. Again, remember to make it clear (if there might be any doubt) whether computer-printed staves are intended for live musicians or sequenced synthesizer sounds.

Computers can make the task of producing parts from the score for live players very much quicker, but remember that your performers will need page turns in suitable places and players of transposing instruments will require the part to be in the correct key. Also, try to use a decent quality of paper for printing the parts since flimsy computer-printout paper will never stay upright on a music stand.

In the end you may not be surprised to learn that some people find it quicker, and more satisfying, to use traditional pen and ink!

Composition checklist

Use the following list to ensure that you haven't overlooked any important points when it comes to submitting your work.

- ✦ Have you given the composition a meaningful title?
- ✦ Is there an indication of the tempo?
- ✦ Have you remembered the time signature?
- ✦ Are all the staves or tracks unambiguously labelled with the relevant instrument?
- ✦ Have you included a key for any parts, such as drum-kit, that use non-standard notation and for any graphic notation that you may have used?
- ✦ Have you included dynamics and other performing directions that you feel are important to the realisation of the piece?
- ✦ If any sections are expected to be improvised by the performers have you provided them with adequate instructions?
- ✦ Are all the pages numbered and in their correct order?

If you are submitting a score in conventional notation, also check:

- ✦ Do all the staves have the correct key signature?
- ✦ Have all articulation and other essential performing directions been included?
- ✦ Are all the notes for each instrument playable?
- ✦ Are phrase marks and slurs clear? They should always begin and end on specific notes – not on barlines or between notes.
- ✦ Does every bar have the correct number of beats? Checking is tedious but essential if you are to avoid this common fault.
- ✦ Have you numbered the bars for easy reference?
- ✦ Are there any blank bars? If a part is not playing it should either be omitted from the system or be given whole-bar rests, since blank bars can be ambiguous.

Finally, remember that you must include a recording of your piece, either performed as intended or in a suitable arrangement (for example for piano, or for sequencer-driven synthesizer) and a completed and signed authentication statement on a form provided by Edexcel. The composition must be entirely your own work, but your teacher is of course allowed to advise in general terms on the various techniques of composition.

Achieving a good mark

Concentrating on the following three aspects of composing should help you achieve a good mark.

Development of ideas

Some minimalist and riff-based music uses a lot of repetition. If you choose one of these styles it may be wise, as mentioned earlier, to consider writing a relatively long piece in order to show that you can achieve some variety and a sense of development in your composition.

Many of us stumble across occasional great musical ideas when doodling at the keyboard or singing to ourselves in an idle moment. The difficulty is always what to do next, after that initial bar or that opening phrase. Many promising openings are spoilt by excessive repetition in the bars that follow, leading to too little variety and no sense of alternating areas of tension and repose. Just as common are openings that are followed by too much diversity – so many new ideas in rapid succession that the piece fails to hang together.

The best way out of this dilemma is to discover what happens in music that you know. Start from:

- the pieces you play and the music you listen to
- the works you study from the *New Anthology*
- the pieces you have chosen to use as models for composing
- the music you enjoy in your leisure time.

Note the techniques used by composers to represent their material in different contexts and to give their music structure. Instead of introducing new ideas, take time to explore your opening idea in more depth. Break it up into smaller motifs and try to give these a life of their own before introducing new material. Above all, aim for a balance of unity and diversity in your work.

Control of texture

Most composition examiners would agree that this is the area in which candidates have the most difficulty and yet varied textures are vital to most types of music. If you assign your melody line to one instrument throughout and condemn the other parts to dull accompanying lines, you risk the wrath of most of your players, the boredom of your audiences and a low mark in your exam.

Try to distribute thematic material among *all* the resources at your disposal, remembering that each instrument in your ensemble can use different parts of its range. Use contrasted dynamics and articulation to help achieve variety. Try to break longer melodies into short motifs that dart from one instrument to another. Accompanying parts will be far more interesting if lugubrious semibreves are replaced with some rhythmic movement or interesting figuration. The use of a countermelody or other simple contrapuntal device can transform an ordinary piece into a work of real interest. Pay particular attention to phrase endings. If phrases often end on a long note try to add some decoration or a link motif in another part to propel the music forwards, or see if the end of the phrase can be overlapped with the start of the next.

Points of tension and relaxation are vital in most music and such moments need careful planning throughout the piece, especially if you are using a repetitive structure such as may occur in a lead-sheet arrangement. Changes in texture play a vital role in defining points of climax, where a thickening of chords, increase of harmonic pace, rise of melody to a high note, addition of extra parts and increase in rhythmic activity can combine to maximise the impact you intend.

Above all, remember that **rests** are the key to achieving good variety of texture. They are essential if singers and wind players are not to expire before the final cadence, but they are also essential to give relief to the ear. Assign solos to different parts of your texture and don't feel obliged to occupy all the instruments in every bar. Experiment with different combinations, such as a melody in the bass or inner part, and remember that occasional moments of totally unaccompanied melody can be ravishingly beautiful.

Refinement of ideas

You would be talented indeed to compose a piece of music and not then need to refine and polish it. At the very least you are likely to have to make adjustments as a result of trialling the work in performance. In addition to matters such as unplayable passages or miscalculated balance, you should be prepared to use a critical ear to identify the passages where the music seems to lose its impetus or direction. Perhaps a long note at a cadence needs to be sparked into life by adding an embellishment in another part, or perhaps a tendency for the piece to sound too sectionalised and predictable needs to be corrected by overlapping the phrases or adjusting the lengths of sub-phrases.

Gnawing away at the details in order to refine the work is a normal and expected part of the compositional process, but there will also be a time when you should let go. Music is not a science, and you will reach a stage at which further change is likely to be counter-productive and could result in inconsistencies of style that detract from your original conception of the piece.

How much should I write?

Most compositions tend to find their own natural length, but examiners will rarely be impressed by Adagio movements in an unvarying C major that attempt to reach the minimum three-minute length requirement by dint of excessive repetition, since these are unlikely to meet many of the criteria for a successful mark.

Composing involves a certain amount of risk, and your efforts are more likely to be successful if you attempt a piece that displays a real sense of character and ambition. The criteria for a high mark require confident and creative handling of a number of aspects of the work.

Finally, remember that while a neat and unambiguous score (in whatever format you choose) is important, it is not the object of the exercise. There is no need to try to impress the examiner by filling it full of Italian directions (English is perfectly acceptable) or by peppering it with a random selection of dynamics and performance directions that have no relation to the musical content. Keep it clear and keep it simple. Some useful books for composers include:

The Composer's Handbook by Bruce Cole. *Schott and Co Ltd*, 1996. ISBN: 0-946535-80-9.

Orchestral Technique by Gordon Jacob. *Oxford University Press*, 1931, 3rd edition 1981. ISBN: 0-19-318204-1.

Rock, Jazz and Pop Arranging by Daryl Runswick. *Faber and Faber*, 1992. ISBN: 0-571-51108-2. .

2. Compositional techniques

For the other half of Unit 2 you are required to produce two coursework exercises in compositional techniques. The tasks are set by Edexcel in a paper issued on 1st February in the examination year and, like the composition, the work has to be ready to reach the examiner by 15th May.

You have to choose two of the following topics, then pick one of the alternatives from each. The two exercises you undertake must come from two different topics:

- **Textures**. *Either* baroque counterpoint (completing an upper part to a given figured bass) *or* minimalism (completing a given keyboard opening to make a piece lasting about one minute).
- **Chords and cadences**. *Either* a Bach chorale (adding three lower parts to a melody to harmonise the cadences) *or* a 32-bar song (realising the middle-eight and turnaround from a given chord chart).
- **Scales, modes and series**. *Either* renaissance counterpoint (adding a part to two given parts) *or* serialism (completing an opening for solo instrument to make a piece of about 12 bars)
- **Timbres**. *Either* extended instrumental techniques (developing one of two given melodic ideas into a piece lasting about one minute that exploits one of the following: vocal contrast such as speech/sprechgesang, prepared piano, woodwind chords, glissandi, vocalising through the instrument) *or* electro-acoustic music (record a given ostinato, then add a second track to make a piece lasting about one minute which exploits one of the following: envelope shaping, filtering, pitch shifting, sampled sounds, reversing, looping).

You are required to copy out the given parts of the exercises you choose and complete the tasks requested. In the case of electro-acoustic music you are required to submit a recording rather than a score.

Your teacher will explain to you the techniques required in the various types of exercise. Before starting on the coursework paper you will need plenty of practice in using the techniques concerned. For example in the case of Bach chorales you might start by experimenting with the different ways that just one chord can be laid out in four parts. Then you could progress to using two chords to form perfect and imperfect cadences, concentrating on how the individual parts must move between the chords in this style of music. Once you can do this confidently in a variety of keys you could then see how a third chord might be used to approach the cadence.

Similar step-by-step work will be needed in any of the topics and of course careful study of suitable music to use as a model for your own work. If you are taking AS in one year, as is common, it is advisable to get through as much ground work as possible in the first term, so that you have a chance to work through some exam-length examples before the coursework paper arrives in February (but remember that you don't have to start work on the paper immediately – you can continue working on practice exercises).

Listening and understanding

There are two parts to this unit:

- ✦ a 45-minute listening test that accounts for just under 40% of the marks for this unit (15% of the total AS mark)
- ✦ a 1½-hour written paper that accounts for just over 60% of the marks for this unit (25% of the total AS mark).

1. Listening test

The test is presented on CD and consists of four questions. There are silences during the recording in which you can write your answers. The four questions require the following tasks:

1. You will hear two passages of music (twice each) for which no notation is given. For each passage you will have to identify such matters as the performing forces and how they are used, and/or comment on the texture of the music. Textures include homophony, counterpoint (including imitation, fugue and canon), melody and accompaniment styles, antiphony, and two-part, three-part, and four-part writing.

Texture, and terms to describe texture, are explained in the glossary of this book, which will refer you to examples of their use in the *New Anthology of Music*. You can then listen to the differences between different types of texture on the CDs that accompany the *Anthology*. We also point out many other examples of these musical textures in later chapters of this guide.

2. You will hear two different performances of a passage of music for which no notation is given. You will hear the pair of performances three times in all and you will be asked to comment on the differences in such areas as tempo, dynamics, ornamentation and instrumentation, and perhaps the impact that these differences make.
3. An excerpt of music will be played five times and the question will include a skeleton score of at least part of this music. You must choose whether to answer questions that require you to add notation to the music (rhythms, melodies and chords) or to answer questions about the music's context (where and when it might have been written, the type of work from which it comes, its style, its purpose, how it expresses any text that may be sung, and so forth).
4. A short passage of music, which will be printed as a single-stave skeleton score, will be played four times. You will be asked about the tonality of the music (such as whether certain passages are major or minor) and how the keys of specific passages relate to each other (tonic and dominant, minor and relative major, and so on). You will be asked to identify simple chord progressions such as different types of cadence, the circle of 5ths, or chords in a tonic/dominant relationship. You may also be asked to identify individual chords (triads in root position and first inversion, Ic, V^7 and the diminished 7th).

The following two books, both of which come with CDs, can help provide practice for questions 1, 3 and 4 of the listening test:

Aural Matters by David Bowman and Paul Terry. *Schott and Co Ltd*, 1993. ISBN: 0-946535-22-1.

Aural Matters in Practice by David Bowman and Paul Terry. *Schott and Co Ltd*, 1994. ISBN: 0-946535-23-X.

2. Written paper

For this part of the unit you must prepare two of the following areas of study:

Music for large ensemble * 20th-century art music * Music for small ensemble * Keyboard music * Sacred vocal music * Secular vocal music *	Music for film and television Popular music and jazz World music

At least one of your two areas of study must be from the western classical tradition (marked * in the list above).

The *New Anthology of Music* is published by Peters Edition Ltd, ISBN: 1-901507-03-3 (CDs, ISBN: 1-901507-04-1), and is available from Edexcel publications (see page 2) or all good music retailers.

The music for each of these areas of study is provided in the *New Anthology of Music* (referred to as *NAM* in the rest of this book) with recordings on a companion set of four CDs. You are expected to use an **unmarked** copy of the anthology in the exam.

In the examination you will have to answer two questions, one on each of your chosen areas of study. All questions have four parts and are arranged as follows:

(a) you will be required to choose two musical terms from a list of four, all of which relate to the music in the area of study, and to give the meaning of these two terms (4 marks)

(b) you will then have to give the precise location in *NAM* of an example of each of the terms you chose for (a) (4 marks)

(c) you will be set a question on the music from the area of study which will require one or more short answers (8 marks)

(d) you will be set a question on the music from the area of study which will require a longer style of answer (14 marks)

A This symbol indicates a List A work, for special attention if you sit the exam in June 2001 or June 2002.

B This symbol indicates a List B work, for special attention if you sit the exam in June 2003 or June 2004.

In the specification (and in this guide) the works in each area of study are designated as belonging to either List A or List B. Questions (a) and (b) above may refer to music in either list (in other words, to any piece in the area of study). But questions (c) and (d) will refer to only music in the list specified for each particular examination year. These lists are designated as follows:

- **List A** for the exam sat in **June 2001** and **June 2002**
- **List B** for the exam sat in **June 2003** and **June 2004**

This means that you need to study all the pieces in the area of study (in order to answer the first two questions) but the main focus of your work should be on List A if you are taking the exam in June 2001 or June 2002, or on List B if you are taking it in June 2003 or June 2004.

Questions will concern only the works in the areas of study and will not require you to know other music. However the specification encourages extensive listening, and *relevant* references to other music that support your answers to the (c) and (d) questions will be credited by the examiner.

Most of the rest of this guide is devoted to an introduction to each of the areas of study and the music it contains. Words printed in **bold** can be looked up in the glossary at the end of the book.

Terminology

The glossary is not a dictionary. It simply explains the terms you are most likely to encounter in the various areas of study. Terminology in music, like any other subject, is merely a means through which it is possible to discuss complicated concepts concisely and accurately so that other people understand precisely what you mean. However it will be of little use if you attempt to memorise the words merely as a series of definitions. In almost all of the glossary entries we have given references to exact locations in *NAM* where you can *hear* the musical meaning of the term by listening to the CD or by playing it for yourself. Once you have done this, try to reinforce the experience by looking for the use and musical effect of the device concerned in the music you play and listen to, and by using it in your own composing.

Try to be sure that you really have correctly understood terms that you might have been using for some years. Examiners often come across references such as 'the theme of bar 1 is imitated in bar 96', where a candidate meant that it was repeated, or 'Haydn sequenced the first theme', when they meant that he used a sequence, not an 18th-century sequencer. If in doubt about the correct technical term, try to explain what you mean in plain but precise English.

During the course of each chapter there are a number of questions designed to help you check your understanding of the topic – these are not necessarily the type of question that you will encounter in the exam. However at the end of every chapter you will find two sets of sample questions to give you some exam practice, particularly in your final weeks of revision.

Studying music

From the very start of your course you need to be clear that the focus of your studies must always be the music itself. It cannot be too strongly emphasised that your work should be based on the *sound* of the music and how it achieves its musical effect.

Some students seem to go to unnecessary lengths to avoid tackling the music head on. They learn long lists of dates, or the number of symphonies Haydn wrote, or quotations of what other people say about the music. This sort of approach is unlikely to be useful. Information *directly related to the piece concerned* can be important in understanding the context of the music – why it was written in the way it was. For example some pieces in the *New Anthology* were written for domestic music-making at home, some were intended for performance as part of a church service, others were written to be heard in the cinema or on television, and some were written to be played in the concert hall. The intended context of the music is one of the important factors that shapes the music itself.

Studying the context in which music was written can help us to see why certain combinations of instruments were used at certain times, why various technical devices were used by some composers but not by others, and how the demands of different consumers of music – aristocratic patrons, government-funded arts councils or even the record-buying, concert-going public – resulted in music adopting the forms and styles it has during different periods of history. Why does a piece written in the 16th century sound different from a piece written in the 18th century, or in modern times? What is it in the music itself that creates these differences and how are they reflected in performing?

It is equally important to understand how musical elements such as melody, rhythm and harmony are used. This is not a matter of mere description of the music – that would have little point. It is more a question of understanding how the piece works as music and how it creates its impact.

So while it is useful to be able to identify a rising sequence, for instance, the real interest is in why it is used and the effect that it has. Perhaps it is a device for unifying the music, but perhaps it is also one of the ingredients being used to build up towards a climax, or possibly the composer is using it as a device to move the music on through new keys and thus provide contrast.

As well as looking at the detail we also need to investigate the wider issue of each work's overall form. Again, this is not just a question of giving something a label, but of trying to understand how music has its own architecture that enables even a long work to sound unified, without becoming repetitive and boring. Why does the middle section of a particular piece sound different, and yet still familiar enough to be part of the same piece? What is the effect of repeating music in a different key?

We may also need to explore how the composer has used the available musical resources: why some groups of instruments were used in preference to others, how the balance between soloists and an orchestra is handled, or the ways in which the text has been expressed in vocal music.

As we peel back the layers it starts to become possible to understand why music seems to reveal patterns and ideas, or to suggest and enhance moods or emotions. Why some music sounds heroic and other music makes us want to get up and dance. Why one top-ten hit sounds corny while another makes us want to play it time and again. Why one piece of music that we are learning to play seems fully to engage our interest yet another bores us stiff. By studying the music in depth we can begin to answer such questions and to find out how the music actually works.

As we explore below the surface of worthwhile music of any kind, more and more detail starts to emerge, detail that we may have scarcely heard in the past, but that now we listen for. New inter-connections emerge each time we listen, new detail that previously escaped our attention is now revealed to have significance to the whole. And thus it is that we begin to understand how and why one work of art can be universally recognised as a masterpiece, while another may do no more than fleetingly engage our attention.

Once our own listening experience is enhanced in this way, we can see how studying music can illuminate performing. It can help us bring to the attention of our audiences the overall architecture of the music, as well as the myriad of fine detail and the web of interconnections we have discovered, thus enhancing their own listening experience. Understanding music in detail can equally inform our work as composers, helping us to explore subtle ways of structuring our music and suggesting ways in which additional layers of detail can reveal themselves to the listener at each new hearing.

Note taking

Get into the habit of keeping clear, well-ordered notes. Be selective and highlight anything that seems important. Leave plenty of space, so you can make additions later.

Your main sources of information will be recordings, scores, guides such as this and reference books, but remember that your best source of information is your teacher. Don't just sit there and take reams of notes, but try to develop a questioning approach. Ask for clarification of anything and everything you don't understand. Your teacher won't mind – in fact, he or she will be delighted if you show an interest in the work and in improving your own performance.

Exam technique

In part (a) of each question you are asked to give the meaning of two of the four musical terms given. Your answer can be brief. For example if the term is 'trill' it would be quite sufficient to write

> A trill is an ornament consisting of the rapid alternation of two notes a step apart.

This is more than enough to gain the full 2 marks available. Notice that the answer is very precise: it is an ornament; the notes alternate; they do so rapidly; and the notes are a step apart.

In part (b) you are asked to link the terms you have defined to a context in the *New Anthology*. Again, this must be precise – you need to name the work, the bar and (for an isolated event like this) the beat, and the instrument or voice involved. You might say

> There is a trill in the first movement of Haydn's Symphony No. 26 in bar 10, on beats 1 and 2 of the first violin part.

This is quite sufficient. You do not need to give more than one example, or to start writing about other ornaments.

In part (c) the nature of the question will require a longer answer. There are eight marks available, so typically you might expect to have to make four accurate and reasonably detailed statements (the questions themselves often indicate the number of points you are expected to make). Answers can be written in continuous prose, or you could use a numbered list, as in the following example:

> *Mention four ways in which the third and fourth movements of Bach's Cantata No. 48 differ.*

1. Movement 3 is in B♭ major, movement 4 is in E♭ major.
2. Movement 3 is a chorale, movement 4 is an obbligato aria.
3. Movement 3 is homophonic, movement 4 is contrapuntal.
4. Movement 3 has no repetition of the words or musical phrases, movement 4 repeats the words and the music at various points.

Notice that although the answer is short, it is precise. The answer doesn't just indicate that the keys and the texture are different, it states how they are different.

Part (d) of the question attracts the most marks and will require the longest answer – although you are not expected to write an essay, and answers in note form rather than continuous prose are acceptable. However the assessment will include the quality of your written communication, so you need to be clear and be prepared to use music terminology accurately and precisely. It is usually best to avoid long sentences because they can easily become so convoluted that the point gets lost.

Avoid digression and repetition – you won't get any credit for it and with 14 marks available you need to pack in a lot of relevant information. There is no need for opening paragraphs to set the scene, or to describe the composers' lives or other works. Dive straight in and tackle the subject head on. For a good mark you should be able to highlight matters of significance, and use your knowledge to interpret and explain bare factual detail. Try to avoid personal opinions of a general nature, such as stating how much you like the music. If you do feel it appropriate to include a personal reaction, make sure that it is backed up by evidence from the music, eg 'the start of the development sounds doom-laden *because* ...'.

Citing evidence for your arguments will give authority to your answer and your main source of such evidence will usually be the music itself. Try to refer directly to something in the music to illustrate each of your main points. Instead of merely writing ...

> Mozart often uses thin textures.

illustrate your point with an example ...

> Mozart's preference for thin textures can be heard in the opening bars, in which he uses just a two-part texture.

Examiners will be looking for well-focused responses that answer the precise question posed and that are supported by specific references to the music itself. However there is no need to write out examples from the music – just refer to bar numbers in the anthology. Questions cannot be answered by trying to memorise 'prepared answers' that you hope might somehow fit the question, like an embarrassed politician in a television interview. Nor can they be answered by responding in vague generalities about what a splendid and moving piece you think you have studied.

The key to success in this unit is to get to know the music very thoroughly, and to understand why, when and how it was written. Take a similarly thoughtful approach to the music you play, using the skills you learn about to inform your performing. Try out the techniques you encounter by playing them, and by using them in your own improvising and composing.

Revision

You need to plan sufficient time for effective revision, and that should include a thorough reappraisal of your notes and marked answers, particularly seeing where any previous errors or misunderstandings need correcting. It can be useful to summarise your notes into just a short list of key issues – notes on notes, as it were.

Practise drafting skeleton answers, as well as working through whatever specimen and past papers are available, preferably under timed exam conditions.

After revising each topic you should aim to feel confident enough to be able to answer questions on it, from whatever perspective they may be set. Always remember that the main focus of the examination is not a memory test, but a means of assessing your understanding of the music in the areas of study you have chosen.

Further listening

Although all of the music in the anthology (except *NAM 54*) is recorded on its companion set of CDs, it can be useful to look out for alternative recordings of the works you study in order to make comparisons between interpretations. This is useful practise for question 2 of the Listening Test, and it can also be very helpful in showing just how different the same music can sound in different interpretations. This is particularly so in the case of early music. For example, it would be instructive to hear *NAM 21* played on the harpsichord and to compare it with the very fine performance on the piano on CD2. Similarly, a recording of Bach's *Brandenburg* Concerto No. 4 (*NAM 1*) played on recorders and period string instruments would make a good comparison with the performance on modern instruments given on CD1.

It will help your understanding of the styles and techniques of the music you study to listen to similar works by the same composer. Many of the pieces in the *New Anthology* are paralleled by extracts in the two books mentioned on page 19, *Aural Matters* and *Aural Matters in Practice*. The extracts in these books are presented as aural tests, which will give you further practise for the Listening Test as well as the opportunity to see how the techniques you have learnt about are used in the context of different but similar works.

Further reading

What to Listen for in Music by Aaron Copland. *Penguin Putnam* (USA), new edition 1999. ISBN: 0-451-62880-2. This justifiably famous guide to the elements of music was written in 1939 by one of America's foremost composers, and has recently been updated and reissued as a modestly-priced paperback.

The Cambridge Music Guide edited by Stanley Sadie and Alison Latham. *Cambridge University Press*, 1985. Paperback edition 1990. ISBN: 0-521-39942-4. A moderately priced and very well-illustrated introductory guide to the history of music with many examples. It includes a useful overview of the development of instruments and the rise of the modern orchestra.

Collins Classical Music Encyclopedia edited by Stanley Sadie. *HarperCollins*, 2000. ISBN 0-00-472390-2. Each chapter introduces a period in music history, and focuses on two or three major composers. There are sections on instruments, and on forms and styles, and the book includes a listening guide.

Music for large ensemble

The concept of an orchestra as an ensemble of musicians who regularly played together developed in the late 17th and early 18th centuries, particularly in the form of small orchestras maintained by royalty and wealthy aristocrats, and in the groups of musicians engaged to play in opera houses. In this baroque period orchestras were founded on a small string group divided into four parts: first violins, second violins, violas and a bass part played by cellos and double basses. This ensemble was supported by one or more chordal instruments (such as the harpsichord or organ) that could fill out the harmony where necessary. Oboes and bassoons were added where resources permitted and sometimes instruments such as the recorder, flute or horn were used for special effect. Trumpets and timpani were often added to the ensemble if the music was of a ceremonial nature.

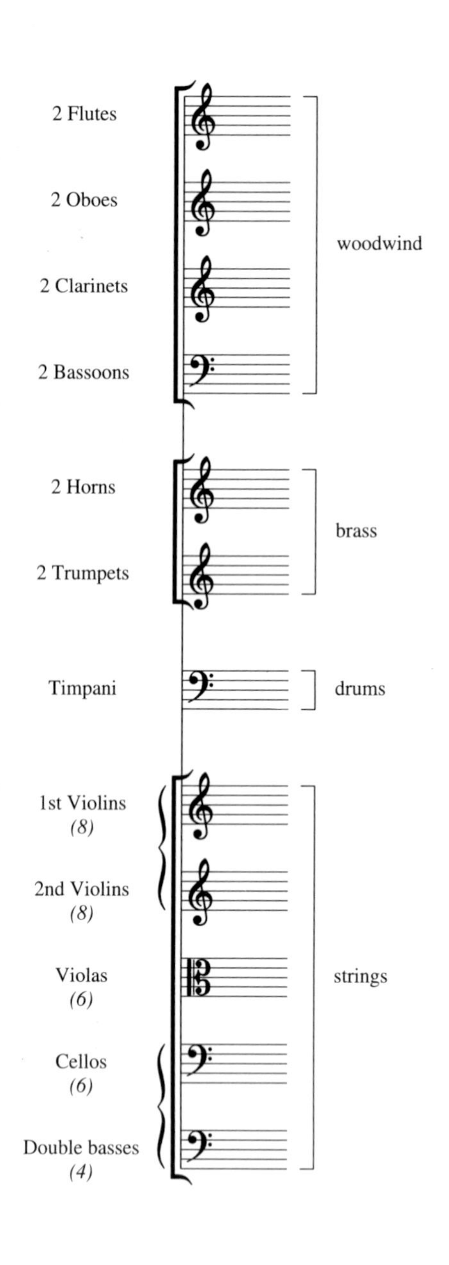

Strings have remained the foundation of the orchestra to the present day but during the late 18th century the woodwind section became a large and self-contained unit, with two clarinets joining the pairs of older instruments, and horns, trumpets and timpani became regular members of the orchestra rather than occasional visitors. To balance this body of sound, the number of string players increased dramatically and a harpsichord or other chordal instrument became unnecessary. The Berlin opera house orchestra of 1772 had 22 string players – by 1841 the same orchestra employed 54 strings. Much of this expansion was due to the main focus of concert life moving away from the private salons of the nobility to the public concert halls, large theatres and opera houses that were starting to appear at this time.

Individual works vary in their requirements but a typical orchestral piece of around 1800 was scored for the instruments shown *left*. The number of string players per part would also vary, but some typical figures for the time are shown in brackets. Sometimes there would be more than one wind player per part – for instance it was common to use four bassoons, two on each part. This diagram also shows the normal order of instruments in a score and will help you follow the layouts of the various pieces in the *New Anthology*.

Composers and audiences alike were thrilled by the rich sonorities available from these larger orchestras and helped stoke the demand for further expansion after 1800. By now instruments previously used mainly for dramatic effect in the opera house started to be used to expand the sonority of the concert orchestra – trombones, 'Turkish' percussion (bass drum, triangle and cymbals), the piccolo and the contrabassoon. And as the string section became larger it was possible for composers to create new textures by sometimes subdividing each string part and by writing double-bass parts that had greater independence from the cello line.

The keywork of woodwind instruments was improved during the 19th century in response to the increasing technical demands that composers were making on performers. Valve mechanisms for horns and trumpets started to appear in the 1820s. Valves gave these instruments a full chromatic compass instead of the restricted sets of notes available on the 'natural' trumpets and horns of earlier times. The number of brass players increased – it became normal to use at least four horns and the tuba joined the orchestra to provide a bass for the brass family. More unusual woodwind instruments such as the cor anglais and bass clarinet started to appear, as well as harps and a greater range of percussion instruments. And the number of strings was, of course, increased again to balance.

This constant expansion of the orchestra continued until the early years of the 20th century, when the harsh economic conditions of the first world war and its aftermath inevitably caused many composers to turn their attention to works for smaller types of ensemble. The changes in the style and complexity of orchestral music over this period is reflected in the works set for this Area of Study:

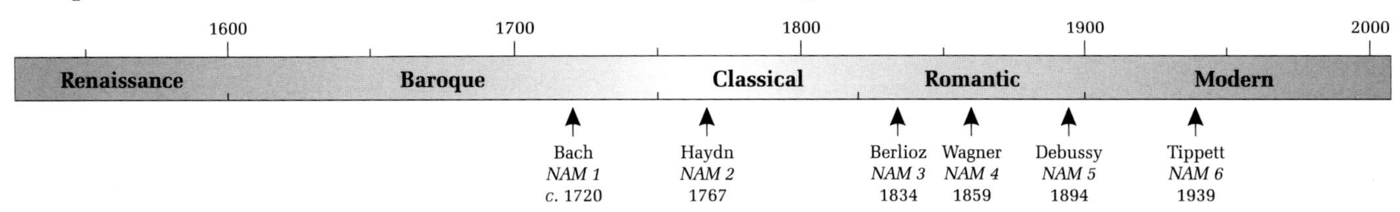

Brandenburg Concerto No. 4, movement 1 (Bach)

A *NAM 1* CD1 Track 1
Northern Sinfonia of England
Directed by George Malcolm

A concerto is a large-scale composition for contrasting musical forces, most commonly a soloist (or group of soloists) and an orchestra. The basic design of three movements in a fast–slow–fast pattern was established in the early 18th century, and was widely used by late baroque composers such as Bach and Vivaldi.

There are two main types of baroque concerto. The solo concerto features one instrument with an orchestra – Vivaldi's set of four violin concertos called *The Four Seasons* are probably the best-known examples. The concerto grosso (or 'grand concerto' as Handel called it) features a group of solo instruments with an orchestra. Bach's fourth *Brandenburg* concerto is of this type.

The first movement of a solo concerto by Vivaldi which uses the same form as *NAM 1* is included in *Aural Matters* (Bowman and Terry) pages 112–113.

Bach's six *Brandenburg* concertos are so called because they were dedicated to the Margrave of Brandenburg, ruler of one of the many small states into which Germany was then divided. They were written by Bach when he was director of music to the ruler of the tiny German principality of Cöthen from 1717 to 1722, and where he had an excellent orchestra at his disposal.

In this concerto the group of soloists, or *concertino*, consists of a violin and two recorders. The orchestra consists, as it almost always did in baroque concertos, of strings and **continuo**. The word *ripieno* at the start indicates that all available violins (and violas) are to play these staves – they are not solo parts.

The recording on CD1 uses flutes instead of recorders. Try to compare it with one of the many recordings that uses recorders and period string instruments.

Listen to the movement and answer the following questions:

1. How does Bach ensure that the recorders (flutes) can be heard in the first 12 bars, despite the fact that everyone is playing?
2. Which continuo instrument can you hear most clearly?
3. There are almost no dynamic markings, but can you hear apparent changes in dynamics? If so, how are they achieved?
4. Why does this music sound so energetic and happy?

The last of these questions will benefit from some discussion within your study group, but when considering dynamics you probably noticed that the contrasts come about because of the changes in texture between the *concertino* and *ripieno*: loud when all are playing (**tutti**), quieter when only the concertino is playing. These contrasts are quite distinct – they don't involve the use of crescendo or diminuendo to change dynamic level. This contrast is known as 'terraced dynamics' and is a characteristic of late baroque style.

Listen again and try to see how the music is put together. It starts with a long opening section (bars 1–83) that begins with a I–V–I chord progression heard four times in the first 12 bars. It ends with the syncopated rhythms and perfect cadence in bars 79–83. Listen to the recording without the score, but use these two features as markers in order to identify what happens in the rest of the music.

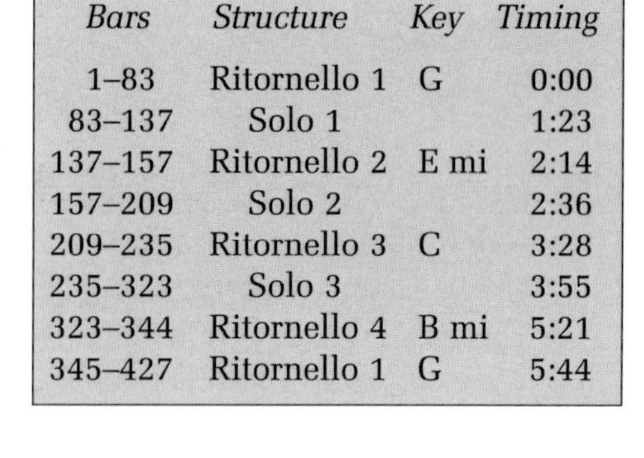

Bars	*Structure*	*Key*	*Timing*
1–83	Ritornello 1	G	0:00
83–137	Solo 1		1:23
137–157	Ritornello 2	E mi	2:14
157–209	Solo 2		2:36
209–235	Ritornello 3	C	3:28
235–323	Solo 3		3:55
323–344	Ritornello 4	B mi	5:21
345–427	Ritornello 1	G	5:44

Did you notice that between the solo sections parts of the opening music return in different keys, and that all of the opening music is repeated in the tonic key at the end? This is known as **ritornello** form. Ritornello means 'a little return' and refers to the use of shortened repetitions (between contrasting episodes) as a structural device. It is a musical form that was widely used in the baroque period, not only in concertos but also in vocal music, such as the last movement of *NAM 28*. This structure is summarised in the table *left* – we have given timings since this may help you follow the music without needing to use the score.

The solo episodes do not stay in one key. Instead they modulate from the key of the previous ritornello to the key of the next. Notice how small fragments of the ritornello punctuate these sections, as in bars 89–91. Because this fragment consists of chords I–V–I Bach can use it as a perfect cadence to highlight the most important keys through which the music passes, as in bars 103–105 where they appear in the dominant, D major. However the orchestra mainly take a background role during the solo episodes, as in the sustained A in bars 125–128. Sometimes the accompaniment is provided by just the continuo instruments. Can you hear the harpsichord improvisation starting at bar 114 and say how this relates to the violin solo that it accompanies?

Bach is famous for his skill in **counterpoint** and a contrapuntal texture is very evident in bars 165–174. In the virtuoso solo that Bach wrote for the leader of the court orchestra (bars 187–208) recorders and ripieno are used in delicate and varied accompanimental textures. First the lower strings play detached chords while recorders play a motif taken from bars 4–5 of the movement. Then roles are reversed in bars 194–197.

? Private study

1. Explain the following terms and state to which instruments they apply in this work: concertino, ripieno, continuo.
2. How does Bach make bars 69–83 sound exciting?
3. Comment on the rhythm of the solo violin part in bars 83–136.
4. What are the main differences between the recorder (flute) parts in bars 125–156 and their parts in bars 165–186?

Symphony No. 26, 1st movement (Haydn)

B *NAM 2* CD1 Track 2
Academy of Ancient Music
Directed by Christopher Hogwood

The type of music that most people associate with the orchestra is the three- or four-movement symphony. It first became popular in the second half of the 18th century and central to its development were the 104 (or more) symphonies of Josef Haydn.

For much of his life Haydn was director of music to the Hungarian Prince Esterházy at a magnificent palace 50 kilometres south-west of Vienna. Here he had a small orchestra and every facility to perfect his craft. He said to his friend and biographer, Georg Griesinger,

> I could experiment, observe what created an impression and what weakened it, thus improving, adding, cutting away, and running risks. I was cut off from the world … and so I had to become original.

The title of Haydn's Symphony No. 26 comes from an inscription on a manuscript of plainsong melodies (possibly dating back to the middle ages) which reads *Passio et Lamentatio* (Passion and Lamentation). This is a reference to the passion of Christ, the story of which is told in the plainsong. Here is its opening:

Pas - si - o Do - mi - ni nos - tri Je - su Chris - ti se - cun - dum Mar - - cum

Translation: The passion of our Lord Jesus Christ according to Saint Mark

This was well known throughout southern Germany and Austria at the time when Haydn composed the *Lamentatione* Symphony (1767). So it is highly probable that the Esterházy household would instantly have recognised the plainsong when they heard it played on oboe and second violins in bars 17–38. The pitches shown above exactly correspond with those in bars 17–21. The various words above the score refer to the plainsong passion. The *Evangelist* is the narrator of the story while the passages labelled *Christ* (bar 26) and *Jews* (bar 35) were direct speech in the original plainsong. When the Jews call for Jesus to be crucified the semiquaver run (bar 37) and the following wild leaps (bars 40–41) suggest the excited cries of the crowd.

Haydn used a wide range of material in his many symphonies. It should perhaps be stressed that the idea of basing a movement on plainsong, as happens here, is highly unusual.

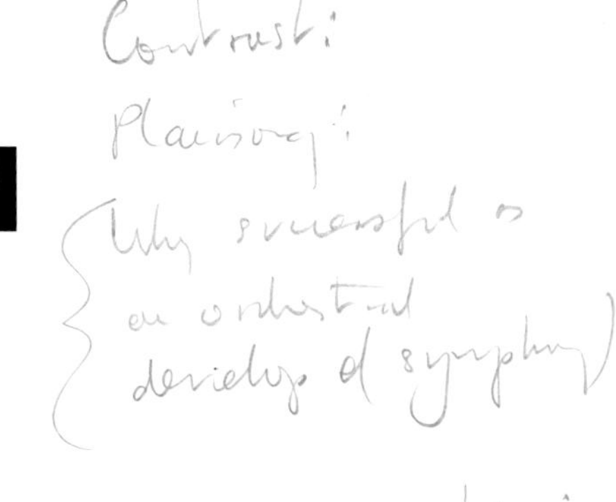

Listen to the movement, making sure you can spot the plainsong quotations, and answer the following questions:

1. Does this have more contrasts or fewer contrasts than *NAM 1*?
2. Does the texture sound as though it is thicker or thinner than the movement from the *Brandenburg* concerto?
3. What makes this music sound so much angrier in mood than *NAM 1*? (Consider key, rhythm and contrasts.)

The size of orchestra is typical of Haydn's early symphonies and is a little larger than that required for *NAM 1*. However you probably concluded that the texture often sounds thinner. This is because:

- the violas mostly double the bass part at the unison or octave
- the two violin parts are sometimes in unison
- the two oboes and bassoon mainly double the string parts.

The two horns in D (which sound a minor 7th lower than printed) are used sparingly until bar 99 because of the limited pitches available on natural horns for which the composer wrote. When the music moves into D major at bar 100 a greater number of notes can be used. The very thin two-part texture of the first eight bars would probably have been filled with chords from the harpsichord (cembalo), but, as the recording on CD1 shows, the bare texture only enhances the fierce mood created by the syncopations and discords (such as the C♯ that crashes into a D♮ in bar 1).

The dramatic style of this music, and of other Haydn symphonies of the same period, later became known as *Sturm und Drang* (Storm and Stress), a term borrowed from German literature of the time. It is characterised by minor keys, syncopation, sudden contrasts, wide leaps and use of the dramatic diminished 7th chord (for example in bar 13).

Now listen to the music again and see if you can follow its structure:

- an opening idea (called the first subject) in D minor followed by a contrasing second subject in F major (the plainsong theme at bar 17) – these 44 bars are then repeated
- a middle section (bars 45–79) in a variety of keys
- a return of the opening section at bar 80, now with both the first and second subject in D; because the second subject is major, its return is in D major (bar 100).

For a first movement in sonata form from a much later symphony by Haydn see *Aural Matters* (Bowman and Terry) pages 126–128.

This is known as **sonata form** and it was one of the main musical structures of the classical period. The first section is called the exposition and introduces the idea of two contrasting keys. Most (but not all) sonata-form movements also use, as Haydn does here, contrasting melodies for the first and second subjects.

Can you hear how the music of the middle section sounds different and yet seems to fit into the whole? This is because it develops ideas from the exposition and is thus called the development. For instance bars 45–52 are based on a variant of the syncopated idea from the first subject, transposed to F major and treated in sequence. The more extended sequences of bars 57–64 are based on a **circle of 5ths** (B♭–E–A–D–G–C♯–F♮–B♮ on the first beat of each bar) that carry the music to the key of A minor. Above a dominant **pedal** in this key (bars 65–68) the oboes play a variant of Christ's plainsong (first heard at bar 26). Of which bars in the exposition are bars 74–79 a development?

The final section recaps (with changes) the exposition and is therefore called the recapitulation. Compare bars 92–99 with bars 13–16 to see how Haydn modifies and extends the end of the first subject to allow the second subject to return in the tonic major (D major). The movement ends with a **coda** (bars 126–133) which is an expansion of bars 43–44 from the end of the exposition.

Private study

1. What is the pitch of the first note sounded by the horns? (Remember that they are transposing instruments.)
2. What helps to make the syncopated opening really rhythmic?
3. Briefly but precisely describe the texture in bars 58–62.
4. Compare bars 100–105 with bars 17–21.
5. Why was Haydn able to make such a significant contribution to the development of the symphony?

Harold in Italy, movement 3 (Berlioz)

A *NAM 3* CD1 Track 3
London Symphony Orchestra
Conducted by Colin Davis

NAM 1 is a concerto, *NAM 2* is a symphony and in some respects *NAM 3* is a combination of both. Although called a symphony, *Harold in Italy* has a solo viola part that was intended for the great violinist Paganini. Since his chief claim to fame was a formidable technique, it is unsurprising that when he saw the simple viola part he refused to play it, despite having commissioned the work.

In 1830 Berlioz had written his *Symphonie fantastique*, a new type of work which illustrates a highly personal 'episode in the life of an artist' (the artist being Berlioz himself) using the medium of the symphony. The composer's beloved is represented by a melody that appears in different guises in every one of its five movements, called an *idée fixe* (a fixed idea, but used in French to mean an obsession). Berlioz wrote detailed notes for publication in concert programmes explaining how this 'programme music' expresses his hopeless fixation with a woman, her rejection of him and the drug-induced nightmare in which he imagines he has killed her and then witnesses his own execution for the crime.

His next symphony was *Harold in Italy* (1834), based on a poem by Byron – this is vaguely reflected in the titles at the head of each of the symphony's four movements, but in general the work is far less programmatic than its very explicit predecessor. Harold also has an *idée fixe* – here it is as it appears near the beginning of the symphony:

Excerpts from the first movement of *Harold in Italy*, including the *idée fixe* printed below, can be found in *Aural Matters* (Bowman and Terry) pages 130–131.

It makes an appearance in every movement, but it is not obsessive like its counterpart in the *Symphonie fantastique* – it simply turns up to represent Harold, the vagabond dreamer, as an onlooker in picturesque Italian locations. The next example shows Harold's theme as it appears in bars 65–80 of *NAM 3* (the viola player needs to use **double stopping** to produce the octaves):

Finally, this example shows how Berlioz derives the theme which starts in bar 34 from from reordered motifs of Harold's theme:

Berlioz is renowned for his superb orchestration. A comparison of this work with *NAM 2* will show how far the orchestra has come since 1767. Berlioz still uses natural horns – but there are four of them, and in three different keys (C, F and E) to cover as many pitches as possible. There are also a number of instruments new to the orchestra. Can you name them?

Virtually all of the melodic interest in *NAM 2* was concentrated in the violin parts. When do the violins first appear in *Harold* and what role do they play up to bar 71? On the other hand, the violas that had such a lowly status in *NAM 2* are here required to divide into two parts to provide important rhythms at the start and end of the movement – and of course the work features a solo viola.

The rhythm of the oboe/piccolo tune is that of the *saltarello*, an ancient Italian dance. Italian folk musicians still descend from the mountains of the Abbruzi to entertain city folk and tourists at Christmas time with *saltarelli* and other dances.

At the start our attention is focused on a realistic impression of Italian bagpipes represented by a double **pedal** in the wind, above which Berlioz introduces the tone colour of an oboe doubled *two* octaves above by a piccolo (two octaves because the piccolo sounds an octave higher than written). Their tune sounds like a folk dance.

At bar 32 Berlioz carefully notes that the speed should halve. A relatively new instrument, the cor anglais (a low oboe, sounding a 5th lower than printed) introduces the main theme of the movement. Notice how bars 37 and 38 sound more like 3/4 than 6/8. The sequel to this melody introduces an oboe playing in octaves with the cor anglais and this double-reed tone becomes even more biting when the bassoon joins in an octave lower at bar 53. Horns in C (sounding an octave lower than printed) take over the first phrase of the main theme of the Allegretto in bar 59. At bar 65 Harold's *idée fixe* enters and is combined with earlier material.

The music becomes more chromatic and the textures become more complex (although the harp chords that enter at bar 72 helpfully show the basic harmonies). Berlioz modulates to D minor for the central climax of the movement in bar 111, after which the music retreats to a long-overdue perfect cadence in C (bars 134–135).

Berlioz frames this central section by returning to the folk dance style of the start (bars 136–166 repeat bars 1–31). But at bar 166 a final section begins – so vanishingly quiet that it must surely be Harold dozing off into another daydream in the hot Italian sunshine. Berlioz combines phrases from the main theme of the Allegretto (on solo viola) with Harold's *idée fixe* (flute, pinpointed with harp harmonics), the folk-dance rhythm (divided violas) and the bagpipe drone (also violas). Gradually instruments drop out to leave us with isolated fragments of the saltarello melody (bars 194–198) and the bagpipe drone (violas ***ppp*** at bar 201). Finally everything winds down to the lowest note of the muted solo viola (C, the tonic) and the movement ends with repeated C-major triads played almost inaudibly on muted strings.

Private study

1. Name the chord played by the violas on the first beat of bar 1. How does this chord relate to the key of the movement?
2. What type of instrument is a cor anglais? What is special about the notation of music for this instrument?
3. What is an *idée fixe*? How does the term relate to this movement?
4. Summarise the structure of this entire movement in a single short sentence.
5. State **two** reasons why Paganini might have found this work unsatisfactory to reflect his talents as a virtuoso string player.

Prelude to Tristan and Isolde (Wagner)

B *NAM 4* CD1 Track 4
Vienna Philharmonic Orchestra
Conducted by Georg Solti

One important aspect of 19th-century romanticism was a desire to bring the arts together and this is seen particularly in the operas of Richard Wagner, who developed what he called the *Gesamtkunstwerk* (total artwork). This was a type of work in which the arts collaborated on equal terms to produce a single all-embracing music drama for which he alone was responsible. To achieve this he wrote his own words, set them to music in a symphonic style for a very large orchestra, supervised every aspect of the production and even designed his own opera house in Bavaria which was dedicated solely to the staging of his music dramas.

NAM 4 is the prelude (or overture) to *Tristan and Isolde*, one of these 'total artworks'. The opera tells a story of medieval fantasy about the love affair of the knight Tristan and the princess Isolde that begins during Isolde's journey to marry someone else. So the central theme of the opera is yearning, longing, burning for a love which, under the conventions of the time, can only be consummated in both their deaths (which is, of course, what happens).

Music from the end of this opera can be found in *Aural Matters* (Bowman and Terry) pages 134–135.

Before listening to the prelude, remind yourself of the opening of Haydn's symphony (*NAM 2*), with its clearly-defined phrases and regular perfect cadences in bars 8 and 16.

Now listen to Wagner's prelude (a basic plan of the music is shown *right*). In addition to the much grander scale of Wagner's music, did you notice that the fragments at the start seem very unresolved and, once it really gets going, there is a continuous stream of music, with very little sign of perfect cadences anywhere?

Bars	*Structure*
1–24	Exposition
26–65	Middle section
66–83	First recapitulation
83–111	Second recapitulation

To see in detail how Wagner generates such unresolved tension listen to the first 17 bars. The opening motif is shown *right*. The dissonance in bar 2 is such a feature of this work that it is known as the 'Tristan chord'. It is followed by V^7 of A minor – but this dominant 7th doesn't resolve on the tonic. It is followed by four long seconds of silence.

'Tristan chord'

This phrase is heard twice more, ending on V^7 of C major in bar 7 and V^7 of E in bar 11 – these dominant 7ths are also not resolved. In bar 12 the harmonic progression is repeated an octave higher, still without resolution. Then just the last two notes of the motif are played without accompaniment on strings, then woodwind.

Bar 16 begins with V^7 of A minor over which these last two notes wind their way up to the leading note (G♯). Surely the tension will now at last be resolved by a tonic chord? But no, with a sudden swelling of sound the resolution is to a chord of F, forming an **interrupted cadence**, while the melodic line passionately overshoots its goal to land on a highly dissonant **appoggiatura** on B before wilting down to its original destination, A.

Similar procedures can be found throughout the prelude and, along with the frequent use of chromatic dissonances (such as the A♯ in the music example above) help give the music its restless, yearning quality.

Equally distinctive are the long stretches of what Wagner called 'unending melody' – the phrases that join and overlap to give a seamless texture of romantic sound. These melodies are often built up from smaller units called **leitmotifs** (leading motifs). These are another fingerprint of Wagner's style. Each strongly characterised fragment is associated with a particular person, place, object or emotional state in the opera.

Grief
cellos

Desire
oboe

Glance
cellos

Love potion
cellos

You can hear this principle at work in the cello melody of bars 17–22 which is based on motif *x* shown in the music *left* (sometimes known as the 'Glance' motif). This leitmotif itself breaks down into two shorter motifs, *a* and *b*. When *x* begins to repeat in sequence motif *b* is changed from a falling 7th to a falling tone. In bars 19–20 the first note of *x* is tied over while the falling 7th of motif *b* is inverted to a rising 7th.

What makes Wagner's system so complex is the way his 'unending melody' mutates with the ease of microbes. So the portion of melody that some call the 'Love potion' (see *left*) is in fact made up of the same two motifs as the 'Glance' motif, but in reverse order and followed by motif *y* from the 'Desire' motif.

The score looks formidable but if you learn to recognise these leitmotifs you should come to a realisation (by listening rather than reading) that many parts double each other and that there are rarely more than two principal melodic lines sounding at once.

If you look at page 81 of the *New Anthology* you will see a forest of notes. But if you listen several times to the music between timings 7:13 to 7:30 on the CD you will hear horns and cellos playing the 'Grief' motif three times, the trumpets playing the 'Desire' motif twice, and the woodwind playing the 'Glance' motif four times.

The score looks complex because Wagner is adding more and more instruments as the music approaches its climax. Notice the upward thrusts of the ascending scales in the violins, and the excited tremolo in the violas (indicated by the strokes through note stems) as the tension builds. And it builds not towards a tonic chord, of course, but to the colossal scoring in bar 83 of the 'Tristan chord' that was heard in bar 2, and a second recapitulation of motifs that were heard earlier.

Towards the end of the prelude the interrupted cadence from bars 16–17 is repeated in bars 93–94. In the remaining bars the 'Glance' motif and 'Grief' motif are easy to spot as the prelude winds its way down to its inconclusive ending on the dominant of C minor (far from its opening key) – which then leads into the start of the opera.

Private study

1. What type of instrument is a cor anglais? What is the sounding pitch of the first note played by the cor anglais?
2. What is meant by an appoggiatura? Which note in bar 37 is an appoggiatura?
3. Briefly explain how Wagner creates a sense of excitement and tension in the prelude.
4. Name some of the features of this music that strike you as characteristic of romantic music, and that are not found in the 18th-century styles of *NAM 1* and *NAM 2*.

Prélude à L'Après-midi d'un faune (Debussy)

B *NAM 5* CD1 Track 5
Concertgebouw Orchestra
Conducted by Bernard Haitink

The faun in Debussy's 'Prelude to the Afternoon of a Faun' is an ancient pagan nature-god, guardian of herds and patron of country pursuits. The inspiration for the prelude was a poem by his friend Stéphane Mallarmé, the great French poet. The faun awakes in the shimmering heat of a summer afternoon and languidly plays his panpipes while watching two nymphs. His passion aroused, he seizes the water nymphs, but they are frightened by his burning kisses and the vision vanishes. As night falls he stretches himself voluptuously on the sand to sleep.

The poem is deliberately obscure, so it is not surprising that Debussy's form should be as fluid as the changing images of erotic dreams. Despite the work's title, it is not a prelude to something else, but a short and self-contained tone poem. Tone poems, or symphonic poems, developed from the programme music of Berlioz and the illustrative music of works such as Mendelssohn's *Midsummer Night's Dream* overture. Their primary purpose was to tell a story in music.

NAM 5 (composed in 1892–94) has a three-part (or ternary) structure in which the languid faun's theme (bars 1–4) is heard in sharp keys centred on E major in the two flanking sections (bars 1–54 and 79–110). The central section is based on a more impassioned theme in flat keys (centred on D♭ major) which is heard three times (woodwind in bars 55–62, upper strings in bars 63–74 and solo violin in bars 75–78). Listen to the music and make sure that you can recognise these main ideas. Try to decide what you feel are the most important features of the music and then see if you agree with our list below:

- complex rhythms that disguise a regular pulse
- melodic variation (rather than the development of motifs)
- rich colourful harmony that often seems to obscure the keys of the music rather than define them
- subtle orchestral textures.

All of these features contribute to a style of music in which the atmosphere created by colour, tone and texture seems more important than clearly-defined phrases and structures. This late romantic style, which looks forward to some features of 20th- century music, is known as impressionism. The term is borrowed from French painting of the period in which there is a similar interest in conveying the impression of light and movement, rather than giving an exact representation of shapes.

Mallarmé was delighted with the result which he said went further than his own poem in representing 'nostalgia and light with subtlety, malaise and richness of expression'.

Debussy's melodic style is very different to the constant development of motifs that we saw in Wagner's prelude. When we examine the way Debussy treats his opening flute melody we find that he:

- repeats it unchanged with an accompaniment of fluttering tremolo strings (bars 11–14)

- lengthens the first note and decorates the melody of bar 3 with demi-semiquaver triplets (bars 21–22)
- ends the phrase with a fast version of the first bar (bars 26–27)
- slows the whole melody down (bars 79-82 and 86-89)

... and so on. At no point does Debussy extract motifs and manipulate them to form new melodies. Instead he presents the same theme in various rhythmic and melodic variants, and in different textures and harmonisations.

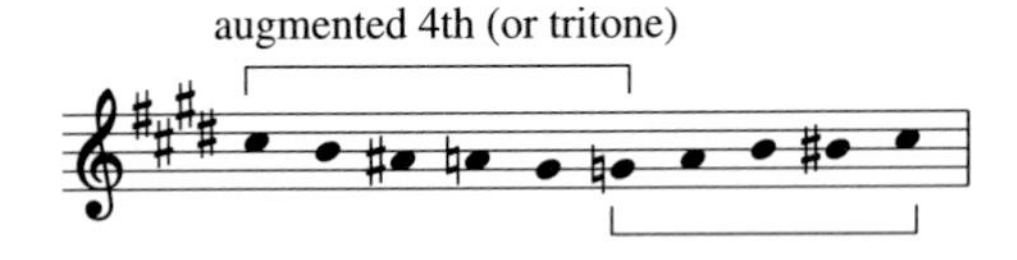

The importance of instrumental colour is apparent in the very first bar, in which the augmented 4th (or tritone) outlined by the opening motif is presented in the distinctive bottom octave of the flute's register. The lower notes of the flute are very quiet and so Debussy leaves the melody unobscured by any accompaniment. The tone colour then changes to that of soft horns, with delicate harp glissando and muted (*sourdine*) string accompaniment.

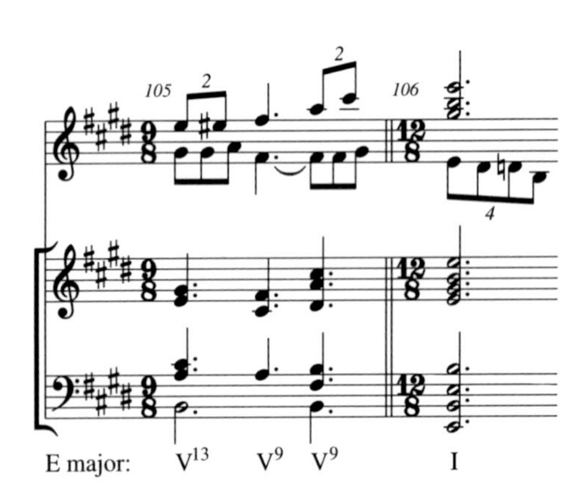

A taste of Debussy's harmonic style can be seen in the final perfect cadence (shown *left*). There is little tonal tension – the cadence seems to be enveloped in a haze of sound. This is partly attributable to the fact that the leading note (D♯) puts in a late and very quiet appearance in the dominant chord, and partly by the diatonic discords (7ths, 9ths, 11ths and 13ths above the dominant) that add sensuous colour rather than tonal direction. Debussy goes out of his way to ensure that a regular pulse will not be apparent by introducing lazy duplets and groups of four, completely disguising the compound-time beat as the music drifts timelessly to a close.

The music of the last five bars contain many examples of instrumental subtlety. Muted strings are divided into 12 parts to play the tonic chord in bar 106, but the two top notes are played by unmuted solo violins. Muted horns subtly colour the middle range and against this chord two harps play the four-quaver groups. In bar 107 two solo muted horns in 3rds are accompanied by muted first violins for the chromatic fragment from the opening motif of the work. In bar 108 the flute adds a 6th to the tonic chord (echoed by a harp harmonic), while the violins play an appoggiatura (A♯) that lasts six beats before it resolves. Tiny antique cymbals sound the root and 5th of the tonic chord and almost inaudible pizzicato cellos and basses bring the work to an end.

Private study

1. What do you think is meant by the instruction to the harpist in bar 1?
2. What is a glissando (harp, bar 4)?
3. The small circles over the last four harp notes indicate the use of harmonics. What does this term mean? (Look it up in a good dictionary of music if you are not sure.)
4. What do you notice about the number of performing directions in this piece compared with NAM 1?
5. Choose two passages that you feel are examples of interesting orchestration and explain why each of them is so effective.

Concerto for Double String Orchestra (Tippett)

A *NAM 6* CD1 Track 6
Academy of St Martin-in-the-Fields
Conducted by Neville Marriner

Tippett's use of two string orchestras in this concerto of 1939 produces contrasts that may remind us of the concertino-ripieno oppositions of the concerto grosso (as in *NAM 1*), although Tippett is contrasting groups of equal size. However the music is in a **modal** style that harks back much further, to the dancing polyphony of late 16th and early 17th-century string music such as the galliard by Anthony Holborne in *NAM 13*. In the galliard there is a constant shift between three minim beats in a bar (bars 1–2 and 4–5) and two dotted-minim beats (bars 3 and 7). This is reflected in the metrical shifts in bars 38–51 of Tippett's concerto – and Tippett even uses ancient devices such as the **phrygian cadence**, found in bars 15–16 of Holborne's galliard and in bars 20–21 of *NAM 6*.

But it is apparent from the start that Tippett's rhythms are more complex than those of Holborne. Listen to the first movement of the concerto (*NAM 6*) and concentrate on the rhythm.

The use of syncopation makes the music sound jazzy, but do you agree that at the start (and for most of the rest of the movement) there is no clear sense of a regular pulse, as you would expect in most types of jazz?

Instead we hear 'additive rhythms' of a type that composers such as Stravinsky and Bartók often used. In this type of rhythmic organisation there is a constant unit of time (the quaver in Tippett's concerto) which is too fast to be perceived as a pulse. These are gathered into irregular units that deny a regular pulse. At its simplest such units can produce the type of 3+3+2 rhythms that are found in Latin-American dances (as in bar 15 and other bars marked 'Beat 3'). At a more complex level additive rhythms can ride rough-shod over the bar lines, such as in the melody in the second orchestra during the first four bars.

At a more complex level still, different additive rhythms in contrasting strands of counterpoint can, in Tippett's own words,

> 'propel the music forward by differing accents, which tend to thrust each other forward'.

This is the case in the two-part counterpoint of the first four bars, and in the much more involved counterpoint at the end of the movement. It is this combination of two or more rhythmically independent strands that gives this movement its tremendous excitement.

The influences on Tippett's music are many and varied, and much of the interest comes from the ways in which he gives new life to traditional ideas by using and combining them in surprising ways.

The structure of the movement uses some techniques that would be familiar to Bach, and others that would be recognised by Haydn. On a small scale there is, embedded within the two contrasting contrapuntal strands of the first four bars, a number of motifs from which most of the rest of the movement is constructed. Take, for example, the oscillating two-pitch figure of the first four notes. In bars 8–12 it becomes a sequence (violins) that is imitated in **inversion** by violas and cellos. In bars 21–30 this syncopated figure becomes an accompaniment to a new motif (marked *scherzando* – jokingly). On a larger scale this two-note figure and the motif introduced by the second orchestra in bar 1, help us recognise the start of a sort of ritornello (bars 1–20) that recurs in whole or in part in bars 68–71, 129–146 and 194–197, rather like a ritornello structure in one of Bach's concertos.

But listen again and you will hear that these ritornellos signal the starting points for something that seems more like sonata form. The first ritornello (bars 1–20) corresponds with a 'first subject' and bars 33–67 serves as a 'second subject'. The 'development' (bars 68–128) does indeed manipulate motifs from the first part of the movement, but it is marked by a passage in which additive rhythms give way to simpler rhythms in 2/2 starting at bar 95. Look at the first orchestra staves and compare the violin parts in bars 95–96 with the cello and and bass parts two bars earlier. Do you see that the violins are playing the inverted theme in **augmentation** at bar 95? Now look at the cello and bass parts of bars 99–102. Can you say how this inverted theme has been changed again?

Eventually forward propulsion begins again and additive rhythms return in bars 107–112 until we reach the recapitulation. Almost the whole of the 'first subject' is repeated in bars 189–146 (compare them with bars 1–18) and the 'second subject' in bars 159–193 (which is a transposed and slightly modified repeat of bars 33–67).

The final 'ritornello', beginning in bar 194, signals the start of a coda in which a lyrical new cello melody (bars 202–208) is combined with earlier motifs, and the descending triadic figures of bars 15–16 are inverted to form the ascending figures in bars 210, 212 and 215. The movement concludes with a contrapuntal fireworks display that ends with a cadence on the note with which the movement began.

Private study

1. Why does Tippett use 8/8 and not 4/4 as the time signature?
2. Compare the music played by the three lowest parts of the first orchestra in bars 5–6 with the music in bars 1–2.
3. How is the opening motif from bar 1 treated when it returns (a) in bar 8 and (b) in bar 10?
4. What is the signficance of the instruction 'Beat 3' in bar 15?
5. Briefly mention some of the variety of string-orchestra textures that Tippett uses in this work.

Sample question 1

(a) Explain what you understand by any **two** of the following:

cembalo coda syncopation circle of 5ths

(b) Link each term you have chosen in your answer to question (a) to a context from a specific work. Name the work, the precise location and the instrument or voice parts involved.

Answer the following two questions only if you are taking the exam in 2001 or 2002.

(c) Mention four features of *NAM 1* which identify it as baroque music.

(d) Contrast the style of the solo viola part in *NAM 3* with Bach's writing for soloists in *NAM 1*.

Answer the following two questions only if you are taking the exam in 2003 or 2004.

(c) State what you understand is meant by impressionism in music and mention three features of *NAM 5* that could be described as impressionist.

(d) What are the important differences in the size of the orchestra, and the way in which it is used, between Haydn's symphony (*NAM 2*) and Wagner's prelude (*NAM 4*).

Sample question 2

(a) Explain what you understand by any **two** of the following:

sturm und drang leitmotif appoggiatura concertino

(b) Link each term you have chosen in your answer to question (a) to a context from a specific work. Name the work, the precise location and the instrument or voice parts involved.

Answer the following two questions only if you are taking the exam in 2001 or 2002.

(c) Mention four features of *NAM 3* which support the argument that Berlioz was particularly skilled at orchestration.

(d) Contrast the concerto movement by Bach (*NAM 1*) with the concerto movement by Tippett (*NAM 6*).

Answer the following two questions only if you are taking the exam in 2003 or 2004.

(c) Describe four different ways in which the opening motif of *NAM 4* is used later in Wagner's prelude.

(d) What are the main features of sonata form? Choose examples from *NAM 2* to illustrate your answer.

20th-century art music

One of the most characteristic features of 20th-century art music is its sheer diversity. With the invention of recording and radio, the ease of international travel, and the marketing of popular music on a global scale, people began to encounter a much wider range of music than ever before. This led to the co-existence of many new styles of music, including some that resulted from a rich cross-fertilisation between different musical cultures.

In the early decades of the century composers such as Mahler, Puccini, Rachmaninov, Elgar and Richard Strauss perpetuated the lush harmonies of the late 19th century. But other composers felt that the romantic style of previous years had become exhausted and bloated, and sought entirely new means of musical expression. For some this involved abandoning the idea of key and exploring new ways of organising pitch, for others it meant experimenting with the use of two keys at a time. For many it meant a much freer use of dissonance and an emphasis on new and exciting rhythms.

Some composers found inspiration in jazz, folk music or the styles of earlier times, others in the sounds of music from different cultures, such as the gamelan of Indonesian music. A number of composers experimented with new and unconventional sounds produced from traditional instruments and with various kinds of electronic music. At the other extreme, there were composers who thought that art music took itself far too seriously and who, like Erik Satie, drew on styles such as circus music and incorporated sounds such as rattling typewriter keys, gun shots and fog horns for deliberately satirical effect. And there were also those who felt that composers had come to exercise too much control over their music, and who therefore introduced random elements, dictated by chance events, to avoid predictability in their works.

This search for a new musical language was not always welcomed by the concert-going public, but audiences were also well supplied with music that invested more traditional types of music with the style and modernistic tone of the 20th century by composers such as Prokofiev, Shostakovich, Ravel, Walton and Britten.

In the late 20th century there was a reaction against the dissonance and preoccupation with technique that characterised much of the more modernist music of the preceding decades. Composers started to write in ways which seemed much more familiar to audiences than earlier **avant-garde** music, not least because they used many traditional techniques (such as a return to mainly **diatonic** harmony) presented in new and often very sparse ways. This type of music is referred to under the umbrella word of post-modernism, a term borrowed from the contemporary style of architecture that rejected the cold concrete structures of 1960s' buildings for forms that put the aesthetic and practical needs of people first.

Equally attractive to audiences in the late 20th century has been the new style of music known as minimalism, in which a small number of musical elements are hypnotically repeated with interlocking rhythms and slowly-changing textures (as seen in *NAM 16*).

Pulcinella Suite (Stravinsky)

A *NAM 7* CD1 Tracks 7–9
Academy of St Martin-in-the-Fields
Conducted by Neville Marriner

Stravinsky spent his early years in Russia where his music came to the attention of the impressario Diaghilev, who commissioned him to write a new work for the Russian Ballet to perform in Paris in 1910. *The Firebird* was a huge success and was followed the next year by *Petrushka* and in 1913 by a third ballet, *The Rite of Spring*. This was a much more revolutionary work and the highly rhythmic and very dissonant nature of the score was greeted with noisy protests during its first performance. However it was soon recognised as one of the most important works of its age, opening up new directions for the development of 20th-century music.

The first world war and the Russian revolution of 1917 prevented further visits of the Russian Ballet to Paris until the 1920 ballet season, for which Diaghilev suggested Stravinsky might arrange a score from the music of the 18th-century composer Pergolesi for a ballet. The result was *Pulcinella* – not so much an arrangement as a total reworking of the music in a new idiom, in which Stravinsky uses subtle dislocations of the phrasing and harmonies, unexpected countermelodies and thoroughly modern instrumentation. Stravinsky said Diaghilev was so shocked 'that he went about for a long time with a look that suggested "The Offended 18th Century"'.

Pulcinella was highly successful and in 1922 Stravinsky arranged some of the music from the ballet for chamber orchestra, in a suite suitable for concert performances. It is from this that the three movements in *NAM 7* are taken. Stravinsky later recycled some of the music in various suites for violin and piano, and cello and piano.

In the years after 1920 Stravinsky stayed mainly in Paris, then settled in America in 1939. *Pulcinella* had suggested new ways in which music could avoid the overbearing emotional grandeur of the late-romantic style – a more detached approach that emphasised clear textures, light orchestration, short forms and counterpoint. These principles were developed by Stravinsky and others into a style of composition known as neo-classicism (another example of which can be seen in *NAM 25*) – a confusing term, for many of the techniques derive more from baroque music than classical.

Sinfonia

The sources for *Pulcinella* were much wider than just the music of Pergolesi. The opening sinfonia (a baroque term for a piece of instrumental music, often at the start of a longer work) is based on a trio sonata written around 1750 by an Italian composer named Domenico Gallo. It was published in 1780 in an edition (probably the one that Stravinksy knew) which wrongly ascribed the music to Pergolesi, who had died in 1736 and who wrote in a rather earlier style than Gallo.

The use of oboes, bassoons and strings lends a baroque tone to the music, although the high bassoon writing in bars 7–13 is a much more modern touch. Horns were starting to appear in music around 1750 but they were used sparingly because only limited notes were available on 18th-century horns – they could never have attempted anything like the horn solo in bar 33.

Stravinsky's use of solo strings contrasting with the full body of strings echoes the similar divisions between soloists and tutti in the baroque concerto grosso (see *NAM 1*) and the movement uses the **ritornello** structure found in much baroque music – listen to the sinfonia and see if you can spot where the opening music (the ritornello) returns at intervals throughout the sinfonia.

There is also much to indicate that this is not baroque music. The **syncopation** in bars 1 and 3 is emphasised by appearing in all of the upper parts and Stravinsky adds extra dissonances to the harmony that would never be used by 18th-century composers. For instance the G-major chord at the start of bar 3 has an added A, allowing the second violin to use the bright sound of all three open strings (G, D and A) simultaneously. The differences become less subtle after bar 10, where a bar of 2/4 then 3/4 momentarily disrupts the quadruple pulse. Second violins take over the syncopation in bars 17–18, the open 5ths being emphasised by successive down bows (indicated by the signs above the notes).

Baroque composers generally write long, linear parts – but notice how Stravinsky uses just a few bass notes from the solo strings to give a surprising highlight to the second bassoon part in bar 14. The sequence in the cello at bars 24–26 is a device frequently heard in baroque music, but in the accompaniment a descending scale in crotchets is set against a descending scale in semibreves (and minims in the violas) to produce a succession of warm but very unbaroque dissonaces.

Gavotte with two variations

Aural tests on this movement and on the original gavotte, are given in *Aural Matters* (Bowman and Terry) pages 111–112 and 148–149.

This movement is a reworking of a gavotte for harpsichord by Giovanni Martini (known as 'Padre Martini'), dating from 1742. You can see the relationship between Stravinsky's music and its 18th-century original if you look at the following music, which is the start of Martini's baroque dance:

Compare this music with the first 14 bars of the gavotte in *NAM 7* and make a detailed note of precisely how Stravinsky has interpreted and added to the two-part texture of Martini's original. Remember that the horn in F sounds a 5th lower than written. What is the musical effect of the changes Stravinsky makes?

Like most baroque dances the gavotte is in **binary form**. Stravinsky scores it entirely for wind instruments. Notice the instrumentation of the varied repeat at the end – bassoons and horns at bar 25, and then a hint of the original two-part texture in a delicate duet for flute and bassoon four bars later.

The first variation introduces the combination of oboe and horns in two, three then four-part textures. Trumpet and trombone support the fuller texture in bars 43–50 and the variation concludes with purely double-reed tone. Notice how unexpected dissonances continue to remind us that this is modern music – at the start of bar 44 the woodwind sound a chord of G, but the brass resolutely stay on a chord of D, while in bar 51 the two oboes start a semitone apart before moving away in opposite directions. The second variation starts with exchanges between flute and horn while the bassoon adds a bubbling accompaniment of **alberti**-bass figures and arpeggios. Baroque music was frequently ornamented, but the rapid flute scales in bars 73, 76 and 78 are a decidedly modern interpretation of such embellishment.

Vivo

The original of this movement is a sonata for cello and **continuo** by Pergolesi, which Stravinsky rhythmically alters to create an amusing satire in circus-music style. The trombone introduces the main theme, with prominent use of glissando (produced with the trombone slide) doubled an octave lower by solo double bass (which sounds an octave lower than printed). Later the bass takes over the solo role and some **virtuoso** playing is needed in places such as bars 24–25. The double bass takes Pergolesi's cello part at bar 46, where the music briefly plunges into the tonic minor (F minor), the very high **tessitura** producing a thin tone which sounds like a parody of the original cello writing.

Did you notice that the snappy cadences in bars 33 and 37 sound like perfect cadences that have gone wrong? The first is essentially the progression D^7–G, but the off-beat and heavily accented D^7 includes a G, thus anticipating the tonic, and the tonic chord itself is thrown away – most of the strings don't even bother with it.

Private study

1. Compare bars 37–39 of the sinfonia with bars 24–26.
2. What are the main similarities between the gavotte and each of its two variations?
3. Comment on the chord progression in bar 37 of the vivo.
4. What do you notice about the way Stravinsky uses the orchestra in this work?
5. How can you tell that this is not baroque music?

Quartet Op. 22, movement 1 (Webern)

A *NAM 8* CD1 Track 10
Jacqueline Ross (violin),
Ruth MacDowell (clarinet),
Jan Steele (saxophone),
Mark Racz (piano)

One of the features of late-romantic music from the time of Wagner onwards was a tendency to fire up the emotional tension by using successions of chromatic dissonances over complex chords that seldom resolve on simple tonic harmony – a technique that can be clearly heard in *NAM 4*. Composers such as Mahler and Schoenberg followed in Wagner's footsteps, their dissonances becoming longer and their resolutions ever briefer, such familiar signposts as tonic and dominant chords becoming ever rarer.

By 1908 Schoenberg realised that by abandoning the concept of key entirely he could use expressive dissonance as freely as he wanted. Without key centres to act as focal points such **atonal** music at first proved difficult to structure and it was sometimes hard to avoid one particular note sounding like a home note. To help avoid this problem Schoenberg in the early 1920s adopted a technique known as serial music, in which a series of notes replaces tonality as the most important element of the music.

Serial music

The basis of the system is the arrangement of the 12 notes of the chromatic scale into a particular series called a note row. Each note can appear only once in the row, thus helping to avoid the sense that any individual note is more important than the others. The row can be used forwards, backwards (known as retrograde), in melodic **inversion** or in retrograde inversion. It can be transposed and in addition any note may be used in any octave. However in strict 12-note music the pitches must always appear in one of these predetermined patterns – and that is what gives such 12-note (or dodecaphonic) music its sense of unity and order.

Schoenberg, Berg and Webern all lived in Vienna and are collectively known as the second Viennese school – the first including composers such as Mozart and Haydn who worked in and around Vienna in the classical period. The word 'school' simply refers to similarities in style and not to any sort of educational establishment!

Although serialism sounds coldy mathematical it produced some highly concentrated, expressive, but very dissonant music. The technique was used by Schoenberg's pupils, Berg and Webern, as well as by Stravinsky (in the later part of his life) and by composers such as Boulez and Stockhausen.

Webern was particularly interested in the contrapuntal techniques of renaissance music, which permeate his own compositions. He mainly avoided anything which hints at romanticism, so do not expect to find sequences, familiar chords or lyrical melodies – his preference was for angular leaps of 7ths and 9ths. Webern's compositions are highly condensed and very short, and often written for unusual combinations of instruments, as in this quartet (which consists of *NAM 8* and just one other movement).

Now listen to the movement from Webern's quartet (written in 1930) and discuss your reactions with your teacher and the rest of your study group.

Structure

It takes time to get to grips with Webern's sound-world, but did you notice the overall shape? The music doesn't really seem to get going until bar 6, as if the first five bars are just an introduction, and the middle section (bars 16–23) seems to be differentiated by more activity, louder dynamics and wider leaps. At the end of bar 22 the five octaves between the violin's high C and the low C in the left hand of the piano forms the widest range of notes anywhere in the piece – it is clearly a central climax. If you compare bar 28 with bar 6 you might spot that there are similarities – in fact the final part is a varied repeat of bars 6–15.

Bars	*Structure*	
1–5	*	Introduction
6–15	A	Exposition
16–23	B	Development
24–27	*	Link
28–39	A	Recapitulation
39–43	*	Coda

This gives us the structure shown *left* – an introduction followed basically by a **ternary form** (ABA). The three sections marked * all use related material. In fact a more precise (if rather less obvious) description of the structure would be a modernised version of **sonata form**. The main parts of this are labelled in the diagram: the principal ideas are presented in an exposition, manipulated in various ways in a development, and then return in altered form in a recapitulation. This is a very traditional structure, although in classical music, sonata form essentially concerns the relationship between different keys and that is clearly not the case here.

Next take a look at the rhythm. Can you spot that almost every rhythm is derived from the three printed at the top of the next page?

The first of these rhythmic cells is played in bar 1 by the saxophone, and is immediately repeated by the violin in bar 2. The second is introduced by the left hand of the piano in bar 3 and is immediately repeated in the right hand. The third starts at the end of bar 3 in the violin and is immediately repeated by the saxophone and then the clarinet. While the rhythms themselves sound very modern the technique of basing a piece on a small number of repeated rhythms is very common in the music of J. S. Bach and many other baroque composers. Another more subtle reference to Bach comes in the length of the piece. *NAM 8* appears to show 43 bar numbers, but Webern himself numbered the second-time bars on the last page as variants of the first-time bars, giving 41 bars in all. The significance of this, and the potential homage it pays to the name of J. S. Bach is show in the margin note, *right*.

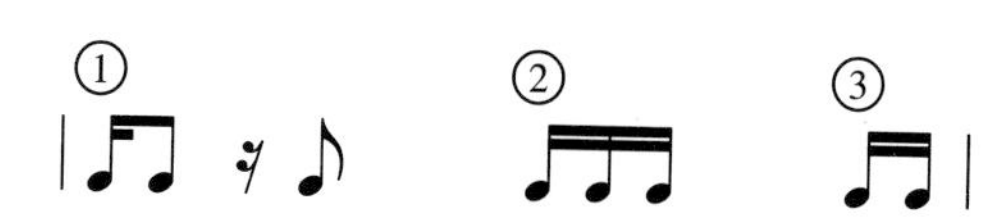

J. S. Bach had a fascination with the study of numerology – the meaning of numbers – and it is clear that he was aware that if the alphabet is translated into numbers (a=1, b=2, and so on) the name Bach can be represented by 14 (2+1+3+8) – a number that he often incorporated into his music in various ways. 'J. S. Bach' adds up to 41, the reverse of the digits 14 (I and J being the same in the Latin alphabet with which he was familiar). This interest in numbers was shared by Webern and it seems unlikely that the 41-bar length of the movement was mere coincidence.

Now let's turn our attention to the note row. The basic series of 12 pitches (called the prime order) is most easily seen in the saxophone part of bars 6–10. The pitches are printed *right* (but without the changes of octave). This is the melodic material from which the entire work is constructed.

Prime, bars 6–10:

The row returns in bars 28–32, at the start of the recapitulation, but here it is split between the instruments so that the tone colour is constantly changing. This sort of melody of differing tone colours is known in German as *Klangfarbenmelodie* (*Klang* = sound or tone, *farben* = colour, *melodie* = melody). The texture of the whole movement is very sparse – tiny groups of notes appear from out of the many rests as tiny dots of colour. This is sometimes described as *pointillist* – a French word used in art to describe paintings formed from tiny dots of colour.

Prime, bars 28–32:

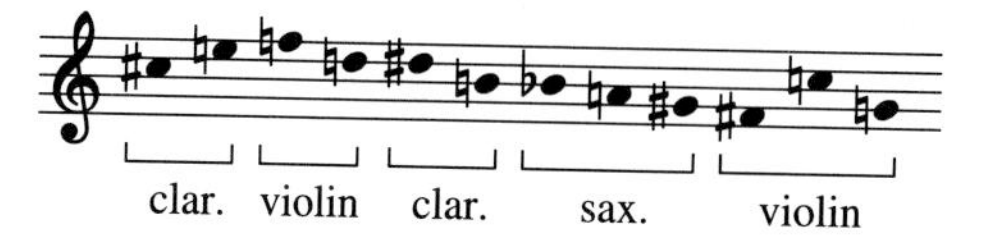

The stave *right* shows the inversion of the row. In other words, whereas the original series rises a minor 3rd, then a semitone, then drops a minor 3rd the inversion replicates all the intervals in the opposite direction – it falls a minor 3rd, then a semitone, then it rises a minor 3rd ... and so on. It can be seen in bars 1–5, divided among the instruments shown on the lower stave below:

Inversion:

Prime (transposed):

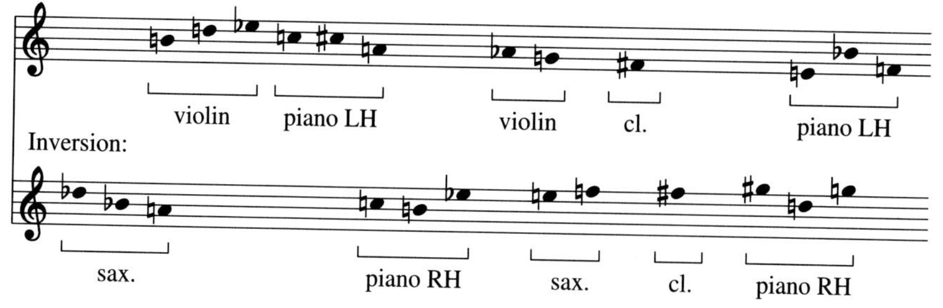

Do you recognise the pattern on the top stave in this example? It is the original prime order of the note row, transposed down by a tone. The combination of the two versions results in a type of **canon** known as a mirror canon because all of the intervals on the bottom stave are reflected on the other stave by the same intervals in the opposite direction. This is another technique found, in an entirely different musical context, in the music of Bach and it is a technique that Webern uses throughout this movement.

Earlier we mentioned that the note row and its inversion can both be used backwards in serial music. These versions both occur in the link passage (bars 24–27), which is essentially a retrograde version of the introduction. Notice how the saxophone pitches in bar 27 are the reverse of those in bars 1–2, and how the violin pitches in bars 26–27 are the reverse of those in bar 2. The following staves shows the complete retrograde versions (and the way they are laid out) and indicates how they compare with versions in the introduction (the various octave displacements have again been ignored for clarity):

Prime (transposed), bars 1–5:

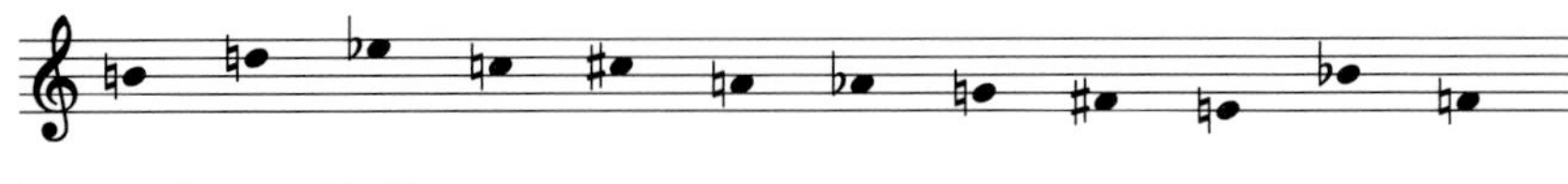

Retrograde, bars 24–27:

Inversion, bars 1–5:

Retrograde inversion, bars 24–27:

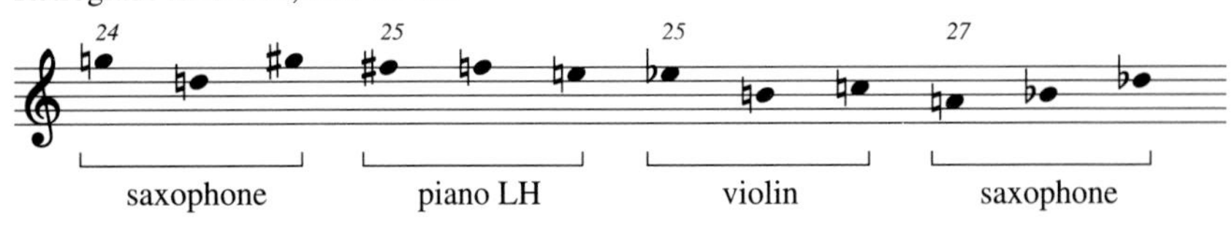

With typical attention to symmetry, Webern reworks this passage one more time to form the Coda (bars 39–43). However be aware that in many editions there is a missing treble clef before the last two saxophone notes.

We have touched on only a few of the complex interrelationships in this movement. Every note is derived from various forms of the note row, every rhythm from the basic rhythmic cells and canonic structures permeate the entire, intensely concentrated work.

If serialism is one of the compositional techniques you have chosen for Unit 2, this movement will repay close study. And if you have suitable performing resouces it would be well worth attempting your own performance of the movement – it is slow moving, but it will require very careful counting!

Private study

1. What is meant by the term atonality?
2. What is a note row?
3. What are the main ways in which a note row can be transformed in serial music?
4. What is a mirror canon?
5. How does Webern unify the use of rhythm in this movement?
6. Which piece do you feel relies more on traditional techniques of the past, this movement or the movements from *Pulcinella* in *NAM 7*?

String Quartet No. 8, movement 1 (Shostakovich)

B *NAM 9* CD1 Track 11
Coull Quartet

Shostakovich lived all his life in Russia, where he was one of several prominent composers who periodically suffered harsh criticism from the communist state. His opera *Lady Macbeth of Mtsensk* was denounced in 1936 (possibly by Stalin himself) as a representation of 'chaos instead of music' and banned for its decadent western modernism. Shostakovich toed the party line by supplying suitably heroic and wholesome music to glorify the state – only to be denounced again in the cultural purges of 1948. 'I know the party is right,' he humbly replied, 'I am deeply grateful for the criticism.'

An excerpt from Shostakovich's cello concerto is given in *Aural Matters* (Bowman and Terry) pages 152–153.

Shostakovich's relations with the all-powerful state became easier after Stalin's death, but he was deeply humiliated by being forced to join the Communist party in 1960 – the price he paid for the removal of the ban on some his earlier works. In July that year Shostakovich visited Germany where he saw the remains of the city of Dresden after its intensive bombing in the second world war. This experience directly inspired his eighth string quartet, completed in just three days and dedicated to the 'memory of the victims of fascism and war'.

There can be little doubt that he saw himself as one of the victims – he planned to commit suicide after being forced to join the Communist party and the quartet is full of quotations from his earlier works, almost as if he was reliving his earlier experiences. In addition Dmitry Shostakovich identifies himself with the music through a four-note cell, first heard in the opening cello notes: D–E♭–C–B♮. In German these pitches are known as D–Es–C–H and they transliterate to D Sch(ostakovich), a musical encryption of the German version of part of the composer's name. He used this motto in other works, but in the eighth quartet it permeates the music and from its use the quartet derives a powerful sense of unity.

Russian is written in the cyrillic alpahabet and this can result in inconsistency when names are transliterated. You may find books refer to 'Dimitri' and German scores that call the composer Schostakowitsh.

The autobiographical nature of the work is confirmed by a touching moment in the final movement when the DSCH motif is heard in counterpoint with a theme from that fateful work of so long before, *Lady Macbeth* – a theme depicting a convoy of prisoners en route to Siberia.

Shostakovich was obliged by circumstances to be a conservative composer, and this is reflected in his choice of the traditional instrumentation for a quartet – two violins, viola and cello – contrasting strongly with the more novel instrumentation of Webern's quartet. It is also reflected in some of the techniques he uses in this first movement. Listen to it now and comment on the way the DSCH motto is introduced by the four instruments.

You probably noticed that the rhythms are very simple and that each instrument enters in turn, low to high, with the same motif, but starting on different pitches in a series of imitative entries. What do you notice about the **tessitura** of the string parts? Do you agree that the tessitura helps make the opening sound sombre?

At the end of bar 11, DSCH is heard in an entirely different texture – three parts in octaves against a viola G. In the first violin part the last note of the motto overlaps with the first note of a quotation (in greatly expanded note-lengths) of the opening theme from the composer's first symphony (bars 13–22), the work that had established his reputation some 34 years earlier. DSCH then returns, to be followed by a descending chromatic scale over a long-held double **pedal** on a bare 5th.

Another reference to DSCH (cello, bar 46) leads to a central section in which the simple idea introduced by the first violin in bar 50 is developed into a second violin **countermelody** to the long, slow first violin theme that begins in bar 55. This duet is accompanied throughout by more long pedals, this time in octaves, on C and G.

The return of DSCH in **augmentation** at bar 79 heralds the start of a restatement of material from the first section, but now with a number of changes. Instead of imitative entries the opening motif is presented in an entirely **homophonic** texture, harmonised with three simple but unrelated root-position triads (G major, E♭ minor and F major) and then a biting dissonance in bar 82. This section is greatly curtailed and Shostakovitch reverses the order of the remaining sections so that the chromatic melody appears next (bar 87). It is transferred to the cello above which the violins in 3rds at bar 89 hint at a warmer harmonisation. DSCH is heard in the violins (bar 104–106) again overlapping with the quoted theme from the first symphony (bar 106). The DSCH motto appears one final time in bar 118 and then all of the instruments sink to their lowest notes. The second violin briefly refers to the accompanying motif from the central section (bar 122). On the last repetition of this the A♭ is notated as G♯ (known as an enharmonic change) to form a link to the second movement, which is in the remote key of G♯ minor.

Private study

1. What are the only two pitches played by the viola in bars 50–79?
2. Compare bars 87–92 with bars 28–33.
3. What effect do you feel the long pedal notes have on the character of the music?
4. Briefly describe some of the different types of texture used in this movement.

Sonatas and interludes (John Cage)

B *NAM 10* CD1 Tracks 12–14
Joanna MacGregor

It should be mentioned straight away that, while it is tempting to mount a performance of this work, serious damage can be done to expensive pianos by even touching the strings with a sweaty finger, let alone pushing objects between its strings. Resist the temptation unless you have permission to use a suitable instrument in this way.

The American composer John Cage studied with Schoenberg and initially used techniques derived from serial music. However his employment as composer for a modern-dance company soon led to an interest in the rhythmic possibilities of music and works for percussion, including the percussive potential of the 'prepared' piano. This is an ordinary piano that is transformed into a multi-purpose percussion instrument with a range of different **timbres** by means of inserting various objects between the strings.

Although the three movements in *NAM 10* are short, the complete work of 16 sonatas (separated by four interludes) is substantial, taking over an hour to perform. It was finished in 1948, at a time when Cage was becoming interested in eastern philosophies such as Zen Buddhism. Cage himself said that the 16 sonatas were intended to express the eight traditional Indian emotions – mirth, sorrow, fear, anger, the heroic, erotic, wondrous and odious. However if you compare *NAM 10* with *NAM 58–59* your impression is likely to be of how closely the prepared piano reflects not the music of India but another characteristic sound of the east – the music of the Indonesian gamelan.

Cage was a pioneer in many aspects of the **avant-garde** music of his day, including electronic music, graphic notation and music that is determined as much by chance events as by the will of the composer (aleatoric music). His pursuit of the last of these led to a certain notoriety, not unlike artists who present dead animals preserved in chemicals as works of art. Most famous is *4'33"* (the title referring to the duration of the piece) which contains nothing but performance directions and rests. The work therefore consists of whatever sounds happen to occur in and around the auditorium during this period of time, usually embarrassed coughs and muffled giggles from the audience. Other works included music determined by whatever happened to be being broadcast on simultaneous radio channels and music determined by the throw of dice.

Cage's instructions for preparing the piano are printed at the start of the piece. He explained why these needed to be so precise:

> I learned many essential things about the prepared piano, only in the course of the years. I did not know, at first, for instance, that very exact measurements must be made as to the position of the object between the strings and I did not know that, in order to repeat an obtained result, that a particular screw or bolt, for instance, originally used, must be saved.

It is clear that Cage originally regarded the precise timbre of each note as an essential element in the work. However in 1973 he said that that the table of preparations need not be followed and that pianists could determine their own ways of preparing the piano, thus introducing a significant random element into performances of the *Sonatas and Interludes*.

Because the prepared piano can produce sounds of indeterminate pitch, Cage bases the construction of the pieces on rhythmic rather than melodic ideas. An important part of this is the way the entire piece relates to its component parts. For example in the first sonata an opening phrase of 28 crotchets (bars 1–7) is made up of rhythmic cells in the following order.

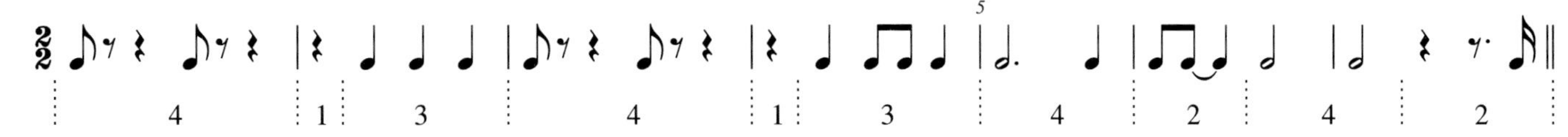

The seven-bar pattern consisting of units in the proportions 4–1–3 repeated, followed by 4–2 repeated, determines the proportions (although not the rhythms) of the entire sonata:

Bars 1–7	28 crotchets	= 4 × 7
Bar 8	7 crotchets	= 1 × 7
Bars 9–12	21 crotchets	= 3 × 7
Bars 13–19	28 crotchets	= 4 × 7
Bars 20–26	14 crotchets	= 2 × 7

The indication *una corda* at the head of the score refers to the left pedal of the piano. The figure 8 above a treble clef indicates music to be played an octave higher than written, while 15 instructs the performer to play two octaves higher than written. The end of these transposed sections is indicated by the word *loco*, meaning 'place' (that is, in normal position).

Cage's concept of a sonata derives from the baroque keyboard sonatas of composers such as Scarlatti. Each of the three sonatas in *NAM 10* is a short, single-movement work in **binary form** in the pattern ‖:A:‖:B:‖. Each sonata establishes its own mood. The first is mainly chordal and includes chord clusters (groups of adjacent notes sounded simultaneously) in bar 10. The second is built on mainly **monophonic** and two-part textures, and makes prominent use of the tritone (three whole tones) between A and E♭. The third establishes a more contemplative mood with the tolling of a single note in the left hand throughout its first section.

Private study

1. Comment on Cage's use of dynamics in the sonatas.
2. Is every aspect of this piece totally new or does Cage's music relate to existing musical traditions in any way?
3. How do the first and third sonatas contrast in texture?
4. What are the two main structural devices used in the sonatas?

Sequenza III for female voice (Berio)

A *NAM 11* CD1 Track 15
Cathy Berberian

The Italian composer Luciano Berio wrote a number of works for his wife, the famous singer Cathy Berberian, who performs this piece on CD1. The works in his series of pieces entitled *Sequenza* each explore and extend the technique of an unaccompanied voice or instrument, and all make considerable demands on the performer particularly in their speed and requirements for unusual methods of sound production. Berio said that the title is 'meant to underline that the piece was built from a sequence of harmonic fields from which the other, strongly characterised musical functions were derived'.

Berio's other 'Sequenzas' include works for flute, harp, piano, trombone, viola, oboe, violin, clarinet and trumpet.

Sequenza III, written in 1966, includes a strong element of 'performance art' as the composer's opening note makes clear. The soloist may be a singer, an actor or (preferably for this piece) someone who is both. It also encompasses a vast range of vocal techniques, outlined on page 172 of the *New Anthology*. Berio said:

> I have always been very sensitive to the excess of connotations that the voice carries, whatever it is doing. From the grossest of noises to the most delicate singing, the voice always means something, always refers beyond itself and creates a huge range of associations.

These associations are intensely concentrated in *Sequenza III*, which highlights the extreme flexibility of the voice and the way in which human states (tense, witty, urgent, giddy and so on) can change in a moment. Laughing transforms itself into operatic high notes, for instance, or a cough becomes a part of the vocal expression. The three main elements of the piece are formed by:

- ✦ fragmenting the text, often into single vowel sounds
- ✦ using vocal gestures such as muttering, coughing or laughing
- ✦ creating a range of expression through abrupt shifts in mood.

The transitions between these, and between the various levels of speech and song, happen very fast – so fast, in fact, that you can get the impression that all occur at once.

The use of graphic scores became popular in the 1960s. The type of score used here allows the composer to specify the order of events and their timing. The indications of pitch and rhythm are relative and allow the performer some freedom of interpretation.

Remember that this work will provide a useful model for both Timbres (extended techniques) and Theatre Music in Unit 2.

Private study

1. In what ways does this piece make greater demands on the performer than *NAM 10*?
2. Is *Sequenza III* merely a showpiece for the voice, or does it make more profound statements as a work of art?
3. Why do you think Berio wrote this specifically for a female voice?
4. In what ways might *Sequenza III* challenge an audience used to listening to more traditional music? Do you think that such a challenge to orthodox views can have beneficial results?

New York Counterpoint (Reich)

B *NAM 12* CD1 Track 16
Roger Heaton

An extract from a minimalist work by Steve Martland, dating from 1990, is included in *Aural Matters* (Bowman and Terry) pages 155–156.

Steve Reich is an American composer who studied with Berio and the French composer Milhaud. He also studied drumming with the Ewe tribe in Ghana (see *NAM 62*) and played in a Balinese gamelan (see *NAM 59*).

New York Counterpoint was written in 1985 and is an example of the music of the post-modernist movement of the late 20th century, which has seen a move away from the complex intellectual ideas and dissonance of earlier generations. Reich's work is minimalist – it uses a small number of entirely **diatonic** ideas, woven into a repetitive tapestry of counterpoint. Unlike *NAM 11*, the movement has a clear pulse and the **syncopated** themes give the work a popular appeal. Indeed Reich's music is sometimes referred to as a cross-over style. It is as likely to be found in the pop fusions section of a CD shop as in the classical-music department and his music has often been used for television advertisements.

Like *NAM 11 New York Counterpoint* is written for a solo performer, but the use of pre-recorded backing tracks to support the live soloist enables the texture to build up from the two-part texture of the opening to a full 11 parts at bar 27. 'New York' refers to the hectic city life reflected in the music (*NAM 12* is just the slow middle movement of the work). 'Counterpoint' refers to the repetitive free **canons** formed by the staggered entries of the parts. The hypnotic nature of this repetitive texture is punctuated by three pulsating chords, entering in bars 27, 33 and 39. These are used again in bars 47–65, thus providing not only a **homophonic** contrast with the counterpoint, but also a simple means of structuring the piece.

New York Counterpoint is a useful model for several options in Unit 2, including Post-modernism, Fusions and compositional techniques using minimalist textures.

Private study

1. How do the parts in bars 1–2 relate to each other?
2. How do the parts played by clarinet 5 and the live clarinettist in bars 3–6 relate to the music in bars 1–2?
3. In which bar does the live clarinettist start playing material unrelated to the backing tracks?

4. What is the difference between a contrapuntal texture and a homophonic texture?

Finally, remember that although questions on this Area of Study will only require you to know the works discussed in this chapter, there are many other 20th-century works in the *New Anthology* that will help inform your study of the topic, including *NAM 6, 19, 25, 31, 32, 40* and *41*.

Sample question 1

(a) Explain what you understand by any **two** of the following:

imitation   tremolo   retrograde   binary form

(b) Link each term you have chosen in your answer to question (a) to a context from a specific work. Name the work, the precise location and the instrument or voice parts involved.

Answer the following two questions only if you are taking the exam in 2001 or 2002.

(c) State four ways in which *NAM 11* is identifiable as a work of music rather than as purely a piece of experimental theatre.

(d) In what ways do *NAM 7* and *NAM 8* illustrate two very different approaches to the use of techniques that derive from earlier music?

Answer the following two questions only if you are taking the exam in 2003 or 2004.

(c) Describe four different types of sound available from the prepared piano, indicating how each contributes to the overall effect in *NAM 10*.

(d) Explain the significance of the first four notes of *NAM 9* and explain how they are used in the rest of this movement.

Sample question 2

(a) Explain what you understand by any **two** of the following:

canon   Klangfarbenmelodie   ritornello   double pedal

(b) Link each term you have chosen in your answer to question (a) to a context from a specific work. Name the work, the precise location and the instrument or voice parts involved.

Answer the following two questions only if you are taking the exam in 2001 or 2002.

(c) Indicate **four** aspects of *NAM 8* that identify it as a 20th-century work.

(d) Comment on Stravinsky's use of instruments in *NAM 7*.

Answer the following two questions only if you are taking the exam in 2003 or 2004.

(c) Identify and describe four different string textures used by Shostakovich in *NAM 9*.

(d) Compare Cage's use of a solo performer in *NAM 10* with Reich's use of a solo performer in *NAM 12*.

Music for small ensemble

The ensemble music in this Area of Study ranges from pieces intended for domestic performance by amateurs, such as *NAM 13*, through spendid ceremonial music (*NAM 14*) to **chamber music** written for professionals to perform and listeners to enjoy (most of the later pieces in this chapter). The pieces also reflect a wide range of musical styles:

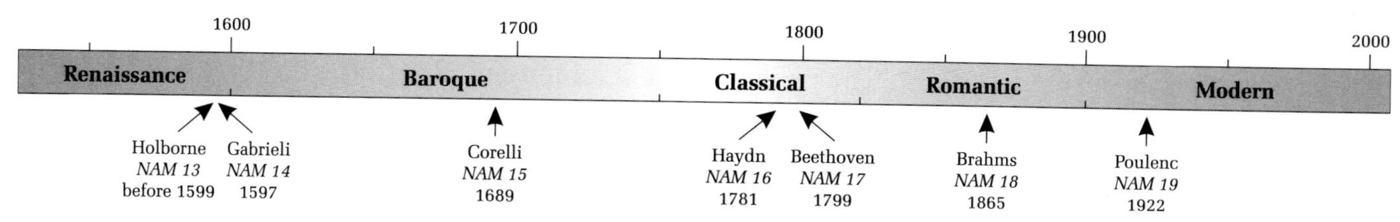

Try to study at least some of this music by performing it. Look for ways in which parts can be adapted for other instruments or filled-in with the help of some music technology if you don't have all the necessary resources.

Pavane and Galliard (Holborne)

A *NAM 13* CD2 Tracks 1–2
Rose Consort of Viols

Life in Elizabethan times is often described as 'merrie England' but it might just as well be called 'melancholy England'. While the educated classes were happy enough to 'sing we at pleasure, content is our treasure' (*NAM 34*) there also runs through the literature and music of the time a deep strain of melancholy and an awareness that death was never far away.

This preoccupation with sadness is clear in Dowland's song *Flow my tears* (*NAM 33*) which starts with a motif that was associated with tears – a **stepwise** descent from tonic to dominant, outlining the interval of a 4th and flowing from an initial dotted note. This motif can also be heard at the start of Holborne's pavane *The image of melancholy*, published in 1599, and at the start of Sweelinck's 'Tearful Pavane' (*NAM 20*) composed only a few years later.

Holborne's other titles in the same collection include *The Sighes*, *The Funerals* and *The Teares of the Muses*.

The pavane (or paduana) was a moderately slow courtly dance in duple time that was often paired with a more sprightly triple-time dance called the galliard. By the late 16th century these basic dance rhythms were often obscured by dense **counterpoint**, as is the case in Holborne's pavane and galliard. This is music for the ear rather than for the feet. It would have been played domestically for the delight of the amateur performers themselves, so they are all given parts of independent melodic interest.

In England at this time an ensemble of solo instruments was called a consort. Music for such consorts was usually played on whatever instruments were available, as indicated in the note printed above the score. On CD2 Holborne's dances are played by a consort of viols of different sizes. These cousins of the violin family were bowed and fretted instruments, held on the lap or between the knees. They were popular from the 15th to the early 18th centuries. A consort of five viols was the most popular medium for the performance of chamber music, but wind instruments (such as a consort of recorders) were also used. If the ensemble included instruments of different types it was called a 'broken consort'.

When following the score, notice that the middle stave uses the alto C clef – the middle line of the stave is middle C and consequently the first note is A. Also be aware that the parts frequently cross each other so, for example, the highest notes in bar 41 are played by the middle part.

Dances at this time usually consisted of several sections, each repeated. The pavane has three sections, the first and last ending with a perfect cadence in the tonic key of D major and the second ending with a perfect cadence in the dominant key, A major.

Today we write D minor with a key signature of one flat, but at this time it was usual to flatten the 6th degree of the minor scale (B♭ in this key) only where needed.

The galliard is in D minor and also falls into three sections. The first and last end with a perfect cadence and **tierce de Picardie** in the tonic key of D minor, while the second ends with a **phrygian cadence** (IVb–V) in the same key.

Both dances share features common to much Elizabethan music:

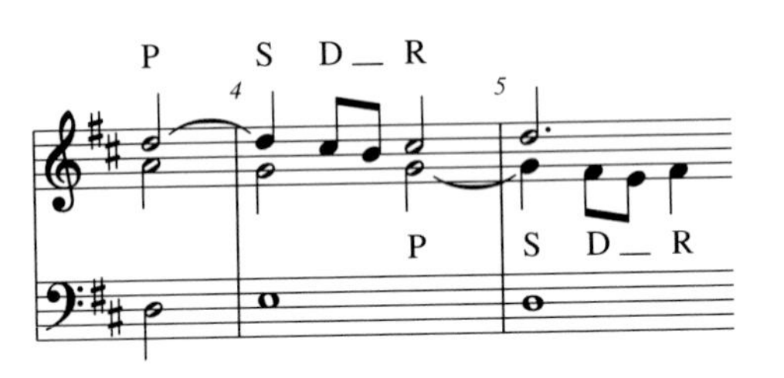

- ✦ All of the chords are in root position or first inversion.
- ✦ The only on-the-beat discords are **suspensions**, often decorated as they resolve and sometimes overlapped with suspensions in other parts. In the example *left* you can see how the dissonant 7th between the top part and the bass at the start of bar 4 is prepared (P), suspended (S) decorated (D) and resolved (R). As it resolves to C♯ the second part down starts a similar process with a note that is to form a 4th above the bass in bar 5. Be aware that not all tied notes are suspensions: those in bars 1 and 2 of the pavane do not form discords. There are only three suspensions in the galliard: can you find them?
- ✦ In the pavane there are prominent **false relations** between C♯ and C♮ in bar 11 and between G♮ and G♯ in bar 13. These add to the sense of melancholy and so, not surprisingly, there are no false relations in the rather jollier galliard.
- ✦ Frequent use of **imitation**. For example the 'melancholy' falling figure in the uppermost part at the start is imitated in the second half of bar 1. At the start of the second section this figure is adapted to make a longer motif, imitated by the second part down in bars 18–19. At the start of the third section each part except the lowest enters with a scalic figure that is an **inversion** of the initial 'melancholy' motif, again treated in imitation.

The texture of Holborne's pavane is unrelentingly thick: the parts form a web of five-part counterpoint with only a couple of rests.

The Latin title, *Ecce quam bonum*, means 'Behold how good' (the opening words of psalm 133). Its significance to the music is not entirely clear, but many of the non-English titles in Holborne's collection refer to the literary works of Dante written some 300 years earlier, and this particular psalm quotation is found in Dante's *De Monarchia*, a medieval treatise on government.

Despite a similar lack of rests, the texture of the galliard is more varied, with imitation in the first and last sections and a largely **homophonic** central section. But the most obvious feature of this dance is the **syncopation** in its first section. There are two types. The first is caused by the off-beat entry of the rising dotted figure in the fourth voice down. This syncopation is evident every time the rising figure enters (the second crotchet of bars 2, 5 and 6).

The second type of syncopation is caused by alternating bars of 3/2 and 6/4 time. There are clearly three minim beats in each of the first two bars, but in bar 3 the metre changes to two dotted-minim beats. This is caused by the rhythms of each of the five parts and by the change of chord halfway through the bar. This sort of metrical interruption is called a **hemiola**, and it is a characteristic of many triple-time dances written in the baroque as well as the renaissance (see page 58).

Notice that Holborne gives no performing directions, not even tempo or dynamic markings. This was normal in music of this period. However the performers introduce variety by adding ornamentation when each of the sections is repeated, some of which is shown *right*. Decoration of this sort was an important performing convention at the time this music was written. Can you identify other places where the music is ornamented in the repeats?

Upper 3 parts (bars 9–10)

Second part (bars 13–15)

Private study

1. What is a false relation? Identify the location of a false relation in bars 17–33 of the pavane.
2. In bar 1 of the galliard, how does the music played by the fourth part down relate to the music played by the top part?
3. Where does a hemiola occur in bars 4–8 of the galliard?
4. Why is this music for the ear rather than the feet?
5. What are the main similarities and differences between the pavane and the galliard?
6. Briefly describe how the sounds of viols on CD2 differ from the sounds of modern string instruments.

Sonata pian' e forte (Giovanni Gabrieli)

B *NAM 14* CD2 Track 3
His Majesty's Sagbutts and Cornetts
Directed by Timothy Roberts

Although Venice is a tiny city, situated on a group of islands in a lagoon at the head of the Adriatic, it accrued enormous wealth through trade with the middle and far east, including China. As a result Venetians were able to erect palaces and churches of the utmost splendour to line the banks of their city's canals, and to impress visitors with the scale of their entertainment and music.

Most magnificent of all was the palace of their elected leader (the Doge) and its chapel, now the cathedral, of St Mark. It was at this church that Giovanni Gabrieli was organist. Motets such as *NAM 27* for two or more choirs, instrumental ensembles and organs resounded from the four galleries that surround the central dome.

The *Sonata pian'e forte* comes from a collection of works by Gabrieli published in 1597. These are all ensemble compositions for eight to 15 instruments. The *Sonata pian' e forte* is famous because it is among the first works in which the composer indicated dynamic levels (*pian'* is an abbreviation of *piano*).

Instruments

Gabrieli also specified the instruments that make up the two four-voice 'choirs' (*coro* means a choir – here a choir of instruments). The *cornetto* (cornett in the score) should not be confused with the cornet, which is a brass-band instrument, or an Italian ice-cream. It is a wooden wind instrument with a mouthpiece similar to that on a brass instrument, but it has a softer tone than the trumpet.

'Violin' in the 16th century could refer to several sizes of the violin family. In this sonata its range dictates that it could be played on a viola (in bar 28 it descends to E a minor 3rd lower than the modern violin's lowest note). A viola is used for this part on CD2.

The parts for trombones 1 and 2 are printed with a tenor C clef. This indicates that the second line down on the stave is middle C. Thus the first note of the sonata is the D a tone above middle C.

Both choirs contain three trombone parts and on CD2 each choir also includes a chamber organ (they can only just be heard). Gabrieli did not write parts for them, but by 1597 it was becoming common practice for an organ to be used to support sacred music, both vocal and instrumental.

Textures

The texture is dominated by the dark sonority of the six trombones, instruments associated with solemnity and priestly ritual. It has been suggested that the *Sonata pian' e forte* might have been played during the most solemn part of the Latin mass. It was certainly intended for a building such as St Mark's, where the choirs of instruments could be positioned in opposite galleries for maximum stereo effect in the echoing acoustic. It is the opposition (bars 1–13 and 14–25), combination (bars 26–31), **antiphonal** exchanges (bars 37–40) and echo effects (bars 45–49) of these choirs that are the main feature of the sonata.

Several other features add to the solemnity of this music:

- the textures are never less than four parts (one complete choir)
- although mostly contrapuntal, the only obvious imitation occurs in the last ten bars (eg the entries marked *forte* in bars 71–72)
- there is a preponderance of root-position triads, such as those in the **circle of 5ths** in bars 36–41
- the music is more **modal** than much written at this time.

The dorian mode is similar to D minor, but it uses B♮ and C♮ rather than B♭ and C♯.

This last point requires explanation. The sonata is in the dorian mode: this mode can be found by playing an octave of white notes on the piano from D to D. The mode is here transposed to G, giving the notes G–A–B♭–C–D–E–F–G. However accidentals are frequently used to avoid awkward intervals, to form a tierce de Picardie at the end of an important section or to construct cadences such as the phrygian cadence in bars 44–45 and the final plagal cadence.

Many of the main stylistic features of the music can be seen in the following quotation of bars 12–17 and most should be familiar from your study of *NAM 13*, which was written at much the same date:

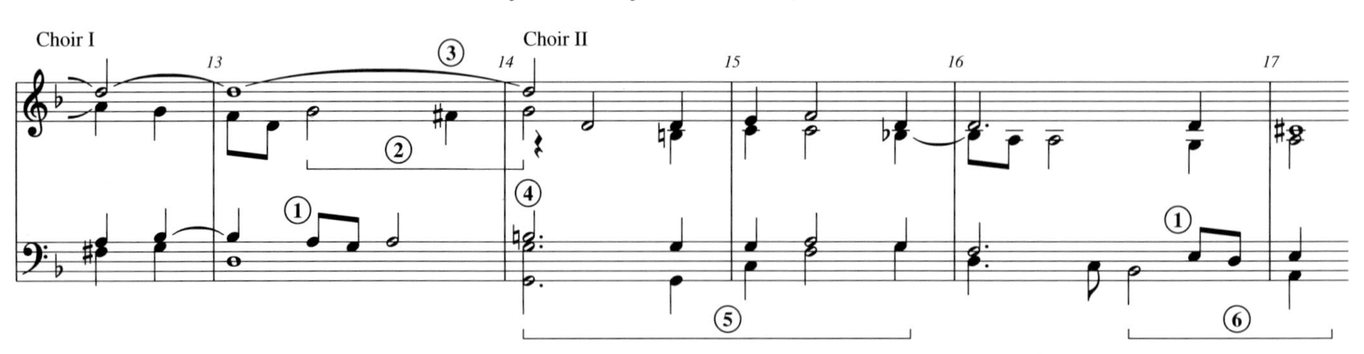

① passing dissonances
② a suspension
③ F♯ is outside the mode but it allows a perfect cadence on G
④ a tierce de Picardie
⑤ a progression of modal root position triads
⑥ two chords (IVb–V in D minor) that form a phrygian cadence.

Private study

1. Why is St Mark's Venice significant to this composition?
2. How many suspensions are there in bars 22–25?
3. When both choirs first play together in bar 26 on what chord do they start?
4. What do you notice about the rhythm on pages 198–199?
5. With what type of cadence does the sonata end?
   How is the final chord of this cadence modified?
6. What is a cornett?

Trio sonata in D, 4th movement (Corelli)

A *NAM 15* CD2 Track 4
Fitzwilliam Ensemble

When Gabrieli wrote *NAM 14* the word sonata simply meant a work that should be played rather than sung. By the late 17th century 'sonata' had come to mean something more specific. For the most famous musician of the period, the Italian composer Arcangelo Corelli, it meant the four-movement *sonata da chiesa* (church sonata) or the multi-movement *sonata da camera* (chamber sonata).

Both types of trio sonata were written for two melody instruments (always violins in Corelli's trio sonatas) supported by a **continuo** group comprised of a bass instrument, such as a cello, and a harmony instrument. Corelli specified that the latter should be an organ in his church sonatas while in 12 of the chamber sonatas a harpsichord is mentioned. Most of the church sonatas contain four untitled movements in the order slow–fast–slow–fast, while most of the chamber sonatas begin with a prelude which is followed by a number of dance movements. However dance movements also appear in the church sonatas – in style if not in name. This movement is essentially a gigue (see page 70), the dance which Corelli and many other baroque composers often used to conclude their multi-movement compositions (see *NAM 21*).

For another movement from a trio sonata by Corelli see *Aural Matters* (Bowman and Terry) pages 110–111. For a movement from a solo sonata by Corelli see *Aural Matters in Practice* (Bowman and Terry) pages 38–39.

If possible try to perform *NAM 15* with your fellow students. If you don't have violinists available it would work very well on two flutes. Experiment with different ways of realising the figured bass, using a piano or a soft pipe-organ voice on a synthesizer.

Corelli's string writing is idiomatic. This means that each part is conceived in terms of the instrument for which it is written rather than being a melodic line that could equally well be played on any available instrument (as in Holborne's pavane and galliard). The range covered by these parts is larger than in earlier periods. This can be seen in bars 34–35 where the first violinist is required to play in third position (that is with the left hand moved further up the fingerboard).

NAM 15 is the last movement from a trio sonata in a collection of 12 *Sonate da chiesa a tre* (church sonatas in three parts) published in 1689. The numbers and other symbols below the bass stave indicate the type of chords that should be improvised by the organist. For example, 6 indicates a first-inversion chord while no number means a root-position chord. Most of these figures were added by a 19th-century editor of this music. Nevertheless this **figured-bass** part reveals that Corelli's harmony is largely confined to root position and first-inversion triads seasoned with dissonant suspensions that usually resolve by step to a consonant note. Thus nearly every 7 (which indicates a dissonant 7th above the bass) is followed by 6 – a consonant 6th above the same bass note.

The fact that there are three parts explains the term 'trio sonata' but, as we have seen, the continuo normally needs two players so, paradoxically, the trio sonata is usually music for four performers.

Corelli's **diatonic** harmonic progressions clarify the **binary form** 𝄆A𝄇𝄆B𝄇 of the movement. The movement starts in D major and then modulates to a perfect cadence in the dominant key of A major in bars 10–11, in which key it remains until the first double bar. The B section returns to the tonic after which, beginning with the A♯ (the leading note of B minor) in bar 26, it passes through several related keys until the tonic is regained in bars 36–37. This wider range of modulations in the B section is typical of binary form.

The texture of the music is often widely-spaced, with the violins high and often crossing, and the bass sometimes three octaves lower (as in bar 12), the gap between them being filled by the organ.

The movement begins like a fugue, based on the subject heard in the first two bars. This is followed by the real **fugal** answer played by the second violin ('real' because it is exactly the same melody as the subject, 'answer' because it sounds a 4th below the subject). The final entry comes in the bass at bar 6. At the start of the B section the fugal subject is heard in free **inversion** with the imitative violin II and bass parts now entering only a bar apart so forming the fugal texture known as **stretto**. Most of the melodic material derives from the quaver and semiquaver motifs in the subject.

The hemiola in bar 26 as it is written:

The hemiola in bar 26 as it sounds:

In bar 27 Corelli enlivens the rhythm with a **hemiola** in which the beat effectively changes from a dotted crotchet to a crotchet (as shown *left*). This type of syncopation adds to the dancing rhythms of a movement that must surely have been played as the congregation joyfully left the church for more pleasurable pursuits!

Private study

1. Name the instruments required for a trio sonata such as this.
2. What is meant by a figured bass?
   Briefly describe what the organist plays in this piece.
3. What type of dance music is this?
4. What are the main characteristics of binary form?
5. In bar 18 the violins create a point of tension by being a tone apart. What is this device called?
6. Where in bars 28–35 is there a hemiola?

B *NAM 16* CD2 Track 5
The Lindsays

String quartet 'The Joke', movement 4 (Haydn)

The thick-textured counterpoint of Holborne's pavane and galliard is typical of much late-renaissance chamber music, just as the lighter texture of Corelli's trio sonata, with its support from the continuo, is typical of much baroque chamber music. The four-part texture of the string quartet (two violins, viola and cello) is equally typical of classical chamber music, and it was a **genre** brought to perfection by Haydn.

For a minuet from a string quartet by Haydn see *Aural Matters* (Bowman and Terry) pages 120–121.

Haydn's earliest quartets perpetuated the light textures of baroque music; the first violin usually had most of the interesting material and the viola spent much time doubling the cello. But by the 1770s he had established a four-movement format that was to become the norm (two fast movements flanking a slow movement and a minuet) with all four instruments treated as equally important.

In 1781, after Haydn had completed the six quartets of opus 33, he wrote to potential purchasers describing them as 'written in a new and special manner'. They are lighter in style than some of his earlier quartets and often deliberately humorous: *NAM 16* comes from a quartet nicknamed 'The Joke' and one of the nicknames for the whole set is *Gli Scherzi* (the jokes) because they all contain a fast scherzo rather than a stately minuet as either the second or third movement. The melodies are often folk-like in their dancing simplicity and the structure of each movement is crystal clear. To add to the directness of the music individual movements are often **monothematic** (based on just one theme and motifs from it).

All of these features are evident in the finale from *The Joke* Quartet. The tempo is very fast, but the melody of the first eight bars is as simple and memorable as a jig (aided by the balanced tonic and dominant harmonies shown *below*). The music is in a symmetrical **rondo** structure: the opening eight bars (**A**) form the refrain, and this returns after each of the intervening episodes (**B** and **C**):

The diagram below shows one possible way of identifying the rondo structure, but you may feel that the whole of bars 1–36 forms the refrain, repeated in full in bars 71–106 and repeated in part after that. Don't lose sight of the fact that Haydn wrote the movement to be enjoyed, not analysed!

Bar	*8*	*28*	*36*	*71*	*79*	*99*	*107*
|: A :|	|: B	A :|	C	A	B	A	*Coda*

The principal key is E♭ major in all sections except **C**, where the music modulates through A♭ major and F minor before coming to rest on the dominant of E♭.

Nearly all of the thematic material derives from motifs in the refrain:

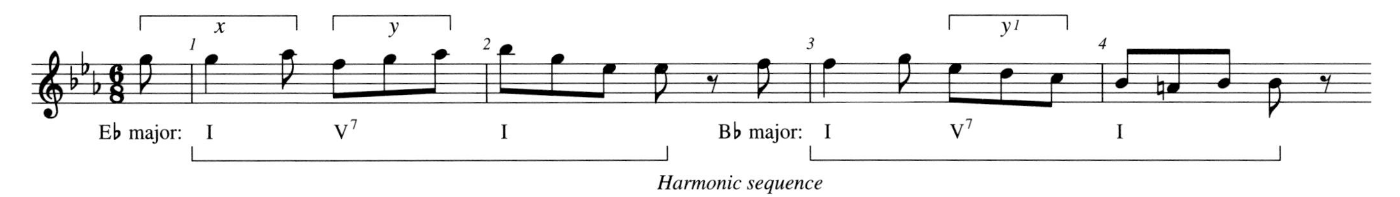

In the theme itself motif *y* is inverted (*y*[1] *above*) then repeated to form the rising scale in bar 6. In bars 9–13 chromatic notes are added to both motifs, and in bars 22–24 the middle note of motif *x* is shortened to produce playful slurred quavers. This new version of *x* is then repeated to form the chromatic **sequence** in bars 24–27.

Many more manipulations of this material occur throughout the movement – try to spot some for yourself.

The jokes

The nickname should be 'the jokes' for there are many of them in this movement, some more obvious than others, but all dependent on the structure and motifs discussed above. Here are just a few.

After only seven bars the first episode lands on the dominant **pedal** of E♭ at bar 16 and remains there for 13 bars creating expectancy for a terrific musical event. Instead what follows is the tiny eight-second musical squib of the refrain (bars 28–36).

The central episode begins with another dominant pedal, this time in the key of A♭ major (bars 36–47). But instead of resolving to chord I in bar 41 the music gets stuck on chord Ic, not once, but four times. Every time this happens chord Ic is marked ***sf*** (as though Haydn were venting his fury at being unable to find the tonic chord of any key other than E♭ major). Having failed to find chord I of E♭ major, Haydn moves down to F minor with a similar lack of success

Notice that the ***sf*** accents in bars 41 and 43 are emphasised by **double-stopping** from the first violin.

(bars 48–53). Finally he gives up, returns to E♭ major and, after two abortive attempts (bars 55 and 57) at last achieves a perfect cadence in bars 58–59). To celebrate he uses motif x in a rising sequence which leads to ... another dominant pedal (bars 64–68)!

By the time we get to the **coda**, 54 out of 107 bars have featured prolonged dominant pedals so it is a relief to hear a tonic pedal (bars 107–111) and what sound like conclusive perfect cadences (bars 120–123). But Haydn hasn't finished – the jig continues to another dominant pedal (bars 128–140) and more fun with the truncated version of motif *x*. A total silence and melodramatic **appoggiaturas** (bar 139) lead to a dominant 7th (note the pitch of the viola in bar 140). After another dramatic silence that catchy refrain sneaks in yet again.

Could this be the end? No! A loud dominant 9th ushers in an *Adagio* – almost as if we're in for an extra slow movement, just when we thought it was all over. But all movement stops and the by now almost irritating refrain starts up yet again. But this time it is in its death throes – chopped into pieces by the G.P. (general pause) that interrupts every two bars.

That's it! Bar 166 and the end of the refrain, so it must be all over. But no. There is now a silence for three bars (a long time when you are trying not to giggle) after which Haydn pulls his last rabbit out of the hat in the shape of the first two bars of the movement (which you will remember contained a perfect cadence within it, as shown in the example on the previous page).

Private study

1. What is a pedal? In which bars does a pedal occur (a) in the viola part, and (b) in the violin 1 part? How do these differ?
2. What is double stopping? Where is it used on page 206?
3. What is meant by (a) coda, and (b) monothematic?
4. Where on page 205 does Haydn use imitation?

Can music really express humour? Discuss this question with your teacher and fellow students.

Septet in E♭, movement 1 (Beethoven)

A *NAM 17* CD2 Track 6
Berlin Philharmonic Octet

Although the septet was first performed privately (like most 18th-century chamber music) it was repeated a few weeks later at a public concert in the Royal Imperial Court Theatre, Vienna, where it shared the programme with the premiere of Beethoven's first symphony.

When reading the score remember that the clarinet sounds a tone lower than printed, the horn in E♭ sounds a minor 6th lower, the double bass sounds an octave lower, and the viola uses the alto clef.

Beethoven was taught for a short time by Haydn, and it is said that the only work of the pupil to earn Haydn's unqualified praise was this septet. This is not surprising for it is stylistically one of Beethoven's most classical works, written in 1799 when he was 29. It is a large-scale piece (seven players and six movements) and it perhaps lacks the intimacy of true chamber music such as *NAM 16*.

The movement begins with a slow introduction that moves from the opening tonic chord of E♭ major to chord V in bar 8. Notice the dramatic contrast between the loud **tutti** opening and the solo violin. The four violin notes starting after the rest in bar 8 will dominate much of the rest of the movement. Bars 8–10 are repeated in the tonic minor (E♭ minor, bars 10–12) and the major mode returns for the ornate violin melody that ends on a dominant 7th chord, decorated with a very characteristic clarinet arpeggio.

The *Allegro con brio* is in **sonata form**, the usual choice for classical first movements. First try to listen for its main features:

Bars	18	53	111	154	188	233
	Exposition		**Development**	**Recapitulation**		**Coda**
	1st subject	2nd subject		1st subject	2nd subject	
Keys	**E♭ major**	**B♭ major**	**Various**	**E♭ major**	**E♭ major**	**E♭ major**

The harmony is generally simple and **diatonic**, although decorated with chromatic passages such as bar 26. There is often a slow rate of chord change, speeding up towards the cadences. This is evident in the first subject (bars 18–29) in which the first four bars are harmonised with chord I, then the chords change every bar in bars 23–26, then every half bar in the next two bars.

Exposition

The first subject starts with a version of the four-note motif we noticed in the introduction, treated in sequence in bars 18–20. The whole of the ten-bar violin melody is repeated on the clarinet, supported by a **syncopated** accompaniment in the strings.

The second subject, which starts at bar 53 in the dominant key of B♭ major, initially has a very different character: a **homophonic** texture of three-part strings, at first in minims although when this four-bar phrase is immediately repeated by wind the lively quavers return as an accompaniment in the strings. Another second subject theme appears in bars 61–68, shared between violin and clarinet doubled by bassoon; this is also immediately repeated in a different scoring. Finally Beethoven introduces a third idea (also part of the second subject) – the staccato chordal phrase in bars 86–88. This is repeated in **sequence** and (in bar 90) at the original pitch but with varied harmony. A **cadential 6–4** (in the classical progression Ic–V–I) concludes the second subject in bars 97–98.

Bars 98^3–111 form a codetta (a small coda) that reinforces the establishment of the dominant key. The one-bar phrase at the start of this section (based on the four-note motif) will later assume considerable importance. It is repeated in sequence over a reiterated tonic pedal (B♭ played by horn then double bass until bar 106). The exposition ends with three perfect cadences (bars 107–111).

Development

The development of ideas from the exposition begins with the opening of the first subject and a rapid modulation to C minor. In this key the melody from the codetta is heard on the clarinet (bars 116–120). The same theme is then heard in sequence on the horn and the music starts to modulate through a wider range of keys, as is usual in a development section. At bar 125 Beethoven draws on another earlier idea (from bar 40) which alternates with the codetta theme until the music settles on a dominant **pedal** in bar 140, heralding the imminent return of the tonic key. Over the pedal is heard more of the codetta phrase, as well as the minim theme from bar 53 and our four-note motif which appears in the rising sequences of bars 148–151.

Recapitulation

The recapitulation starts with a rescored repeat of bars 18–30, but a sudden modulation to A♭ major in bars 170–172 leads to more development of earlier material until, at bar 182, Beethoven returns to E♭ major for a repeat of bars 47–98 in the tonic key.

Coda The coda begins at bar 233 with a repeat of the codetta, but it is greatly expanded by further development of the four-note motif (starting in the cello at bar 249). This accompanies a variation of the codetta theme played on the horn, together with a syncopated dominant pedal on the violin. At bar 258 the two melodies swap positions, the four-note motif now in the treble and the codetta theme in the bass, the latter imitated by woodwind in bar 260. Arpeggios and scales lead to a conclusive cadence in E♭ major (bars 276–277). The movement ends with a new trill figure, compressed in rhythm to increase excitement from bar 285, and harmonised by no less than nine perfect cadences in the last 11 bars.

Private study

1. On what chord does the movement begin?
2. Compare bars 2 and 4.
3. In bars 161–164 the key is E♭ major. Which of these bars are diatonic and which include chromatic writing?
4. What is the name of the ornament in the violin part of bar 163?
5. What precisely is meant by the phrase 'a syncopated dominant pedal' in the above description of the coda?
6. Compare bars 53–56 with bars 188–191. What is the main difference between these two passages?

B *NAM 18* CD2 Track 7
Guarneri Quartet with
Peter Serkin (piano)

Piano Quintet in F minor, movement 3 (Brahms)

Brahms was a romantic composer with a great respect for earlier music. He studied baroque counterpoint, helped to edit the music of Handel and wrote variations on themes by Handel and Haydn. He was also strongly influenced by Beethoven's music, especially its intensive use of short motifs and its use of tonality (keys) to structure large movements. These influences led some of his contemporaries unfairly to dismiss Brahms' music as conservative, but in other respects such as lyrical melody and lush harmony, he was as romantic as most late-19th century composers.

Many of these features of Brahms' style are evident in the scherzo from his piano quintet. Like Beethoven, he often revised his music many times before he was satisfied; this work was first composed as a string quintet in 1862 then rewritten for piano duet in 1864. *NAM 18* is the third version, composed in 1865 for piano quintet (that is a piano plus a string quartet).

Brahms clearly intended this work for highly skilled performers. The music is fast and technically demanding, and all of the instruments use a wide range. This is particularly evident in bars 146–157 (compare the string writing throughout with that in *NAM 13*).

The trio is a section which contrasts with the outer parts of the movement. Its name derives from the fact that such sections were once written for just a trio of instruments.

NAM 18 consists of a scherzo followed by a trio, after which the scherzo is repeated. This gives the overall movement a **ternary** (ABA) structure. A scherzo (meaning a joke) was a fast triple-time movement in the classical period, but Brahms uses both 6/8 and 2/4 metres, and his style is much more serious than that found in the light and witty of scherzos of earlier times.

First listen for the three themes of the scherzo:

A (bars 1–12)

The first is a rising melody in C minor and compound time. It is characterised by frequent syncopations and is *pianissimo*. Brahms' interest in counterpoint is evident at bar 9 where the theme played in octaves by violin and viola is imitated by the piano.

B (bars 13–21)

The second is a jerky melody (staccato notes separated by tiny rests) also in C minor but in simple time. It revolves obsessively around the dominant and is also played *pianissimo*.

C (bars 22–29)

The third is a very loud march-like theme in C major with strong second-beat accents (marked *forzando*). It is immediately repeated at bar 30, where Brahms adds variety by using the piano to imitate the strings two beats later (starting at the ***ff*** in bar 31).

Notice how the motif in bars 22–24 is an **augmentation** of the semiquaver figure in bar 14, now in the major.

Brahms then repeats A (bars 38–56) and B (bars 57–67), modulating rapidly in the process. This leads to the distant key of E♭ minor and the central section of the scherzo, in which counterpoint becomes the most important element.

Fugato (bars 67–100)

Brahms uses a **fugal** texture in which the viola treats the first four bars of theme B as a fugue subject (bar 67). This is answered by the piano (right hand, bar 71). There are further entries of the subject starting in bars 76 (violin) and 84 (viola). These are combined with no less than three countersubjects, introduced as follows:

1. piano left-hand, bar 67 (next heard in viola, bar 71)
2. piano left-hand, bar 71 (next heard in viola, bar 76)
3. viola, bar 80 (next heard modified by violin 2, bar 84)

In bars 88–100 all of these melodies are fragmented into tiny cells in a complex five-part contrapuntal texture. The example below shows how, in the first-violin part, the first ten notes of the subject are detached (*a*), then just the first five notes (*b*), then just the first three notes (*c*). Notice how the pitches rise through the use of sequence until the climax at bar 100.

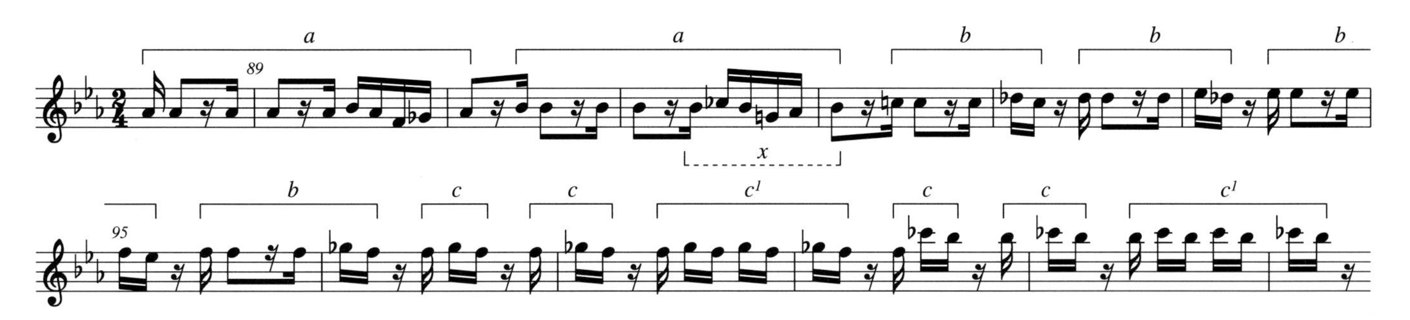

Can you spot similar processes at work in the cello and piano parts in the same passage? These fragments (and those of the viola from bar 92) are heard in a type of close imitation known as **stretto**.

The fragment marked *x* above is a motif that will recur in various transformations, imparting a sense of unity to the structure.

After this central section Brahms repeats the themes of the first part in the following order:

B (bars 100–109): E♭ minor
C (bars 109–124): E♭ major
A (bars 125–157): E♭ minor modulating to C minor
B (bars 158–193): C minor (greatly extended to form a coda and using a tierce de Picardie to end on a chord of C major).

Shown *left* are just two of Brahms' transformations of motif *x*. The first is an **augmentation** of *x* (every note is four times longer than before). The second is in E♭ major instead of E♭ minor and an ornament has been added to its fifth beat (at *y*).

The entire work is unified by devices of this sort. The falling semitone that constantly appears in the final bars of the example printed on the previous page is heard prominently throughout the scherzo. Even the contrasting trio is linked with the scherzo by several common motifs, the most obvious being motif *y* (*left*) which becomes an integral part of its main melody (bars 197 and 199).

Trio (bars 193²–261)

The trio is in ternary form:

A Bars 193-225: A broad 16-bar melody in C major, modulating to B major in the last five bars. Introduced by piano and then repeated by strings, it contrasts strongly with the episodic nature and contrapuntal textures of the scherzo.

B Bars 225–241: Legato melody with staccato bass; in bars 233–241 these parts are then reversed – melody in the bass with staccato accompaniment above. The harmony is chromatic but it is anchored to C major by the dominant pedal (on G).

A Bars 242–261: The first 11 bars of the melody from the first section return, in a dark texture in which all instruments are in a low **tessitura**. This leads to a plagal cadence in C (bars 253–254) and a tonic pedal (bars 254–261).

The performers are then instructed to repeat the scherzo – *Scherzo da Capo sin al Fine*, meaning repeat the scherzo as far as the word *Fine* (the end).

Private study

1. What in the music suggests that this movement was written to be played by professional performers in the concert hall rather than by amateurs at home?

2. Describe some of the ways in which the main themes of the scherzo (up to bar 193) are contrasted.

3. Look at the texture in bars 15–17, 57–59 and 88–90. Use an appropriate word or phrase to describe each of these textures.

4. How is the trio contrasted with the scherzo?

Sonata for Horn, Trumpet and Trombone (Poulenc)

B *NAM 19* CD2 Track 8
Nash Ensemble

Francis Poulenc was a French composer who achieved considerable success in such diverse areas as music for stage and film, church music, songs and chamber music. The latter includes a number of sonatas for wind instruments of which *NAM 19* (the first movement of a sonata written in 1922) is among the first.

Movements from Poulenc's flute and clarinet sonatas are often performed by young wind players. If anyone in your study group is learning one of these this would be an ideal opportunity to hear and get to know some more of Poulenc's music.

Much of Poulenc's early music is characterised by its light, witty qualities, as was that of his friend Georges Auric (composer of *NAM 42*). Both composers, like the others in the group of contemporary French composers known as *Les Six*, were influenced by the satirical style of the French composer Erik Satie.

Poulenc greatly admired the music of Stravinsky, whose ballet *Pulcinella* (see *NAM 7*) had received its first performance in Paris in 1920. *Pulcinella* draws on the music of baroque composers but Stravinsky reinterpreted this material with syncopated rhythms, pungent 'wrong notes' and unusual instrumentation.

In Poulenc's own music, melody is of supreme importance. His use of harmony is less adventurous than many early-20th century composers – it often consists of adding unexpected dissonances to spice-up fairly conventional progressions.

Poulenc wrote in 1942, 'I am not one of those composers who have made harmonic innovations ... I think there's room for *new* music which doesn't mind using other people's chords'.

All of the above features and influences are found in *NAM 19*:

- simple diatonic melodies (opening trumpet theme)
- syncopation (bars 13–14)
- tonal harmonies (chords I, IV and V in bars 1–4)
- discords that spice-up conventional progressions (see *right*)
- humour, in short-winded phrases that constantly change metre and speed (the recording on CD2 brings this out particularly well – listen to how the brass make a headlong dash towards the first cadence in bar 4)
- classical phrasing (bars 1–4 answered by bars 5–8) disrupted by a cadence in the 'wrong' place in bar 8 (on the weak fourth beat).

Satire is also evident, particularly in the use of the title sonata. Traditionally sonatas are works of some magnitude, with tightly integrated ideas worked out over substantial time spans. Poulenc happily pokes fun at such serious ideas, presenting a movement of short, amusing sections that have no such pretensions of grandeur.

Until valves were invented in the early 19th century the trumpet and horn could play only a limited series of notes, produced through the use of different lip pressures. The horn was therefore only occasionally used in solo and small ensemble works, and the trumpet hardly at all, until the romantic period. The use of valves gives both of these instruments a full chromatic range, which Poulenc fully exploits in this work.

The opening trumpet figure, based on the tonic triad of G, sounds just like a motif by Haydn ripe for development. But when it recurs in bars 21^4–25 it loses all its energy and its accompaniment, and even its shape, as it fragments among the trio. The horn gets the rhythm of the first two notes 'wrong' (quavers instead of semiquavers) and the trombone slows it down further by augmenting this rhythm to crotchets. They then try it more quietly in G minor. Exasperated, they give up any further development for the moment and instead embark on the middle section of this **ternary** (ABA) form. The fast sections (bars 0–25 and 57^4–85) are in G major while the slower B section (bars 26–39) is in E♭ major and B♭ major.

The contrast of key and speed is matched by a change in style, with quiet dynamics and legato phrasing, but this mood is suddenly disrupted by the loud outburst and wild trumpet leaps in bars 36–38. A short cadenza for trumpet consisting of a downward scale leads to a dramatic pause followed by some very fast and silly hiccuping variations of the opening melody in bars 40–55.

When the A section returns Poulenc begins with the opening theme (bars 58–65) but he then interpolates material from the B section (bars 66–71 are taken from bars 48–53) before continuing with the rest of the A section (bars 73–85, which are taken from bars 9–21). Both of these last two passages are transposed, re-scored and reharmonised. The **coda** (bars 86–89) consists of an obstinate B$\flat$ against a very discreet chromatic scale, followed by a cheeky reference to the opening notes of the movement.

Private study

1. Check that you understand all the directions in French.
2. Which of the three instruments is given the smallest share of the melodic material?
3. What are the sounding pitches of the last three notes played by the horn (remember the transposition)?
4. Briefly state how this movement compares with the first movement of Beethoven's septet, *NAM 17*.
5. Which aspects of this movement refer to older styles of music and which are more contemporary?
6. How does Poulenc's writing for the horn differ from Beethoven's horn part in *NAM 17*?

Sample question 1

(a) Explain what you understand by any **two** of the following:

imitation   antiphonal   suspension   G.P.

(b) Link each term you have chosen in your answer to question (a) to a context from a specific work. Name the work, the precise location and the instrument or voice parts involved.

Answer the following two questions only if you are taking the exam in 2001 or 2002.

(c) Briefly explain the significance of the numbers and other symbols below the bass stave in *NAM 15*.

(d) In what ways do *NAM 17* and *NAM 15* illustrate two very different approaches to chamber music?

Answer the following two questions only if you are taking the exam in 2003 or 2004.

(c) Why is the quartet from which *NAM 16* is taken known as 'The Joke'?

(d) Compare Brahms' use of instruments in *NAM 18* with Gabrieli's use of instruments in *NAM 14*.

Sample question 2

(a) Explain what you understand by any **two** of the following:

ternary form   monothematic   dominant pedal   viol

(b) Link each term you have chosen in your answer to question (a) to a context from a specific work. Name the work, the precise location and the instrument or voice parts involved.

Answer the following two questions only if you are taking the exam in 2001 or 2002.

(c) Indicate **four** aspects of *NAM 19* that identify it as a 20th-century work.

(d) Compare Corelli's string writing in *NAM 15* with Holborne's string writing in *NAM 13*.

Answer the following two questions only if you are taking the exam in 2003 or 2004.

(c) What do you notice about the use of performing directions in *NAM 14, 16* and *18*?

(d) How can you tell that NAM 16 was written in the classical period?

Keyboard music

Organs and harpsichords

The earliest keyboard instrument was the pipe organ. Organs with keyboards resembling the familiar layout of modern instruments are known to have existed by the 14th century. At about the same time a new instrument appeared in which a range of strings could be plucked by a mechanism driven from a keyboard. This was the harpsichord and it remained one of the main types of keyboard instrument until the late-18th century (and it has enjoyed a revival of interest in more recent times). The virginals and spinet are names for small harpsichords.

Harpsichords proved popular because they enabled a single player to play chords and multiple lines of music – treble, bass and inner parts. However like the organ, but unlike most other instruments, they could not vary the dynamic of individual notes.

This problem did not arise with the clavichord, an instrument in which each string is not plucked but hit by a small piece of metal attached to the key. The player can vary the dynamic through the force used to strike the key and can even produce vibrato by waggling the key while in contact with the string. The overall dynamic range is small, though, making the clavichord an instrument for the home rather than for public performance.

The piano

Most of these problems were addressed by the piano. Invented in the early 18th century its original names (*fortepiano* or *pianoforte*) immediately describe what it can do best – play either loudly or quietly, allowing the player to use dynamics for the expressive shaping of phrasing as well as for dramatic contrasts. By the late 18th century the piano had replaced the harpsichord as the preferred keyboard instrument for domestic and public performance.

The late 18th-century piano, the type of instrument Mozart would have known, had a wooden frame like the harpsichord. This can support only a relatively low string tension, resulting in a gentler tone than modern instruments. The invention of the iron frame in the 19th century allowed the use of high-tension strings capable of a much wider dynamic range and greater sustaining power. At the same time the compass of the keyboard was extended and numerous improvements were made to the mechanism, particularly to facilitate the type of virtuoso playing that became popular in the romantic period.

In 1700 the typical compass of the harpsichord was five octaves. By 1800 the piano usually had six octaves and by 1900 seven octaves was normal. The modern piano has a range of at least seven octaves plus a third.

The keyboard music in this Area of Study covers a span of more than three centuries:

1600 | 1700 | 1800 | 1900 | 2000

Renaissance | Baroque | Classical | Romantic | Modern

Sweelinck	Bach	Mozart	Schumann	Debussy	Shostakovich
NAM 20	*NAM 21*	*NAM 22*	*NAM 23*	*NAM 24*	*NAM 25*
1615	1728	1783	1838	1894	1950–51

NAM 20 and *NAM 21* would probably have been intended for the harpsichord or clavichord, although Sweelinck's music could have been played on the organ – and the recording of *NAM 21* shows how well Bach's music transfers to the modern piano. The other four items are all piano music.

B *NAM 20* CD2 Track 9
Peter Seymour (harpsichord)

Pavana Lachrimae (Sweelinck)

In the last quarter of the 16th century there was an explosion of interest in music-making among the educated classes in England and its continental neighbours. Many of these cultured amateurs could sing madrigals and play domestic instruments such as the recorder, viol, lute and harpsichord.

Because this piece is so closely based on *Flow my tears* we recommend you read the section on NAM 33, starting on page 95, before studying Sweelinck's variations on Dowland's song.

Another pavane that begins with a falling-4th figure similar to the start of Dowland's song is *NAM 13*. Its title, *The image of melancholy*, clearly echoes the imagery of *Flow my tears*.

For an example of keyboard variations by William Byrd see *Aural Matters* (Bowman and Terry) page 102.

Among the most popular types of instrumental music were sets of variations on dance tunes and secular songs. Of many new songs composed around 1600, Dowland's *Flow my tears* was perhaps the most famous (*NAM 33*). Dowland himself wrote variations on it, as did his fellow Englishmen Byrd and Farnaby. All three entitled these works *Pavana Lachrimae* for two reasons. Firstly the song is in the style of a slow processional dance of the late renaissance known as a pavane. Secondly *Lachrimae* (meaning tears) refers to the image of falling tears that is central to the words of the song.

A number of English composers, including Dowland, travelled and worked in Europe at this time. English keyboard variations were widely known and became one of the principal sources for the development of variation techniques in northern European music. The minor English composer John Bull spent eight years as organist at Antwerp Cathedral and while in the Netherlands he became a friend of Sweelinck (organist at the Old Church in Amsterdam for over 40 years). There can be little doubt that Bull introduced Sweelinck to Dowland's lute songs and the variations written on them by English composers of keyboard music. Sweelinck, in turn, influenced generations of pupils, laying the foundations for the magnificent late baroque keyboard music of J. S. Bach.

Lute song and pavane

Exam questions will not ask you to compare Dowland's lute song with Sweelinck's variations, but knowledge of the relationship between the two works may help gain you credit if such information is relevant to the answer you offer.

Sweelinck's *Pavana Lachrymae* (1615) follows the structure of Dowland's song but instead of the repeat of each of the three sections there is a variation, and the printed note values of *Flow my tears* are doubled in the *Pavana*. This means that:

- bars 1–8 of the song = bars 1–16 of the pavane
- bars 9–16 of the song = bars 33–48 of the pavane
- bars 17–24 of the song = bars 65–81 of the pavane.

The example *below* shows the first phrase of Dowland's song in its original note values and Sweelick's free transcription of it.

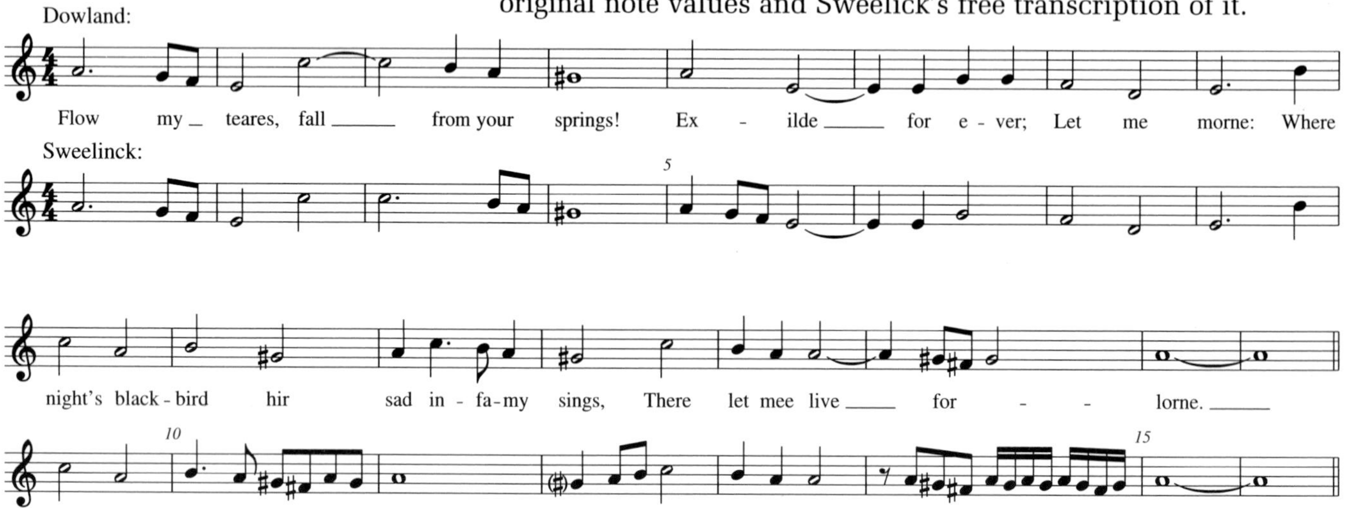

Sweelinck leaves Dowland's harmonies mainly unchanged in these bars, including the **false relation** between G and G♯ in bar 10, but

he embellishes the cadences in bars 8 and 14–15. At bar 17 instead of repeating the first part of the song to new words, as Dowland did, Sweelinck writes a variation on it, in which mainly **stepwise** semiquavers replace the longer notes of the vocal melody, bass and sometimes an inner part. The next example shows how, in bars 17–20, he retains all of the pitches of the melody of bars 1–4:

The remainder of the pavane follows a similar pattern: first a free **transcription** of eight bars of the song (forming 16 bars in *NAM 20* due to the longer note values) and then a variation on it in a more keyboard-like style. The form could be expressed as $AA^1BB^1CC^1$ where the little figure 1 indicates a variation.

Notice how the rising 3rds in bars 12–13 of Dowland's song are filled with **passing notes** in bars 39–41 of the pavane and how these grow into four-note figures in the variation of phrase B (bars 55–57).

The *Pavana Lachrimae* is played on a harpsichord on CD2 but it is equally suitable for organ, on which instrument the expressive suspensions in bars 90–92 would be sustained and thus more clearly heard.

Composing and performing

If you decide to write variations for Unit 2, study Sweelinck's variation technique in this piece. Try to perform the piece, either on the piano or in an arrangement for a quartet of instruments. As an exercise try writing another variation, either in a similar style or in a style of your own choice.

Private study

?

1. What sort of a dance is a pavane?
2. Why was English music so well known in Europe at this time?
3. Compare the openings of *NAM 33* and *NAM 20* printed *opposite*. What is the significance of Sweelinck's changes in bars 3 and 5? What rhythmic effect does he choose to omit in bar 11?
4. Explain what is meant by a **tierce de Picardie** and state the number of a bar number in which this is used.
5. Listen to the recording and describe how Peter Seymour plays the opening chord. Can you spot any other types of ornamentation he uses in the performance?

Sarabande and Gigue from Partita in D (Bach)

A *NAM 21* CD2 Tracks 10–11
András Schiff (piano)

The Italian word *partita* normally meant a set of variations in the baroque period, but it was also occasionally used to refer to suites such as this, published in 1728. The baroque suite normally included a number of stylised dances in **binary form**, sometimes preceded by an introductory movement, and usually all in the same key. Bach's keyboard Partita in D conforms to the norm that he

NAM 21 describes this partita as *BWV 828*. *BWV* stands for *Bach Werke-Verzeichnis* which is a catalogue of his compositions.

himself established in containing five dance types (allemande, courante, sarabande, minuet and gigue) together with an air and a massive French overture at the start.

Sarabande

The two dances in the *New Anthology* could not be more contrasting in style. By Bach's time the sarabande had lost all connection with its wild youth in Spain and had become a stately, if not solemn, movement in triple time, often with a stress on the second beat of the bar. You can hear this rhythmic feature clearly in Debussy's Sarabande (*NAM 24*) but Bach's music only fleetingly refers to this feature (the minims in bars 1–2) before embarking on a series of complex rhythms that sound as free as an improvisation.

The ornament above the last beat of bar 1 is an upper mordent and implies a few rapid alternations of C♯ with the note above, D.

The first section of this binary-form movement modulates to the dominant key of A major (notice the G♯s in bars 5–8). The music remains in this key until the cadence in bars 11–12, where a chromatic F♮ adds colour to the ending.

If your copy of the *New Anthology* has a tie between the first and second beats of bar 13, it is a misprint. The rhythm should be the same as in bars 1 and 29, and this is how it is played on CD2.

The longer second section begins with a reworking of material from the first section modulating through the relative minor (B minor, bars 19–20) and E minor (bars 21–24) before returning to the tonic key for the last ten bars. In these final bars Bach recapitulates most of the first section: bars 29–30 are the same as bars 1–2 and bars 31–32 and 36–38 are slightly modified and transposed versions of bars 6–7 and 9–12 respectively. Movements that are rounded off with repeats like this are appropriately described as 'rounded binary form'. In keeping with baroque performing conventions András Schiff adds ornaments to the repeats of both sections of the sarabande – see how many you can hear.

Gigue

The French word gigue (which is related to the English jig) is pronounced with a soft initial 'g': *zheeg*.

As was customary in baroque suites Bach ends with a rollicking binary-form gigue in compound time. The 9/16 time signature indicates that there are nine semiquavers per bar – three dotted-quaver beats per bar, each divided into three semiquavers.

Also conventional is the **fugal** style of the first 21 bars (compare this passage with *NAM 15*). The fugal subject (bars 1–6) is followed by a fugal answer (the same tune as the subject, but transposed up a 5th) in the left hand of bars 7–12. After a passage of free **counterpoint** there is a final entry of the subject in the left hand, starting at bar 16. But Bach does not intend this to be a serious fugue. As early as bar 20 counterpoint gives way to a whirling semiquaver melody accompanied by cheeky two-part chords.

Teasingly Bach introduces what sounds like another entry of the subject in bar 27, but it evaporates after only a bar. A version of the subject reappears in bars 36–41, but the opening arpeggio is wilfully turned upside down. The end of this version of the subject guides the music to the expected key of A major and the perfect cadence that marks the end of the first section.

The second section begins with a new melody which continues the constant semiquavers of the first section. This too is treated in a fugal style, with an answer that occurs in the right hand of bars 55–60. However beneath it Bach ingeniously fits a complete restatement of the first fugal subject from the start of the gigue. After this the second fugal subject is heard in modified form in bars 64–69 and 74–77 (the latter without its ending) and the first fugal subject (without its first bar) is allowed a final appearance in bars 86–89.

Private study

1. What two features are common to all the dances in a baroque suite?
2. What sort of dance is (a) a sarabande and (b) a gigue?
3. Why are both of these dances said to be in binary form?
4. What happens at bar 29 in the sarabande?
5. On what instrument(s) would Bach have played this music?

Piano Sonata in B♭, first movement (Mozart)

A *NAM 22* CD2 Track 12
Alfred Brendel (piano)

By 1783, when Mozart wrote his Sonata in B♭, K333, the late baroque contrapuntal style of Bach had given way to the elegant charms of the classical style, and the piano had started to replace the harpsichord as the keyboard instrument of choice in both the concert hall and the home. It was sufficiently powerful for Mozart to be able to show off his virtuosity in the piano concertos he wrote for the purpose and it was also capable of delicate dynamic effects, making it ideal for domestic performances of the series of piano sonatas that he wrote for himself and his amateur pupils.

You will often see Mozart's works identified as K followed by a number, such as K333. The letter refers to Köchel, an Austrian who catalogued Mozart's surviving music in the 19th century. The numbering system helps to differentiate works that have identical titles, such as the various piano sonatas in B♭, which include K333, K358 and K570.

Mozart's mature classical style was a development of the **galant** style that he had used in his youth and features of it are apparent throughout the first movement of K333. The most obvious are:

- Melody-dominated **homophony**. Throughout most of the movement the chief focus of the music is the ornate right-hand melody that is supported by the broken chords of the left-hand accompaniment. The melodies include frequent **appoggiaturas**, both **diatonic** (the first B♭ in bar 88 which clashes with the dominant 7th chord beneath it) and **chromatic** (C♯ in bar 110).
- Thin, crystal-clear textures. The first 22 bars use an almost entirely two-part texture. When full chords are used they draw attention to the beginnings or endings of important sections (as in bar 23).
- Broken-chord accompaniments. These are evident in the first four bars where Mozart achieves a delicate effect by beginning each left-hand pattern after the first beat of the bar. Elsewhere (notably bars 71–80) he uses an **Alberti bass** accompaniment.
- Clear harmonic progressions with regular cadence points that define keys. Mozart starts with the chords shown *right* and reaches a perfect cadence in B♭ major in bar 10. The modulation to the dominant (F major) in bars 11–22 is equally clear – notice how E♮ occurs with increasing frequency in these bars. But Mozart uses galant techniques as a launch pad for his expressive classical style, so we should not be surprised by the poignant harmonies in passages such as bars 43–49 and 139–146.

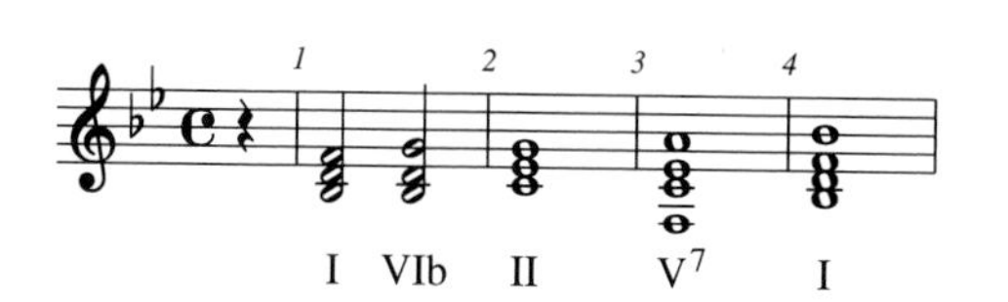

- **Periodic phrasing**. Pairs of equal-length phrases sounding like questions and answers abound in galant music. The eight-bar phrase starting at bar 23 ends with an imperfect cadence in F major, and the eight-bar answer starting at bar 31 ends with perfect cadence in F. In fact most of Mozart's phrasing is more subtle than this – again Mozart is using galant techniques only as a launching pad for his mature classical style.

✦ **Sonata form**. In this movement the home key is B♭ major, a key firmly established by the first subject in bars 1–10. The next 12 bars move towards the contrasting key of the dominant (F major) and in bar 23 Mozart presents the first of several ideas in this key (the second subject group). This exposition section ends with a **codetta** (bars 50–63) in which F major is affirmed by a succession of perfect cadences (bars 53–54, 57–59 and 62–63).

The development (bars 63^4–93^3) begins with the melody of the first subject in F major but soon veers off to pass through the keys of F minor, C minor, B♭ major and G minor until it eventually reaches V^7 of the home key of B♭ major in bars 87–92.

In the recapitulation (bars 93^3 to the end) the material of the exposition returns, but now centred on the home key of B♭ major. The conflict of keys has been resolved in a perfectly balanced sonata-form structure. This is not, of course, the end of the complete sonata – a slow movement and a final fast movement follow this opening allegro.

?

Private Study

1. In bars 1–10 which are the only bars that do not start with an appoggiatura?
2. Where does Mozart use an Alberti bass in the exposition?
3. The first subject is ten bars long. What are the phrase lengths?
4. What is the principal way in which the recapitulation differs from the exposition?
5. Unlike earlier pieces, the mood of this music seems to vary almost by the second. Choose a section of about 24 bars and explain some of the techniques Mozart uses to create such lively variety without the music sounding disjointed.

B *NAM 23* CD2 Tracks 13–15
Alfred Brendel (piano)

Kinderscenen 1, 3 and 11 (Schumann)

Musical romanticism expressed itself in extremes – gargantuan symphonies and tiny piano compositions. The latter (often called character or characteristic pieces) were intended to express intense emotional experiences in the most intimate manner. Schumann's *Kinderscenen* (Scenes of Childhood) were composed in 1838 – the music was written first and the titles added later. But he had always intended the 13 pieces to be reminiscences of childhood that would be played by adults, unlike his *Album for the Young*, written for his seven year-old daughter (and for all young pianists) to play.

Schumann's titles deliberately encourage us, as we listen or play, to allow memories to float across our minds: images of distant lands and people, a game of blind man's buff and spooky childhood experiences. These programmatic interpretations are typical of much romantic music and are quite different from the absolute music of *NAM 22*, where Mozart makes no suggestions about how anyone should experience his sonata movement – its elegant patterns and musical architecture stand on their own and can be enjoyed in as abstract a fashion as the listener wishes.

Even more characteristic of early romanticism is the fragmentary, suggestive nature of many of the pieces in *Kinderscenen*. Thus the melody of 'Vom fremden Ländern' ends inconclusively on the mediant rather than the tonic, and the accompaniment runs on through the final bar, as though the pianist had intended to continue but instead drifted off into a romantic daydream.

The reverse happens in 'Fürchtenmachen' in which the music slides in as though it had been going for some time and had only just become audible. This effect is enhanced by the chromatic writing in the first two bars which disguises the tonic key. Compare this with the opening of *NAM 22*.

Von fremden Ländern und Menschen

The first eight bars are repeated at the end, after a six-bar middle section, forming the pattern ‖:A:‖:BA:‖ – this is a miniature version of the rounded binary form we saw in *NAM 21*. The simple form, many repetitions of the opening two-bar phrase and the short **sequence** in bars 9–12 give the *impression* of a children's song. But this is an adult's recollection of childhood, so do not be surprised by sophisticated chromatic harmonies such as the diminished 7th in bars 1 and 3, and the artful left-hand **countermelody** based on a **circle of 5ths** in bars 9–12.

Schumann's piano textures are also far from childlike. Notice the way the broken chords are shared between the hands, the contrast between the legato melody and semi-staccato bass at the start, the two-part counterpoint between the outer parts in bars 9–14, and sustained notes in inner parts (bars 5–6 and 14).

Hasche-Mann

Repetition is even more evident in the binary-form structure of 'Hasche-Mann'. The first two bars are repeated in sequence and both of these two-bar phrases are then repeated in bars 5–8. So, like the A section of 'Von fremden Ländern', these bars never move out of the tonic key (in this case B minor). The rising sequence of bars 1–4 of 'Hasche-Mann' becomes a falling sequence in bars 9–12, so carrying the music to the unexpected and unrelated key of C major. The piece ends with yet another repetition of the first four bars.

Fürchtenmachen

'Fürchtenmachen' seems to be only a distant memory of childhood fear, recalling how the disjointed images of a dream can be scary. Schumann approaches these recollections through a mist of chromaticism, the image becoming clearer when the left hand presents a diatonic version of the opening melody in bar 5. This soothing eight-bar phrase in G major alternates with two highly contrasting sections (both containing off-beat syncopated chords) to reflect the disjointed images: bars 9–12 in E minor (repeated in bars 37–40) and bars 21–28, in which the constant modulations give an unsettling quality. In total this forms a symmetrical rondo structure: ABACABA.

Schumann emphasises the contrast by marking bars 9 and 37 *schneller* – faster. On CD2 Alfred Brendel extends this idea to the other contrasting section at bar 21.

Private study

1. What features of the music suggest that *Kinderscenen* was intended for adults, not children, to play?
2. In what key is 'Von Fremden Ländern und Menschen'?
3. What type of scale occurs in bar 16 of 'Hasche-Mann'?
4. Compare bars 1–8 of 'Fürchtenmachen' with bars 1–8 of *NAM 22*. What differences do you notice? Can you spot any similarities?

Performing and Composing

If you are a pianist, or if there is a pianist in your group, try to mount your own performance of at least the first of these pieces. Try to explore some of the other items in *Kinderscenen* and compare them with the various character pieces in Schumann's *Album for the Young* (pieces from which are often set for graded piano exams).

Any of these pieces will form excellent study material and useful models if you choose to write a romantic miniature for Unit 2.

A *NAM 24* CD2 Track 16
Zoltán Kocsis (piano)

Pour le piano: Sarabande (Debussy)

Debussy's suite *Pour le piano* (for the piano) consists of three pieces which revive and inject new life into 18th-century forms – a prelude, a sarabande and a toccata. It was published in 1901 although the sarabande dates from 1894, soon after Debussy's use of other historic dances such as the minuet and passepied in his *Suite bergamasque*.

It seems certain that Debussy would have been thinking of the great age of French baroque music, and the sarabandes of composers such as Couperin, when he wrote this work. The performance direction at the head of the score ('with slow and solemn elegance') captures the stately, triple-time mood of the baroque sarabande, with its characteristic accent on the second beat of the bar (bar 2, 4, 8 and so on). Also similar to baroque dance movements (including those in *NAM 21*) is the binary structure in which a short A section (bars 1–22) is followed by a longer B section (bars 23–72).

When we listen to the sarabande, though, it is clear that Debussy is not seeking to copy the style of 18th-century music, but merely using some of its features as a springboard for his own ideas.

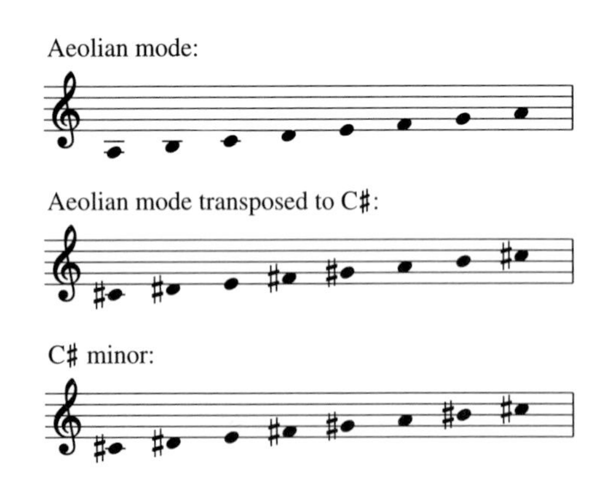

Debussy's handling of key is nothing like the clear-cut tonality that we have seen in the three previous works from the *New Anthology*. The key is C♯ minor, but there is no sign of conventional cadences with sharpened leading notes (B♯) to define this key. Much of the music is in fact modal. It uses the aeolian **mode** (which you can find by playing an octave of white notes on the piano starting from A as the home note) transposed to C♯. The difference between this mode and C♯ harmonic minor is shown *left*.

The first eight bars are entirely modal, with cadences on the fifth note of the mode (G♯) in bar 4 and the seventh note (B) in bar 8. The melody throughout the first 22 bars is modal, although the harmony becomes richer and more chromatic after bar 8.

The use of modality harks back to music of a much earlier era, and this ancient quality is underlined by the chant-like parallel 4ths and 5ths of the opening bar (a technique of early medieval church music). However these notes are just part of the series of lush parallel 7th chords which enrich Debussy's harmony and form a much more modern feature of the work.

There are many other colourful chords that help to give the work its rich sonority. In bars 11–13[1], for instance, the accompanying harmonies are a series of parallel dominant 7ths that never resolve. In fact they are built on a series of notes each a whole tone apart (D–E–F♯–G♯–A♯); such whole-tone scales were used by Debussy in a number of later works. In bars 23–26 he builds his gently dissonant harmony on chords constructed from superimposed 4ths (known as quartal harmony). This technique returns in the last six bars where the bass rises up through a C♯ minor triad to the final modal cadence (B natural rising to C♯ in the outer parts).

The piano textures are equally varied, ranging from the bare octaves of bars 20–22 to the massive ten-part chord in bar 53. The music uses a wide range of the instrument, particularly noticeable in the sonorous bass notes of the final bars.

The letters *m.d.* in bar 72 stand for *main droite* (right hand), indicating that the tied chord must be held with the sustaining pedal so that both hands are free for these bass notes.

Private study

1. What are the main features of a sarabande?
2. Which aspects of Debussy's sarabande are new and forward-looking and which are drawn from older types of music?
3. We have given a translation of the speed direction at the start. Translate all the other French performing directions.
4. List three ways in which Debussy deliberately obscures the C♯ minor tonality of the music.

Prelude and Fugue in A (Shostakovich)

B *NAM 25* CD2 Tracks 17–18
Tatiana Nikolayeva (piano)

Shostakovich lived in communist Russia, where he was publicly humiliated for writing music that failed to glorify the wonders of the party, although in his symphonies and film music he often sought to write music that could readily be understood. Like Bach he was also prepared to write music that amateurs could play. So after he had been to Leipzig as an adjudicator of the 1950 Bach Competition he set to work to write a set of 24 Preludes and Fugues modelled on Bach's two sets of 24 Preludes and Fugues (some of which were composed in Leipzig). As with any of the works in this Area of Study if you (or someone in your group) can play Shostakovich's Prelude and Fugue in A (composed in 1950–51) this would be an excellent way to approach studying the music.

Two aural tests on this work appear in *Aural Matters in Practice* (Bowman and Terry), pages 28 and 29. You may find it useful to tackle these before starting detailed work on the piece.

The idea of modelling new music on older styles, which we also saw in Debussy's sarabande, is known as neo-classicism – although it was more often baroque ideas rather than classical ones that were reused. This can clearly be heard in *NAM 7*, in which Stravinsky decorates his arrangements of baroque music with very modern-sounding dissonances. Neo-classicism was one of many styles to appear in the early 20th century as a reaction to the enormous scale and emotional indulgence of much late-romantic music. Composers who adopted the style used it as a means of recapturing the poise and detached atmosphere of earlier music.

Prelude

The prelude (the word simply means an introductory movement) reflects the style of the prelude in A major in Book 2 of Bach's '48'. To suggest an idealistic image of peaceful country life, both are in 12/8, both are largely diatonic and both make extensive use of **pedal** points which seem distantly to refer to the drones of rustic bagpipes. Shostakovich uses these pedals to define his very slowly changing chords: I in bars 1–3, VI in bars 4–5, and V in bars 8–9.

However Shostakovich also makes use of some very un-Bachian techniques. Gently dissonant notes are freely introduced without preparation and, while the chords in bars 6–8 remind us of a series of baroque suspensions, their layout does not.

In bar 10 the tranquility of the mainly diatonic tonality is suddenly disturbed by the appearance of a chord of C major over the dominant pedal. It is related to A major only by the common note E (the pedal note itself). Equally unbaroque is the style of the chromatic writing starting in bar 13 and even more remote from A major is the plunge into A♭ major in bars 19–22. Shostakovich slips back into A major with no fuss (bar 23) and ends the prelude with an innocent version of a plagal cadence in the upper range of the piano.

Fugue

Serenity also prevails in the **fugue**. This is in part explained by the fact that the subject (bars 1–4) consists entirely of a broken chord of A major (there are no baroque precedents for such simplicity) and partly by the prevailing consonant harmonic style of the whole prelude. The subject is transposed down a 4th to start on the dominant in the left hand of bar 5. This is known as the answer. Meanwhile the right hand plays a countersubject that is still entirely consonant (all of the notes belong to chord V).

The last voice of this three-voice fugue enters in the bass (bars 11–14), still without any sign of a dissonance. This completes the fugal exposition which is followed by an episode (bars 15–20) and then the first middle entry of the subject (stems down, treble stave, bars 21–24) which outlines chord VI of A major, still without a single discord in sight. Well you have probably guessed it by now – there is not a single discord throughout the entire fugue.

In bar 70 Shostakovich begins a stretto: a section of a fugue in which the parts are telescoped together so that the entries of the subject come closer to each other than they originally were. Bars 86–92 are based on a massively extended progression of the chords VI–Ib–V–I that leads to the final, inevitable statement of the fugue subject above the sustained tonic in the last four bars.

Private study

Identify the following features in bars 26–99 of the fugue:

1. A section which uses an entirely two-part texture.
2. Two middle entries of the subject.
3. A modulation to a key a 3rd away from the tonic (this type of key change is known as tertiary modulation).
4. An eight-bar dominant pedal.

Composing

One of the options for Unit 2 is to write a composition in neo-classical style, for which this piece (and works such as *NAM 7*) will form a useful model. However it takes courage to renounce dissonance totally as Shostakovich does in the fugue. It is, after all, probably the most expressive resource available to any composer in any period. The diatonic style of the music seems to anticipate post-modernist music – and that is another option for Unit 2, as is Fusion, which could include the fusion of baroque and modern styles found in such neo-classical music as this.

Performing

Throughout this chapter we have stressed the value of studying keyboard music through performance. This need not be limited to the pieces in the *New Anthology*. See if you can relate any of the music you perform to the styles and techniques in pieces you study. Try to use the work you do in Listening and Understanding to enhance your awareness of the music you sing and play.

Sample question 1

(a) Explain what you understand by any **two** of the following:

imitation compound time false relation countersubject

(b) Link each term you have chosen in your answer to question (a) to a context from a specific work. Name the work, the precise location and the instrument or voice parts involved.

Answer the following two questions only if you are taking the exam in 2001 or 2002.

(c) How can you tell that Mozart's sonata movement (*NAM 22*) was written in the classical period?

(d) What are the main similarities and differences between *NAM 24* and the sarabande in *NAM 21*?

Answer the following two questions only if you are taking the exam in 2003 or 2004.

(c) On what type of keyboard instrument might *NAM 20* have originally been played? Briefly mention any advantages or disadvantages there might be in playing it on a different type of keyboard instrument.

(d) Why can the style of *NAM 25* be described as neo-classical?

Sample question 2

(a) Explain what you understand by any **two** of the following:

binary form diatonic appoggiatura tierce de Picardie

(b) Link each term you have chosen in your answer to question (a) to a context from a specific work. Name the work, the precise location and the instrument or voice parts involved.

Answer the following two questions only if you are taking the exam in 2001 or 2002.

(c) What is a gigue? How does Bach convey the mood and style of a gigue in *NAM 21*?

(d) What are the main features of sonata form? Choose examples from *NAM 22* to illustrate your answer.

Answer the following two questions only if you are taking the exam in 2003 or 2004.

(c) Explain why the three short pieces in *NAM 23* can be described as character pieces.

(d) What are the main features of a fugue? Choose examples from *NAM 25* to illustrate your answer.

Sacred vocal music

All of the works in this Area of Study were written for the Christian religion, which has for centuries inspired a huge quantity of music. They include works designed to be sung as part of church services (both Catholic and Protestant are represented) as well as music that has been inspired by religion but that is intended for the concert hall. The works are taken from a wide range of musical styles:

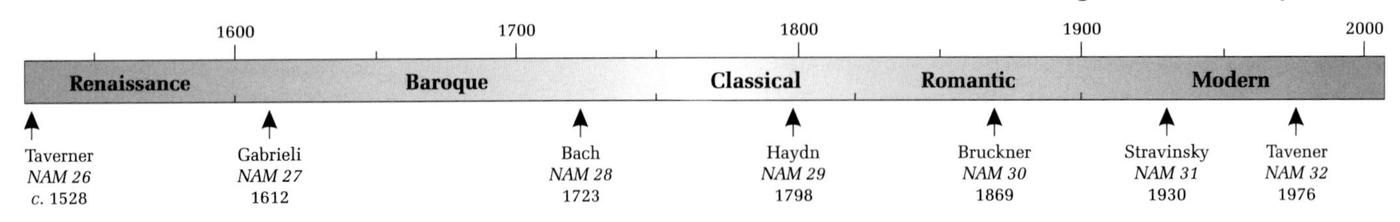

A *NAM 26* CD3 Track 1
Christ Church Cathedral Choir Oxford
Conducted by Stephen Darlington

O Wilhelme, pastor bone (Taverner)

In 1526 John Taverner, the greatest English composer of the early 16th century, was appointed to the prestigious post of Master of the Choristers at the newly-founded Cardinal College in Oxford. At that time the established church in England was still Roman Catholic, and services in the chapel of the college (now known as Christ Church) were sung in Latin.

For another Latin antiphon by an English composer of the 16th century, see *Aural Matters in Practice* (Bowman and Terry), page 12.

Cardinal Wolsey, the founder of the college, Lord Chancellor of England and Archbishop of York, stipulated that after the service of Compline (which was held at about 4pm in this college) three 'antiphons' should be sung – these were settings of religious texts for unaccompanied choir. *O Wilhelme, pastor bone* is addressed to St William, one of Thomas Wolsey's predecessors in the office of Archbishop of York. St William is asked to help all members of the college to 'banish the sins of this life' and to bring each of them 'the joy of a heavenly crown'. This general plea is followed by a special request for the protection of the founder, Cardinal Thomas. Alas, at least to human eyes, these prayers went unheeded, for Wolsey soon fell foul of King Henry VIII, was arrested on a charge of high treason and died in 1530 on the way to his trial. John Taverner left Cardinal College in the same year, but in his short term of office he probably wrote much of his most celebrated sacred music.

Notice that the recording on CD3 is sung by the modern-day successors to the Oxford choir for which John Taverner wrote this music some 470 years ago.

O Wilhelme was intended for an all-male choir. Boys would have sung the two top parts ('mean' refers to low treble voices, but this part is sung by male altos on CD3). The counter-tenor part is written with a tenor G clef (notice the little figure 8 below the clef) so the first note is middle C. On CD3 this part is sung by tenor voices.

In music of this period the need to produce an editorial reconstruction of a missing part is not uncommon. The skills involved are reflected in the renaissance counterpoint option in the compositional techniques part of Unit 2.

In the 16th century music of this sort was not normally written out in a score showing all the parts, as it is in *NAM 26*, but in separate books – one for each voice. The note at the start of the music explains that the tenor part of this piece has been lost. It is possible in music of this type to reconstruct a missing part by observing the stylistic conventions of the time. Of course one can never be absolutely certain what was written, so editorial reconstructions are bound to differ – the one in *NAM 26* is one possible version, while that sung on CD3 is another. Notice that this part also uses a tenor G clef (the first note is therefore F below middle C).

Word setting

Taverner uses a **syllabic** setting of the text until he reaches the last phrase (*aeternae vitae praemium*) where the end of the work is highlighted with a **melisma** in the upper parts. Each phrase of the text has its own melody and texture, sometimes separated from the following phrase by a decisive cadence, sometimes joined by overlapping the end of one phrase with the beginning of the next.

Textures

Taverner often varies the texture by dividing the choir into different groups of parts. Thus in bars 1–7 the words *O Wilhelme, pastor bone* are first sung by two parts in a high register, then by three parts in a low register, the melody of the uppermost part being exactly repeated an octave lower. This effect of one group of performers being answered by a contrasting group is known as **antiphony**. It also enables Taverner to keep in reserve the full impact of his five-part texture until bar 10. See how many different examples of antiphony you can spot.

The first three phrases of the text begin with mainly staggered entries of the parts rather than starting together. These entries are too dissimilar to be described as imitation, but the fact that the syllables of the text often do not coincide between the parts helps us to notice that we are listening to a combination of simultaneous melody lines. This type of texture is known as **polyphony**.

By way of contrast, Taverner later writes parts that do mainly coincide in rhythm. This is known as a **homophonic** texture and it is one in which the words can be more clearly heard than in polyphony. So it is not surprising to see it used when Taverner wants to highlight the importance of Cardinal Wolsey in bars 38–42.

Notice how the treble phrase in bars 33–37 is repeated by the bass in the antiphonal response of the next five bars. This same phrase then returns to the treble in bars 43–47.

Starting in bar 56 Taverner sets the words *Aeternae vitae praemium* to a figure beginning with a rising interval (a 3rd, 4th or 5th) and followed by a gentle descent. Each part enters in turn with this figure in a technique known as **imitation** – this is the third kind of texture found in the piece (polyphonic, homophonic and imitative). Notice how in bar 64 the trebles reach top F as the basses descend to the F three octaves below. It is probably no accident that the full range of the five-part choir is reserved for this climactic vision of eternity.

Harmony

Taverner's harmony consists entirely of triads in root position (sometimes without a 3rd) and first inversion. There is not a single on-the-beat discord in *NAM 26*. However the slightly different reconstruction of the tenor part on the recording does introduce a device known as a **suspension** at some of the cadences (see *right*). We do not know whether Taverner intended these discords – note that exam questions will only refer to the printed version, although knowing that other possibilities exist may prove useful to you.

Taverner sometimes makes use of **false relations**, such as the F♯ in bar 28 followed by F♮ in a different part in bar 29. The most pungent of these occurs in bar 41 where E♭ in the bass part is both preceded and followed by E♮ in the countertenor part. The use of this device is an integral part of English polyphonic style of the period.

Private study

1. How does the tenor G clef differ from the normal treble clef?
2. What is meant by a 'mean'?

3. What is the difference between syllabic and melismatic word-setting? Give an example of each type from *NAM 26*.

4. What term describes the texture of bars 48–49?

5. What features of this music (apart from the text) do you think make it suitable for use as church music?

B *NAM 27* CD3 Track 2
Gabrieli Consort and Players
Directed by Paul McCreesh

Before starting this section read the opening paragraphs on Gabrieli's *Sonata pian' e forte* on page 55 and be sure to listen to *NAM 14*.

For another motet by Giovanni Gabrieli, see *Aural Matters* (Bowman and Terry) pages 104–105.

In ecclesiis (Gabrieli)

The wealth of Venice along with the echoing spaces and multiple choir galleries of its grandest church, St Mark's, provided ideal circumstances for the development of a dramatic **polychoral** style of church music. Andrea Gabrieli (organist of St Mark's from 1566 to 1585, followed by his nephew Giovanni Gabrieli (organist until 1612) wrote music that relied for its effect almost entirely on contrasting textures and antiphonal exchanges between spatially separated choirs of instruments and voices.

Instruments

The ensemble for this work includes three *cornetti*, an instrument also heard in *NAM 14*. It is a wooden wind instrument with fingerholes and a brass mouthpiece. Its tone is like that of a soft trumpet and it was often used with trombones at this time.

A full-time instrumental ensemble was established at St Mark's in 1568. At first this would double or even replace vocal parts, but as the performers became more expert, composers began to write for specific instruments in an idiomatic style that contrasted with the style of choral music. You can hear this if you compare the dotted rhythms and repeated notes that start in bar 31 with the simple choral melodies of the *alleluja* which precedes it.

At the same time, solo singers were becoming more accomplished and were often assigned dramatic roles – you can hear this in bars 57–60, where the voices are matched by equally virtuoso cornett parts. By the end of the 16th century all of these forces, vocal and instrumental, were held together by an organ part improvised from a bass part (the *basso per l'organo* in the score). The improvisation can be realised in many ways – the score of *NAM 27* offers one suggestion and the recording on CD3 offers another.

Useful terms

The divided choirs of polychoral music, with singers placed in different parts of the building, are sometimes called *cori spezzati*. Compositions of the early 17th century that combine and contrast vocal and instrumental ensembles, supported by a **continuo** bass part are described as being in *stile concertato* (concerted style).

Structure

The text of *In ecclesiis* is a Latin hymn of praise divided into five sections by repeated interjections of the Hebrew word *alleluja*. Listen to the whole work and see if you agree with the following:

- each of the first four phrases of the Latin text is set for one or two solo voices and has its own distinctive melody
- the choral interjections of *alleluja* are the same each time they appear (though different groups of solo voices and instruments are added to the chorus parts on each occasion)
- the last sentence (*Deus adjutor noster in aeternum*) and the final *alleluja* section are scored in 14 parts for all three choirs
- there is an instrumental interlude (sinfonia) which divides the two vocal solos from the two vocal duets.

The result is a **rondo** structure built around the central sinfonia, with *alleluja* (B) as the refrain: A–B–C–B–sinfonia–D–B–E–B.

The new style

Gabrieli and some of his contemporaries used a number of new techniques in a style that at the time was described as the **seconda prattica** (the second practice, the first practice being the polyphonic style of the 16th century). These new techniques are ones that we now associate with baroque music. The combination of solo voices, choir and instruments supported by a continuo group is the most obvious such feature, but there are more specific examples. The **ostinato** bass figure that starts in bar 3, and the rhythmic repeated phrase above it, is another hint at the new style, as is the use of various types of **sequence** in bars 13–19. The striking chromatic chord (an augmented triad) on the third beat of bar 31, and the strings of dotted rhythms that follow are also typical of this new trend.

When the combined choirs and instruments enter with a massive homophonic setting of *Deus* at bar 102, Gabrieli uses the dramatic effect of two unrelated chords a third apart (F major and D major). New ways of using harmony are evident in this closing section. For instance there are unprepared discords, such as the D♮ sounding against G♯ in bar 104, and the climactic effect of a dominant **pedal** in bars 115–117.

There are, of course, more traditional techniques in the piece as well. The change to triple time for the *alleluja* sections was common in earlier music, as was the use of a **tierce de Picardie** in the final cadence (although the rather neat idea of finishing the piece with the same four chords with which it began is a more novel effect). You should be able to spot points of imitation (bars 10–11) and the use of contrapuntal textures – although the counterpoint suggesting the teeming life of eternity in bars 115–118 is much more rhythmically complex than the flowing polyphony of *NAM 26*.

Private study

1. How does the vocal solo in bars 26–31 differ from the vocal solo in bars 7–12?

2. Look up the terms **melisma** and **syllabic** in the glossary and then give an example of each type of word-setting in this piece.

3. Why does the harmony sound so dramatic in bars 108–109?

4. With what type of cadence does *In ecclesiis* end?

5. Why does *NAM 27* sound more modern than *NAM 26*?

Cantata 48, movements 1–4 (Bach)

A NAM 28 CD3 Tracks 3–6
Yorkshire Bach Choir
Fitzwilliam Ensemble
Clare Mathias (alto)
Conducted by Peter Seymour

A cantata is an extended piece of music for one or more voices with accompaniment. Most use forms borrowed from opera although they were not generally intended for stage performance.

Extracts from another Bach cantata may be found in *Aural Matters* (Bowman and Terry) pages 116–118.

In protestant Germany the cantata was adapted for use in the long services of the Lutheran church. German composers, most notably Bach, often included accompaniments for a small orchestra and added choral movements of a kind that had developed from the *stile concertato* that we saw in *NAM 27*. In addition one or more German hymn tunes (known as chorales) are incorporated in most of these church cantatas – in straightforward harmonisations and sometimes also as the basis of more elaborate movements.

Bach's main responsibility as director of music in Leipzig's principal church was to compose and direct the performance of nearly 60 cantatas a year for Sunday services and church festivals. Like most of his music, these works were not published in Bach's lifetime; more than 200 survived in manuscripts, but at least 100 were lost after the composer's death. They include a huge variety of music, from solo cantatas without choir (probably sung by one of Bach's many unfortunate sons when the choir was on holiday) to the cycle of six festive cantatas that form the *Christmas Oratorio*. They also encompass almost every type of music known to Bach, from the most serious counterpoint to the jolliest of dance styles.

The complete cantata, which is printed in the old *London Anthology of Music*, has three more movements: a recitative and an aria for tenor soloist and then the chorale on which the first movement is based.

In the four movements from Cantata 48, which was probably composed in 1723, we see two operatic forms – the **recitative** (page 296) and the **aria** (page 297) – as well as a simple harmonisation of a chorale (page 297) and a version of a different chorale used as the basis of a concerted movement for choir and orchestra.

In the Lutheran church service specific Bible readings focused on a theme for the day and a lengthy sermon explained the significance of the readings to the congregation. The cantata was sung before the sermon and would include a setting of a key text from one of the readings. In Cantata 48 this biblical text is heard in the first movement. The anonymous texts of the recitative and aria are personal meditations on the biblical text of the first movement, and are accordingly given to a soloist. The chorale makes the sentiments expressed in the other movements relevant to the whole congregation (although whether they sang it with the choir is not known).

Movement 1

Listen to this movement and then state where the opening 12 bars are repeated exactly. Did you notice that these bars also appear in abbreviated versions in other places? This is known as **ritornello** form. Ritornello means 'a little return', the term reflecting the use of shortened repetitions (between contrasting episodes) as a structural device. It is a form that was widely used in the late-baroque period, especially in concertos such as *NAM 1*. The ritornello here is characterised by minor keys, sequences and discords (on the first beats of bars 1, 2, 6 and 8) that underline the rather grim text.

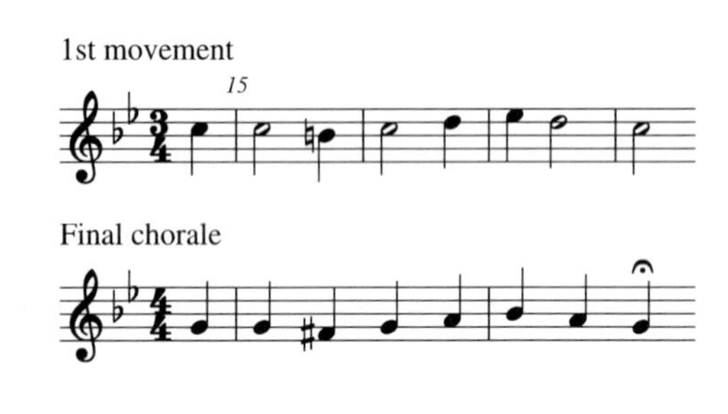

An adaptation of the chorale melody with which the cantata ends is played in **canon** by the trumpet and oboes (see *left*). A pre-existing melody (such as this) against which other tunes are set in counterpoint is known as a cantus firmus. Around this the choir declaims the text in a succession of imitative entries (often canonic in style, but not strictly in canon), and below both sets of parts the ritornello emerges frequently in a feat of amazing contrapuntal complexity.

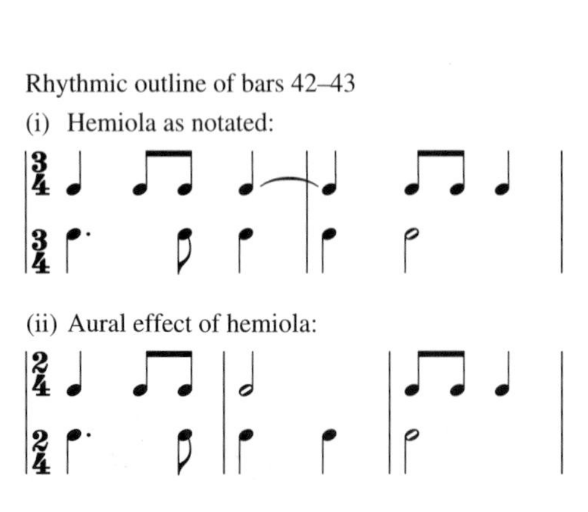

Because of Bach's incorporation of the chorale melody the music is mainly in G minor with modulations to related minor keys (again reflecting the solemn text). Most of the main sections end with a rhythmic device called a **hemiola**. This has the effect of highlighting the cadences by making two bars of 3/4 time sound like three bars of 2/4 (see *left*) and is found in much triple-time baroque music. Notice the calming effect of the long tonic pedal at the end of the movement, and the tierce de Picardie in the final cadence.

The string parts in *NAM 28* are laid out on two staves, the lowest notes of which are played by the **continuo**. The continuo always includes a chordal instrument – in a sacred work such as this it would be the organ. The figures and other symbols below this part form a **figured bass** to indicate what types of chord the organist should improvise. For example, '7' in bar 1 indicates a 7th above the bass note C, which in this context the organist would realise with a Cm^7 chord. Most of the figures have been added by modern editors – Bach himself wrote very few.

Movement 2

Listen to the word-setting in this movement. Do you notice that it is entirely different to the first movement? The text flows past at a much faster rate and the rhythms seem to reflect those of natural speech. The accompaniment is purely supportive and it modulates very rapidly through a number of keys. This type of music is called **recitative**. Because its accompaniment includes a string ensemble it is known more specifically as accompanied recitative.

Later in the cantata Bach used a different type of recitative in which the accompaniment is provided only by the continuo. This is known as secco ('dry') recitative. An example can be seen in the first eight bars of *NAM 36*.

The somewhat lurid text is of a type very popular among some German protestants at the time and is expressed through:

- detached melodic fragments to highlight the sighs and dramatic expressions of self-contempt ('O the pain, O the misery')
- angular melodic lines with tortured leaps such as the diminished 7th on *Elend!* (misery) in bar 2
- extreme dissonance such as the minor 9th between the singer and the bass on the first beat of bar 2
- modulation to a foreign key at bar 10, where the music suddenly moves to E major at the words *stärkste Gift* (strongest poison).

Listen to the recording of the recitative and see if you can spot how the singer embellishes the repeated quavers at the start of bars 7, 11 and 14. Such decoration is typical of the performing practices of Bach's day.

Movement 3

This is a chorale – and if you are studying chorale harmonisation for Unit 2 it is a valuable opportunity to hear one performed – notice that it is played by instruments as well as sung by four-part choir, and that the double bass sounds an octave below the printed bass.

The actual chorale melody is purely **diatonic**, but it is totally transformed by Bach's **chromatic** harmonisation. The use of chords such as the diminished 7th allow unexpected modulations to G minor (bar 2) and A♭ major (bar 6). Instead of the expected perfect cadence in B♭ major at the end of the chorale melody Bach introduces an A♭ which sparks off a series of anguished **suspensions** (for instance the alto G♭ against the tenor F in bar 9).

Movement 4

The fourth movement is an obbligato **aria** – a song with an equally important (obligatory) instrumental solo. When you listen to it try to note where and how the opening music returns.

Did you spot that sometimes only little fragments of the opening music come back? For instance the singer starts with the opening four bars of oboe music, and in bars 23–24 the oboe itself plays a fragment from bars 5–6. Do you recognise this musical form?

Supporting the duet between singer and oboe is a bass that moves almost entirely in quavers. This type of very regular pattern is known as a 'walking bass'.

The aria is in E♭ major and falls into two main sections. The first ends in the dominant key of B♭ major at bar 38 while the second moves straight into C minor and then, as in most late baroque **binary-form** movements, through a number of closely related keys before returning to E♭ major in the perfect cadence of bars 78–79. The opening ritornello (bars 1–16) is then repeated, as indicated by the performance direction *D.C. al Fine* – repeat from the beginning as far as the word *Fine* (meaning finish).

Private study

1. Which of the four movements would you describe as homophonic and which as contrapuntal?
2. Is the word-setting in the recitative melismatic or syllabic?
3. What is a cantus firmus? How is it used in the first movement?
4. What are the main differences between the recitative and aria?
5. What is a chorale? Name two ways in which Bach uses chorales.
6. What two similarities do you notice between the final cadence on page 295 and the final cadence of *NAM 27*?

Quoniam tu solus (Haydn)

A *NAM 29* CD3 Track 7
Barbara Bonney (soprano)
Anne Howells (mezzo-soprano)
Anthony Rolfe Johnson (tenor)
Stephen Roberts (baritone)
London Symphony Chorus
City of London Sinfonia
Conducted by Richard Hickox

Compared to *NAM 26–28* Haydn's music seems incredibly jolly. When he was criticised for composing masses in a style no different from his symphonies Haydn said that he couldn't help himself, for every time he thought of God his 'heart leapt for joy'. In fact for much of the time the orchestral part makes perfectly good musical sense without the vocal parts. Try playing it and you will find that only in bars 1–2, 5 and 7–8 is the vocal part absolutely essential: for the rest the chorus either sing a simplified version of the orchestral part (bars 3–22 and 57–61) or they double the orchestral parts (bars 22–57). It is not until the last 22 bars that the voices and orchestra have entirely independent roles to play.

The mass is the most important service in the Roman Catholic church. Musical settings of the mass, such as the one from which this extract is taken, generally have five main sections, each sung at a different point in the service. The words of *NAM 29* are the last part of the section called the *Gloria* – a joyful text of praise.

When Haydn wrote this mass in 1798 his original title was *Missa in angustiis* (Mass in time of fear), reflecting the terror of the Napoleonic wars then threatening Europe. That same year Admiral Nelson blew up Napoleon's navy and when in 1800 Nelson visited Austria (and met Haydn) it is likely that this mass was one of the works performed in the admiral's honour. It was certainly at that time that the work acquired the nickname *Nelson* Mass.

As was customary in the classical period, Haydn divides the *Gloria* into three independent sections (*Allegro–Adagio–Allegro*) like a three-movement symphony or concerto. *NAM 29* is the third of these sections and, like the finales of many of his symphonies, contains homophonic textures (bars 1–22), a **fugal** section (bars 22–61) and a **coda** (bars 61–82).

Listen to the homophonic opening (bars 1–22) and try to give specific bar numbers for each of the following features:

- question-and-answer passages between soloist and chorus
- mainly diatonic harmonies, with much use of chords I and V
- a tonic pedal
- passages where a melody sung by the choir sopranos is, at the same time, played in a more ornate version by the orchestra (this is a texture known as **heterophony**).

The fugal section begins with a two-bar subject sung by the basses and accompanied by a countersubject of staccato quavers in the orchestra. Notice that both parts use a short sequence.

When the tenors enter with a slightly altered version of the subject in bar 24 the basses sing the countersubject. This pattern continues until all the vocal parts have entered. The basses have another go at it in bar 30, then the tenors in bar 32.

The terrific sense of excitement in the rest of this section is largely attributable to Haydn's use of **stretto** (a contrapuntal device in which imitative entries are telescoped). Thus the sopranos enter in bar 33, just one bar after the tenors – and all three upper parts enter at one-bar intervals in bars 46–48. The fugal texture fizzles out as sopranos and altos descend through a series of suspensions (bars 57–60) to a perfect cadence in the tonic (bars 60–61).

The completely diatonic coda consists of tonic pedals above which bass and tenor soloists pursue each other in a sort of round, decorated by the soprano's triadic descant. The movement ends with three perfect cadences, the last one brilliantly scored so that both tenors and sopranos end on the 3rd of the tonic chord.

Private study

1. What do you notice about the size of the orchestra compared with earlier works in this chapter? Which type of instrument can you hear which did not appear in any of those earlier works?
2. Compare bars 7–8 with bars 13–14.
4. On pages 303–304 where do you hear (i) a homophonic texture, (ii) a dominant pedal, and (iii) a tonic pedal?
4. What makes this music sound so happy?

Locus iste (Bruckner)

A *NAM 30* CD3 Track 8
Christ Church Cathedral Choir Oxford
Conducted by Stephen Darlington

An aural test based on this work can be found in *Aural Matters in Practice* (Bowman and Terry) pages 18–19.

Locus iste, written in 1869 by the Austrian composer Bruckner, is a motet. The term has had many meanings over the centuries but here it refers (as it did in the renaissance) to a short piece of sacred music with Latin text for unaccompanied choir. It was written for the dedication of a church ('This is a place that God has made') and was possibly performed for the first time in the vast new cathedral of Linz where Bruckner was organist from 1855 to 1870.

The simple C-major melody of the first four bars at first sounds as if it is repeated in sequence, but it is subtly varied so that, having passed through G major, it ends back in C.

For the second phrase of the text ('a wonderful mystery') Bruckner devises an aspiring melodic ascent, first to an imperfect cadence in D minor (bar 16), then to the same cadence in E minor (bar 20). Bar 21 introduces a thinner three-part texture of hushed chromatic harmonies returning to an imperfect cadence in the tonic at bar 29.

In the ensuing repeat of the opening, the cadence originally heard in bars 11–12 is chromatically extended – Bruckner marks this passage with a crescendo leading to a loud chord so that the final chord in bar 42 will echo around large churches in the total silence that follows, before the final *pianissimo* cadence in C major.

The fact that *Locus iste* is Latin church music for unaccompanied choir, with a little use of imitation, can mislead the casual listener into assuming that it must be from the renaissance. However the motet has a number of features which identify it as romantic music if you listen carefully – warmly, expressive melodies, dramatic contrasts of dynamics, some unusual melodic intervals (such as the major 7th in the soprano between bars 9 and 10), chromatic passages, some rich harmonies and lingering dissonances (soprano and alto, bar 46). However all of these devices are used in great moderation by Bruckner and in a far less flamboyant way than most of his romantic contemporaries.

?

Private study

1. Which earlier work in this chapter could be described as a motet?
2. What features of this piece do you feel make it appropriate for use as church music?
3. Compare the soprano in bars 13–16 with the soprano part in bars 17–20. What technical device is Bruckner using here?
4. To what extent is imitation used in this motet?

B *NAM 31* CD3 Track 9
Choir of Westminster Cathedral
City of London Sinfonia
Conducted by James O'Donnell

Symphony of Psalms, movement 3 (Stravinsky)

All of the music we have so far discussed was intended for performance as part of a church service. Even Haydn's elaborate masses would originally have been sung as an integral part of the Roman Catholic liturgy, though they are now most often heard in concerts.

The *Symphony of Psalms* was, as the title suggests, intended for the concert hall, although Stravinsky made it clear that

> 'It is not a symphony in which I have included Psalms to be sung. On the contrary, it is the singing of the Psalms that I am symphonizing.'

The sheer size of the unusual orchestra (in which there are no clarinets, violins or violas) would in any case make the work impractical to incorporate within a church service: 14 woodwind, four horns in F (sounding a perfect 5th lower than printed), a trumpet in D (sounding a tone higher than printed), four more trumpets, three trombones, tuba, timpani, bass drum, harp, two pianos, cellos, double basses (the latter sounding an octave lower than printed) and an all-male four-part choir (although it is often sung by mixed voices). The hard-edged timbres and variety of clear textures that Stravinsky achieves with these forces are as vital to his concept of the piece as the notes themselves.

Despite these formidable resources the *Symphony of Psalms* (composed in 1930) is an understated work. This is particularly apparent in Stravinsky's setting of Psalm 150, which forms the third and last movement of the symphony. He shuns obvious opportunities for word painting. For instance at 'Praise him in the sound of the trumpet' (bars 87–94) the trumpets are very much in the background. When the text mentions *timpano* in bar 152 Stravinsky studiously avoids using timpani, and the *cymbalis* (cymbals) sung about in bar 165 are not even included in his orchestra. Similarly when Stravinsky interpolates the word *Alleluia* (in much the same way as Gabrieli does in *NAM 27*) he sets it softly for unaccompanied voices: the effect is one of rapt adoration rather than the great outburst of joy with which composers usually treat this word.

Stravinsky himself identified two ideas that are central to this movement. The first is a figure of two linked 3rds first heard in bars 29–32 (G–B♭ and A♭–C). This motif recurs at different pitches and on different instruments, for example piano 2 in bars 109–112. It also unifies the movement in less obvious ways. For instance in bar 38 the notes of the motif are presented in a different order in the trombone and piano parts – the first and last notes make the 3rd C–A♭, while the middle two make the third B♭–D).

By a similar reordering Stravinsky constructs the whole melody of bars 4–11, the outer notes of *laudate* being D–B♭, the next phrase using C–E♭. This melody, suggesting E♭ major, is accompanied by a bass part outlining a triad of C major – the technique of using two keys at the same time is known as bitonality and was frequently used by Stravinsky. These clashing chords wonderfully resolve to a plain C-major triad (the tonic of the whole movement) in bar 7 – significantly on the capitalised Latin name for God.

The second of Stravinsky's ideas that dominate the whole movement is the six-note rhythm first heard in bar 24. This is used to generate excitement as it steps up in the horns from a C-major triad (bars 32–36) to a D-major triad (bar 37) then an E-major triad (bars 40–43).

In bar 65 the rhythm is shifted forward a quaver to form the setting of the key words of the movement (*Laudate Dominum*, Praise the Lord). In the recapitulation this rhythm is sung to a series of chords that rise from C major (bars 114–121) through E major (bars 126–128) to B♭ major.

Stravinsky wrote that this movement

> 'was inspired by a vision of Elijah's chariot climbing the heavens … never before had I written anything quite so literal as the triplets … to suggest the horses and chariots.'

He is referring to the triplet figures in bars 40–47 which culminate in the massive D-major chords (with bass G♯) of bars 48–49. In the recapitulation these triplets are overlapped with the rhythmic

Laudate Dominum motif (bars 126–134), but now, propelled by the higher-rising chords, they culminate in massive E-major chords (with bass A♯) in the main climax of the movement at bars 144–146.

Another important element in the movement, and one that helps account for its hypnotic effect, is the measured tread of slowly revolving **ostinato** patterns. There are heard in the accompaniment of bars 14–19 and, most memorably, in the coda. Starting at bar 163 the four-note pattern of 4ths played by timpani, harp and pianos, is heard more than 30 times, underpinning the exquisitely balanced dissonances of this final section. The *alleluia* returns one more time at bar 205, to be followed by the complete resolution of all tonal tension in the plain C-major triad with which the *Symphony of Psalms* ends.

Private study

1. What does the ostinato which starts in bar 163 have in common with bar 4?

2. The time signature of the coda (bar 163) is three minim beats in a bar. What effect does this metre have on the four-beat length of the ostinato figure?

3. In bar 65 do the altos and tenors sing in harmony, in octaves or in unison?

4. (i) From what is the soprano motif in bar 150 constructed?
   (ii) How does the bass entry in the next bar relate to this?
   (iii) What do you notice about the part played by the contra-bassoon and bass trombone throughout bars 150–156?

5. What is unusual about the orchestration of this work?

6. What do you notice about the voicing (that is the spacing and layout) of the final chord of the work? (Remember that the cor anglais sounds a perfect 5th lower than written.)

B *NAM 32* CD3 Track 10
Westminster Abbey Choir
Directed by Martin Neary

The Lamb (John Tavener)

When in 1964 the 20-year old Tavener met Stravinsky (then 82 and in England to conduct his *Symphony of Psalms*) the younger composer managed to show the grand old man of 20th-century music a score of his *Three Holy Sonnets*. After reading it Stravinsky looked intently at Tavener then, without saying a word, he wrote in the score 'I know'.

An aural test on *The Lamb* may be found in *Aural Matters* (Bowman and Terry) page 154.

The influence of Stravinsky's austere religious music on Tavener's style is evident even in a miniature such as *The Lamb* – compare the hushed, unaccompanied *Alleluias* in the *Symphony of Psalms* with the final bars of *NAM 32*.

Tavener's music became increasingly popular in the final decades of the 20th century, and the performance of his *Song for Athene* (1993) that brought the funeral of Princess Diana to its moving close in 1997 ensured that he has become one of the best-known composers of contemporary art music.

The Lamb (1985) is a sacred song written for four-part choir and set to an 18th-century poem by William Blake. It is rather like a motet with English words (a type of music known as an anthem in the Church of England) making it suitable for performance in church services. Blake takes the image of a lamb as a delightful woolly creature and compares its innocence with the traditional metaphor of Christ as the lamb of God in the second verse of the poem. Notice that there is no time signature. Although some bars have a distinctly 4/4 feel others are much freer. As Tavener indicates at the start, the rhythm is always guided by the words and not by a regular pulse imposed on those words, as occurs in *NAM 29*, for example.

Listen to the whole piece, especially noting the textures used by Tavener, and answer the following questions:

1. How does the texture of the opening reflect the simple image of the little lamb?

2. How does Tavener make the texture warmer for the phrase 'Gave thee such a tender voice'?

3. What sort of texture helps give the first statement of the words 'Little Lamb, I'll tell thee' a firm, instructional tone?

The opening bar is not only **monophonic** but it also uses just four notes from the scale of G major, giving the question a very childlike expression of innocence.

Now look at the first entry of the alto part and compare it with the opening melody. Can you see how it is constructed? Every interval of the soprano melody has been reused in **inversion**. The soprano part is in G major, its mirror image in the alto is in E♭ major. Do you remember, from your work on Stravinsky, the term used for music that uses two keys at the same time? The simultaneous use of a melody and its own mirror image is used to express the rhetorical question asked of the lamb – 'Dost thou know who made thee?' – the only possible answer is shown to be reflected in the question itself.

The second melody (bars 3–4), although returning to monophonic simplicity, now combines the keys of G major (at the beginning and end) and E♭ major in the middle. Out of these two melodies Tavener constructs the rest of the anthem.

In bars 5–6 the second melody is repeated and is accompanied by its exact mirror in the alto part. In bars 7–10 the opening melody is presented four times in a homophonic texture in which all four parts are heard for the first time. The harmonisation throws new light on what had previously seemed to be a simple tune in G major, because all the notes are from the aeolian **mode** on E (like E minor, but with D♮ instead of D♯) giving the music a more wistful quality. What do you notice when you compare the rhythm of bar 10 with that of bar 9? This is called **augmentation**, and it gives this last repetition of the bar a sense of finality for the end of verse one.

In the second verse (bars 11–20) the same structure is simply rescored: octaves instead of unison trebles in bars 11 and 13–14, pairs of voices (soprano/tenor and alto/bass) in octaves instead of just trebles and altos in bars 12 and 15–16. The setting of the final four lines of the second verse is exactly the same as the setting of the final four lines of the first verse.

Slow, free rhythms that avoid regular patterns and understated textures in which a minimal number of musical events are used to create a meditative and sensory experience for the listener are features of the contemporary style known as post-modernism. In *The Lamb* Tavener combines diatonic writing, bitonality and modality – with just three bars of melody.

Private study

1. Compare bars 11–14 with bars 1–4.
2. State two ways in which bar 20 is given a more final quality than bar 19.
3. What is an anthem?
4. What term describes the style of word setting in *The Lamb*?
5. What aspects of the music identify it as 20th-century?

Sample question 1

(a) Explain what you understand by any **two** of the following:

imitation   antiphonal   continuo   walking bass

(b) Link each term you have chosen in your answer to question (a) to a context from a specific work. Name the work, the precise location and the instrument or voice parts involved.

Answer the following two questions only if you are taking the exam in 2001 or 2002.

(c) (i) Name and locate three different types of vocal texture in *NAM 29*.
(ii) How does Haydn make the central section of *NAM 29* sound exciting?

(d) Compare and contrast the motets by Taverner (*NAM 26*) and Bruckner (*NAM 30*).

Answer the following two questions only if you are taking the exam in 2003 or 2004.

(c) Compare the style and function of Stravinsky's setting of the word *Alleluia* in *NAM 31* with Gabrieli's setting of the same word in *NAM 27*.

(d) Show how Tavener creates the whole of *NAM 32* from a minimal amount of musical material.

Sample question 2

(a) Explain what you understand by any **two** of the following:

cori spezzati   cantus firmus   obbligato   cornett

(b) Link each term you have chosen in your answer to question (a) to a context from a specific work. Name the work, the precise location and the instrument or voice parts involved.

Answer the following two questions only if you are taking the exam in 2001 or 2002.

(c) Indicate **four** aspects of *NAM 30* that identify it as a romantic work.

(d) Name the four different type of movement used by Bach in *NAM 28* and briefly state the main characteristics of each.

Answer the following two questions only if you are taking the exam in 2003 or 2004.

(c) Mention **four** aspects of *NAM 31* that you feel are particularly musically effective. Refer to specific bar numbers in your answer.

(d) Compare and contrast the style of vocal writing in *NAM 32* with that in *NAM 27*.

Secular vocal music

Secular means non-religious, and secular vocal music encompasses solo songs, madrigals and other pieces for small groups of singers and even excerpts from opera. The nine examples we shall study include a number of different styles of music, from the time of Shakespeare to the early 20th century, and include settings of English, French, German and Italian texts:

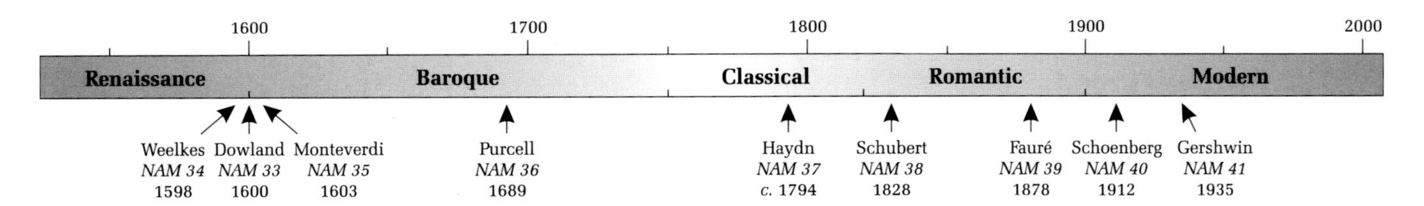

The focus of your study should be the musical techniques used by composers to bring out the meaning of their chosen texts and the ways in which they use the voice as an expressive musical instrument. If you choose to write a vocal composition (for example in the 'Music theatre' option) the study of these techniques should suggest a number of ideas that you could use or adapt in your own vocal settings. If you are a singer this study will hopefully help inform your own performances and you in turn may be able to help the rest of your study group by demonstrating some of the pieces in live performance.

Madrigals

In the 16th and early 17th centuries the madrigal was a musical setting of a poem, composed for several voices. It was usually performed by solo singers, either unaccompanied or supported by a plucked string instrument such as a lute. Sometimes melody instruments such as viols (precursors of the modern string family) would replace one or more of the voice parts if necessary.

The madrigal originated in Italy but soon spread to other countries, notably England where Italian culture was all the rage in the late 16th century. Madrigal singing in the home became an important social accomplishment for educated Elizabethans, as suggested by the quotation *right* from a book published in 1597. The popularity of such amateur music-making was helped by the invention of music printing earlier in the century. Collections of madrigals were usually printed as a set of part books, each containing the music for just one voice part – there was normally no score. Some types of madrigal publications were printed with all the parts at right-angles to each other so that the book could be put in the middle of a table with all the singers sitting or standing around (see *right*).

'But supper being ended, and Musicke bookes, according to the custome being brought to the table: the mistresse of the house presented mee with a part, earnestly requesting mee to sing. But when after manie excuses, I protested unfainedly that I could not: everie one began to wonder. Yea, some whispered to others, demaunding how I was brought up …'

Plaine and Easie Introduction to Practicall Musicke, in which the author and composer Thomas Morley explains how a pupil feels inadequate at his lack of musical skill.

The first collections consisted of translations of mainly Italian madrigals, such as the appropriately named *Musica Transalpina* ('Music from across the Alps') published in London in 1588 and *Italian madrigals Englished* (1590). However English composers soon started to produce great quantities of their own music for the domestic vocal-music market, resulting in a brief but glorious age of English madrigals in the late 16th and early 17th centuries.

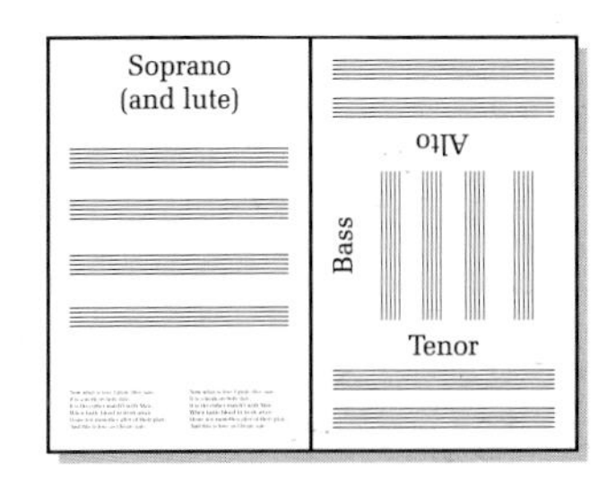

A *NAM 34* CD3 Track 12
Purcell Consort of Voices
Directed by Grayston Burgess

Sing we at pleasure (Weelkes)

Thomas Weelkes was one of the greatest of the English madrigalists. His madrigals range in style from intensely serious works full of poignant dissonances to the carefree jollity of *Sing we at pleasure*, first published in 1598.

Ballett is pronounced like cassette, not like ballet (*bal*-ay), even though both words are clearly related to dancing.

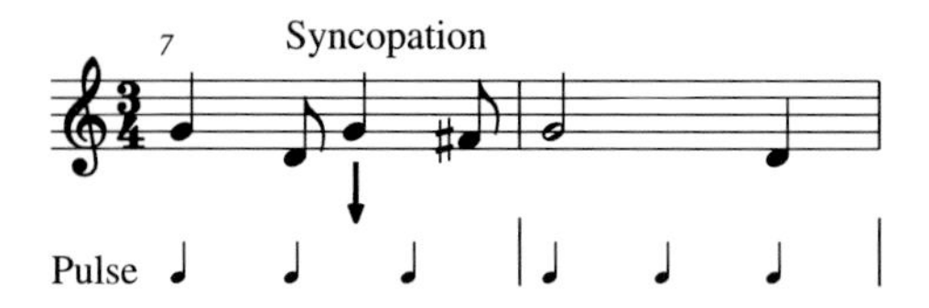

This type of madrigal is known as a ballett and is characterised by a light, dance-like style and a *fa-la-la* refrain. The origin of this **genre** is found in the *balletto*, an Italian instrumental or vocal dance of the 16th century. The dance style is brought out by word setting that is almost entirely **syllabic** (one note per syllable), and lively triple-metre rhythms that are enlivened by **syncopation**, such as in the alto at bar 7, shown *left*.

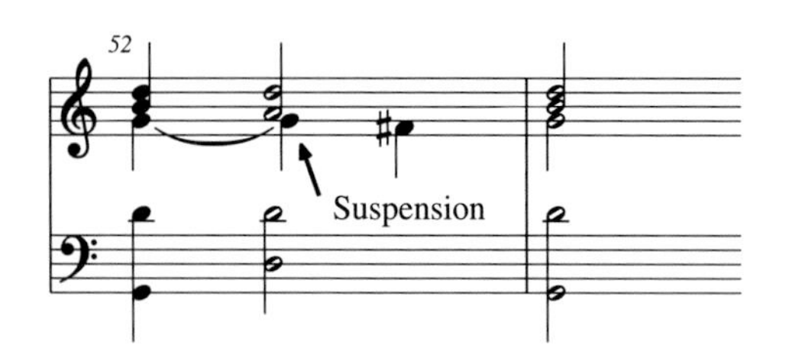

The **consonant** style is largely attributable to the fact that all of the chords are triads in root position or first inversion, most of them major. The only on-the-beat discords are:

- **Suspensions**, sometimes written in crotchets (alto, bar 52, shown *left*) and sometimes in quavers (alto, bar 7). Both are associated with syncopation and give impetus to the dancing rhythms that prevail throughout most of the ballett.
- **Tritones** between the outer parts (at the end of bars 10, 13 and 16) – these are one of the fingerprints of Weelkes' style.

Despite the lack of key signatures these chords, both consonant and dissonant, clearly define the key of G major and suggest passing modulations to D major (bars 9–11^2) and C major (bars 15^3–17). However the idea of using related key centres was still relatively new at this time, and the lingering influence of the modal system is apparent when Weelkes uses a triad of F major, totally foreign to G major, on the last beat of bar 14.

Textures

The ballett divides into a number of contrasting sections that correspond with phrases of the text. Each verbal phrase has its own characteristic melodic shape which is either treated in **imitation** or used as the top part in a contrasting **homophonic** texture.

Sometimes these sections overlap, as when 'Sing we at pleasure' overlaps with 'content is our treasure' on the third beat of bar 3. Every section ends with a perfect cadence in G major, except for 'All shepherds in a ring', which ends with an imperfect cadence in the same key. Some of these cadences mark a break in the flow of the music and a change of texture (as in bar 22, where the counterpoint of the refrain ends and the first homophonic passage begins).

Notice how Weelkes' textures are very fluid. The opening is treated imitatively in the soprano parts while the other parts provide homophonic support. After less than four bars a second **imitative point** ('content is our treasure') employs a different texture. It is announced by soprano 2 and tenor in tenths, and imitated by soprano 1 and bass also in 10ths. When the *fa-la-la* starts in bar 8 the imitation is shared between three parts: bass and both sopranos, while alto and tenor have **contrapuntal** but non-imitative lines.

Weelkes appropriately unites the voices in homophony for the start of 'Sweet love shall keep the ground', but this is immediately followed by very close imitation for 'Whilst we his praises sound' where the entries tumble in only one beat apart.

The voices again come together in homophony and simple root-position triads at 'All shepherds in a ring'. The word underlay of 'Dancing' places the second syllable on an unstressed quaver, giving a syncopated effect, and this tripping dotted rhythm accompanies the word whenever it appears. Notice how the sopranos ascend a seven-note scale to top G as they 'ever sing' in imitation with one another.

Bars 43–53 introduce another new texture. The most remarkable feature of this *fa-la-la* is the **canon** between the two top parts. The second soprano sings the same notes as the first soprano but one bar later until the end of bar 51. The almost continuous quavers shared between the tenor and bass propel the joyful counterpoint forward, but the alto has to be satisfied with an inner tonic **pedal** lasting 7 bars.

Bars 53–84 are a repeat of bars 22–53 with the sopranos exchanging parts in some passages. Notice that these two top parts have the same range and Weelkes capitalises on this by featuring much crossing of their parts throughout the piece so that first one and then the other attracts the attention in the imitative points and on the high notes. The delightful stereophonic effects this can create are evident on the recording.

Performance

If possible, try and sing the madrigal. It will not matter if you have to replace some of the parts by instruments – as mentioned earlier, this was not uncommon in Elizabethan times. The pitch of the recording matches the score, but most scholars believe that pitch at this time was about a tone lower than it is today, so it may not be inappropriate (and it may be more comfortable for singing) to transpose the piece a little lower. Remember that the single most important element of the ballett is its lively, dancing rhythm.

Private study

1. In which country did the madrigal originate?
2. What are the main features of a ballett?
3. How and where might *Sing we at pleasure* have been performed in Elizabethan times? Mention the number of singers you might expect to be involved.
4. The alto part in bar 7 is syncopated. Identify four other examples of syncopation on page 349.
5. Briefly explain the difference between a homophonic texture and a contrapuntal texture, and give an example of each.
6. Which of the following is true about soprano 2 in bars 69–72?

   (a) It imitates the soprano 2 part of bars 36–39.
   (b) It imitates the soprano 1 part of bars 38–41.
   (c) It imitates the soprano 1 part of bars 67–70.
7. Where does a canon occur on page 352?
8. With what sort of cadence does the madrigal end?

A *NAM 35* CD3 Track 13
The Consort of Musicke
Directed by Anthony Rooley

Ohimè, se tanto amate (Monteverdi)

While English composers such as Weelkes continued to write madrigals in a conservative style in the early 17th century their Italian counterparts developed a new madrigalian style governed by the precepts of the **seconda prattica**. This 'second practice' was consciously developed by composers such as Claudio Monteverdi in a desire to create a new style in which music would be the servant of the words. The consequences are evident in madrigals such as *Ohimè, se tanto amate* (first published in Venice in 1603) in which sophisticated poetry is reflected at every point in Monteverdi's equally sophisticated music. Every one of the following stylistic features flow from the principles of this new style:

A translation of the poem is printed on page 539 of the *New Anthology of Music*.

- The word setting is almost entirely **syllabic** for maximum clarity of the text.
- Extremely irregular rhythms change with each new phrase of the poem and closely follow the rhythms of the Italian verse. In bars 5–6, for example, the accented second syllable of *amate* (love) falls on the strong third beat of the bar. Throughout the madrigal Monteverdi constructs his music to mirror the speech rhythms of spoken Italian.
- Expressive melodic lines reflect the meaning of the words. Sometimes these take the form of reflecting the way the voice rises or falls when speaking. Thus the falling 3rds of *Ohimè* ('Ah me') suggest the way the voice falls on these syllables when spoken. In bars 49–52 this falling 3rd is repeated over and over in **sequence** to express the thousand sweet 'Ahs' of the lovers.
- Melodic lines include intervals which were almost never heard in previous styles (a **tritone** in the canto part of bar 12 and a 7th in the bass part of bar 16). **Chromatic** writing was also rare at this time (C–C♯–D in the quinto part of bars 16–17).

The top part, labelled *Canto* (melody) is for first soprano. The lower part on the same stave, which is labelled *Quinto* (fifth part), is for second soprano.

- Extreme dissonance reflects the mock agony of the poem. The unprepared 9ths between bass and quinto in bars 2 and 4 sound harsh even to modern ears. The same is true of the dissonances in bars 16–17 (A against G, A against B, and C♯ against B and D). Other dissonant effects are more typical of late Renaissance music. Thus the **false relation** formed between the B♮ in the **tierce de Picardie** in bar 38 and the B♭ in bar 39 was a cliché of many 16th-century styles. But the whole chain of false relations in bars 49–51 is unparalled in earlier music. The Consort of Musicke wonderfully underlines the pleasure and pain of these thousand 'deaths' the lover hopes to experience with his mistress.

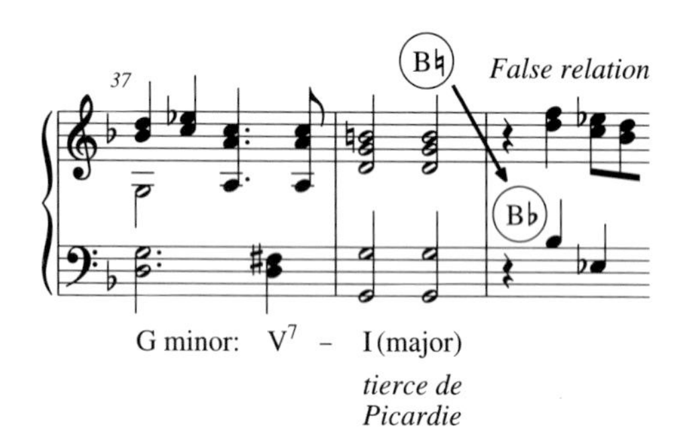

- Contrasts in texture are exploited to the full and again this technique is placed at the service of the words. In the first four bars, for instance, two pairs of voices engage in a dialogue that suggests the sighs of the two lovers.

Like Weelkes in *NAM 34* Monteverdi uses imitative textures, and these too spring from the text. In bars 23–27 the 'sad Ah me' is reflected in the grinding dissonances (for example D, C♯ and E all sounded simultaneously) that are a product of a deliberate use of imitation in such a way that that discords are bound to arise.

This is not vocal music for amateurs to sing in the home, like the madrigals of Weelkes. It was designed for the skills of singers that were only available in the sophisticated courts of Italy and very few other countries.

Notation and interpretation

The main key of the madrigal is G minor and today this would normally be notated with a key signature of two flats (B♭ and E♭). Monterverdi uses just B♭ in the key signature and adds E♭ where needed – this was common practice in minor-key movements until the 18th century. Monteverdi gives no tempo, dynamics or other performing directions in his music – nor did Weelkes (the direction 'With gaiety' at the start of *NAM 34* has been added by a modern editor). This was normal in music at this time, matters of interpretation being left to the performers. Listen carefully to the recordings of both pieces and note the performing decisions that have been made – especially for the endings of both madrigals.

Private study

1. Make a table to show the main differences between *NAM 34* and *NAM 35* using the format shown *right*. Consider key, metre, rhythm, harmony, mood, techniques to express the poetry and the purpose of both madrigals.
2. Why is the change from D major in bar 19 to D minor in bar 20 *not* a false relation?
3. This change to D minor occurs on the words *S'io moro* (but if I die). How does the change in texture at this point also reflect these words?
4. How does Monteverdi express the change of mood in bar 39 at the words *Ma se cor mio volete che vita* (but if, my love, you wish to let me live)? Consider both rhythm and key.
5. What do you notice about the final cadence?

	Weelkes	Monteverdi
Key		
Metre		
Rhythm		
Harmony		
etc.		

Flow my tears (Dowland)

B *NAM 33* CD3 Track 11
James Bowman (countertenor) with David Miller (lute) and bass viol.

The air (or ayre as it is most often spelt at this time) was a type of solo song that had long been popular in 16th-century England. Although related to the contemporary madrigal, John Dowland's airs are now known as lute songs simply because Dowland provided lute parts in tablature. This was a type of notation that showed the performer where to stop each of the strings of the lute (rather like the 'tab' used by some modern guitarists). *Flow my tears* comes from Dowland's *Second Booke of Songs or Ayres*. The first edition, published in 1600, printed the vocal part above the lute tablature (one performer usually performed both parts). Alongside this is a bass part with the same text. This is set out at 90 degrees to the tablature so that a second singer could sit at the same table and read his part from the same book (in the recording on CD3 the bass voice is replaced by a bass viol, a low-pitched bowed string instrument).

The lute is a plucked string instrument which was popular for both solo playing and accompaniment at this time. Dowland himself was an accomplished lutenist and wrote many works for the instrument, often in polyphonic styles that are technically demanding.

Dowland's music was widely circulated in continental Europe during his lifetime and this lute song was the subject of variations by many other composers: *see NAM 20*.

The song is divided into three sections by the three main cadences in A minor:

- bars 1–8, which end with a perfect cadence
- bars 9–16, which end with an imperfect cadence
- bars 17–24, which end with a perfect cadence.

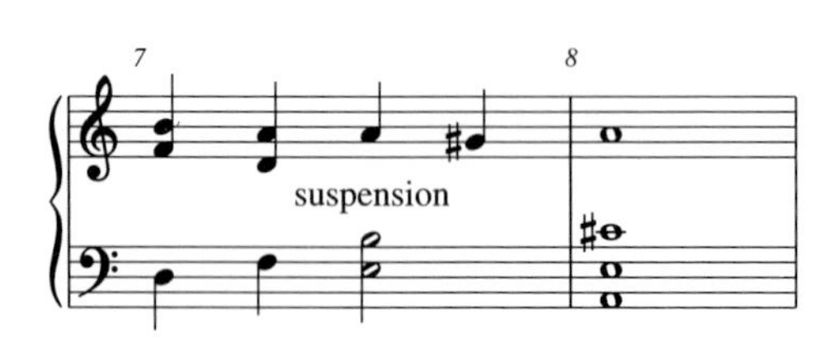

Both perfect cadences use a **tierce de Picardie** in order to end on a chord of A major. Both are also decorated with **suspensions.** (shown *left* in undecorated form). This type of suspension is called a 4–3 suspension because of the intervals it forms above the bass note. Another very common type of suspension is heard at the start of bar 2, where the lute holds a 7th (E) above F in the bass, and then resolves this dissonance by falling to D, a 6th above the same bass note. This is known as a 7–6 suspension for similar reasons.

Like Monteverdi, Dowland uses **false relations** as an expressive device. For example, in bar 5 the lute's G♮ followed by the vocal G♯ creates a particularly poignant effect to reflect the sad words. Rhythm too is used in a very flexible way to give a declamatory character to the word-setting. In the first phrase the word 'fall' seizes the attention through the use of syncopation, as does 'infamy' in bar 6. However at the slow pace this song demands the effect is very different from the dancing syncopation we noted in *Sing we at pleasure* and is used by Dowland more to give natural expression to the rhythm of the words. The word setting is almost entirely **syllabic**, but in the recording on CD3 James Bowman adds a little embellishment in the repeat of bar 15 and in bar 23.

What is most remarkable is the way Dowland, taking his cue from the poetic image of falling tears, unifies the whole song by a falling 4th figure. This is first heard as a scalic descent encompassing a perfect 4th (bar 1), then, with greater anguish, a descent encompassing a diminished 4th (bars 1–2). Elsewhere the falling 4th is heard unadorned (bar 3) and in **sequence** (bars 20–21). See how many other examples of this figure you can find.

In bars 12–14 notice how the vocal solo is **imitated** by the accompaniment in a rising 3rd motive, the rests perhaps expressing the poet's gasping for air between his 'teares, and sighs, and grones' in another passage of vivid **word-painting**.

Private study

1. What is a tierce de Picardie?
2. What word starts on the highest note in the vocal part? How else does Dowland highlight the importance of this word?
3. Give the bar and beat numbers on which you hear suspensions in the middle section (bars 9–16).
4. Briefly describe how the sound of the lute on the recording differs from the sound of a modern (acoustic) guitar.
5. On the recording this song is sung by a counter-tenor. Briefly describe this type of voice.
6. Why is the music on the recording performed a tone lower than notated? (If you are not sure, reread page 93.)

Excerpt from Dido and Aeneas (Purcell)

B *NAM 36* CD3 Track 14
Carolyn Watkinson (soprano)
with the English Baroque Soloists
Directed by John Eliot Gardiner

Dido and Aeneas is an opera that Henry Purcell wrote for a girls' school in Chelsea in 1689. In this excerpt from the final scene, Dido (queen of Carthage) has been deserted by her lover Aeneas and in total despair prepares for death. She stabs herself in the final bars of the excerpt, after which the opera concludes with a final chorus during which cupids scatter rosebuds on her tomb. For such a context Purcell writes highly dramatic music, intended for public performance on stage. We shall therefore encounter some rather different musical techniques from those seen in the more intimate music that we encountered earlier in this chapter.

There are two types of music in this excerpt. The first eight bars form a **recitative** accompanied by **continuo** instruments. The rest of the music is an **aria** accompanied by strings and continuo.

On the recording there are two continuo instruments: the printed bass part is played by a bass viol while the harmonic filling is provided by an archlute – a large bass lute with two necks, one for strings that could be stopped by the fingers and the other for unstopped (open) bass strings.

Thy hand, Belinda

The continuo instruments play from a **figured bass** which outlines the chords to be played by means of numbers and other symbols. The numbers indicate the intervals above the bass note that the chords are to include. You may recognise the 7–6 suspension played in bar 8.

Baroque composers rarely provided complete figuring in their bass parts – they were just a guide to jog the memory. So, in keeping with baroque conventions, you will hear the chord change to C major in bar 2, thus forming a perfect cadence with the F-major chord of bar 3. Similarly a D-major chord is heard at the end of the recitative to prepare the way for the G-minor key of the aria. There are four other major chords not indicated by the figuring – give yourself an aural test by trying to spot them.

If you choose baroque counterpoint for one of your options in the Compositional Techniques part of Unit 2, rest assured that full figuring will be supplied for exam purposes!

Purcell follows every last inflexion of the English text with a strikingly expressive melodic style. In bar 2 he highlights the significance of 'darkness' with a **melisma** on the first syllable. A dark shadow is cast by the chromatic A♭ that so poignantly clashes with the C-major chord of the archlute. Obvious word painting occurs as Dido falls from the opening C to a low D on the word 'death' (bar 7). There are plenty of other expressive devices, such as dissonant intervals between the bass part and the voice: see how many you can find.

When I am laid in earth

The aria uses a **ground bass**, a repeating bass pattern over which melodies and, in this case, different harmonies gradually develop. This variation technique was a speciality of Purcell and, as we shall see, he was skilled in writing vocal and accompaniment phrases that rarely coincide in length with the bass pattern, thus ensuring that the repetitious nature of the form is subtly disguised.

For examples of two other ground-bass arias by Purcell, see *Aural Matters* (Bowman and Terry) pages 114–115 and *Aural Matters in Practice* (Bowman and Terry) page 6.

After the imperfect cadence that marks the end of the recitative the five-bar ground bass is played without accompanying harmonies. Despite the expressive chromatic descent at the start there is no doubt that the key is G minor since the bass pattern ends with five diatonic notes which clearly imply a perfect cadence in that key.

The ground is played 11 times yet there is no sense of mechanical repetition because the cadence points are skilfully overlapped by the vocal melody or string harmonies (or both). For instance the nine-bar vocal phrase starting at bar 16 runs straight through the perfect cadence in bars 20–21 and comes to rest half way through the ground at bar 24.

In the same way the three-bar vocal phrase starting at bar 29 runs across the join between the sixth and seventh statements of the ground in bar 31. At this point the strings move to dominant harmony two beats earlier than expected, thus forming expressive dissonances with the never-changing **ostinato** in the bass (A and F♯ sounding against G on the second beat of bar 31).

Bars 16–24 are a repeat of bars 6–14, but the only added ornamentation on the recording is a vocal slide up to the third beat of bar 22. Can you spot added ornamentation in the first violin part?

The aria ends with an orchestral passage marked *Ritornelle* (a ritornello or 'little return'). Here this simply signifies a passage in which the soloist is silent (she is busy with the dagger at this point). It is characterised by expressive clashes between the upper parts and the bass at the start of every bar. Notice how the melody is unified with the bass in these closing bars by the chromatic descent (first violins, bars 50–55) with which the ground began.

Composing

If you decide to write variations for Unit 2 the ground-bass format may give you ideas for your own music. The basic form can be adapted to almost any style of music (including happy songs), but it readily suits music of a rather oppressive nature in which, as here, there is a sense of inevitable fate dictated by the insistent bass pattern. Remember that ground-bass pieces can be very repetitious and it is difficult to change key, as you may discover if you listen to Pachelbel's famous *Kanon* too many times. Take a leaf out of Purcell's book and think about a bass pattern of an unusual length (such as the five bars he uses here) and the ways in which he disguises the repetitions so they don't become too obvious.

? Private study

1. How does the recitative differ from the aria?
2. Performance directions were still rare in music at this time. Where does Purcell give an indication of the dynamic he requires and what is it?
3. What words in the aria does Purcell highlight with a melisma?
4. What words are set to the highest notes in the soprano part?
5. How does Purcell set the word 'trouble' in the aria?
6. What do you notice about the final chord (bar 56)?

My mother bids me bind my hair (Haydn)

B *NAM 37* CD3 Track 15
Elly Ameling (soprano)
Jörg Demus (piano)

During his first visit to England in 1791–92 Haydn composed a set of songs with lyrics by Anne Hunter, wife of a prominent London doctor. At this time ladies of fashion were expected, among their other social accomplishments, to entertain by singing and playing the piano, an instrument that had become increasingly popular in the late 18th century. Haydn's English songs, with their simple structures and graceful melodies, were aimed at this market.

The song uses the same music for both verses (**strophic** form) but this has some odd consequences. For instance, the halting rhythm that suits the words 'alas! I scarce can go or creep' in bars 27–29 of verse one works far less well when 'vil - lage' becomes divided by a rest in verse 2. Similarly, the descending chromatic scale in bars 22–24 reflects the crying and weeping in verse 1, but seems ill-suited to illustrate the spinning of flaxen thread in verse 2. For a rather more powerful example of word-painting you might compare Purcell's chromatic descent from tonic to dominant at the start of his ground bass with Haydn's use of the same idea.

Many of the features of the early classical style known as **galant** are evident in *My mother bids me bind my hair*:

- motifs based on triads ('My mother bids') and on scale patterns that involve stepwise movement ('rosy hue')
- phrases of regular length (known as **periodic phrasing**), evident in the piano introduction, in which the opening four-bar statement ends with an imperfect cadence and is followed by a four-bar 'answer' which concludes with a perfect cadence
- ornamentation of the melodic line, such as the **appoggiatura** in bar 12, and a slide and acciaccatura in bar 15
- light textures in which the melody predominates. For instance, the second phrase (bars 5–8) begins with just two parts, only thickening in texture at the cadence. Notice that the piano doubles or shadows the voice for much of the song, another indication that it was designed for the amateur singer
- clear tonal schemes, with frequent cadences to outline the structure and main keys of the music. Haydn's vocal part starts by repeating the first phrase of the introduction but then, in bars 12–16, begins the second phrase a 4th lower. This allows Haydn to divert from the tonic key of A major to a perfect cadence in the dominant key of E major.

The expression 'tonal scheme' is a useful way to refer to the arrangement of keys in a piece, such as beginning and ending in the tonic and using related keys such as the dominant or relative minor for contrast.

Private study

1. How does Haydn establish the tonic key at the start?
2. Do the accidentals in bars 3 and 6 indicate modulations to other keys or are they chromatic notes that colour the harmony?
3. How does Haydn illustrate the word 'play' in bar 26 and the idea of being 'away' in the last five bars of the song?
4. What is the main difference between Haydn's accompaniment and that provided by Purcell in the first eight bars of *NAM 36*?

A *NAM 38* CD3 Track 16
Peter Schreier (tenor)
András Schiff (piano)

A translation of this song is printed on page 539 of the *New Anthology*.

The German word *Lied* means a song. The term *Lieder* (songs), pronounced 'leeder', is often used in English to refer to German songs of the romantic period.

Der Doppelgänger comes from Schubert's final collection of lieder, *Schwanengesang* ('swan song'). The preceding song in the same collection can be found in *Aural Matters* (Bowman and Terry) pages 131–132.

The original poem had no title. Schubert chose the word *Doppelgänger* (a 'ghostly double') from the start of the third verse of the poem. A translation is printed on page 539 of *NAM*.

Der Doppelgänger (Schubert)

The contrast between Haydn's galant trifle (written when he was at least 60 and still had many more years to live) and Schubert's terrifying romantic song (written in 1828 when he was 31 and knew that he had only a few weeks to live) could not be more striking.

Like Purcell's *When I am laid in earth* this song makes its initial impact from its very slow (*Sehr langsam*) tempo and minor key. Also like Purcell's song it is based on an **ostinato** figure (in this case four bars long) which is heard in its original form five times.

Although the poem is cast in three verses, Schubert doesn't use a strophic setting as Haydn did for his song in *NAM 37*. Schubert's music is **through-composed** – the music develops throughout the song, although there is some repetition.

The stillness of the night is represented by the extremely low dynamic level, the very static rhythm of the accompaniment and by the F♯ which forms an inner **pedal** on the dominant of B minor throughout the first 40 bars. It is to this note that the tenor obsessively returns in every one of his first nine two-bar phrases.

The opening bars suggest B minor, but the triads are incomplete and the bare 5ths in bars 1, 4, 5 and 8 suggest the empty loneliness of the poet, as does the halting and fragmented vocal line, sounding more like recitative than a song. As the poet fills in details of the scene, so the tolling piano chords fill out until the singer breaks free of the fateful F♯ in bars 29–30. But the piano retains the F♯ and the rising melodic line returns to F♯ in the first climax of the song, marked to be played as loud as possible in bar 31 and underpinned by the chromatic dissonance in the next bar.

The ostinato resumes in bar 34, but this time the tenor claws his way up from F♯ to reach G, the highest note of both the vocal and piano parts. It is at this second climax (bar 41) that the pianist at last relinquishes the dominant note and it is here that the poet realises that the man he saw is a horrifying reflection of himself. He knows that he is doomed, for the person who meets their other self is, according to legend, about to die.

Now begins one of the most remarkable harmonic progressions that even Schubert could devise. While the voice revolves hopelessly around F♯ the piano rises chromatically from B to D♯, retaining an F♯ in every one of these bleak chords. The chromaticism leads to a modulation to D♯ minor, and this unusual and remote key is affirmed by alternate tonic and dominant hammer blows in bars 47–50. This is the only passage not in the key of B minor – it is as if the poet is already gone and his mocking ghost has triumphed.

Another chromatic dissonance (bar 51) at a stroke returns the music to B minor and the last climax of the song, in which the poet recalls the torment of the night so long ago. From this point the singer sinks exhausted back to the tonic. Finally the ostinato returns, but this time the last chord is changed to C major – in the context it seems enigmatic and questioning; the major chord certainly sheds no ray of hope. The piano postlude ends with a plagal cadence and tierce de Picardie – and no ray of hope is shed by that either.

A postlude is a closing section and usually refers to a passage for piano alone at the end of a song.

Private study

1. Compare the introduction to this song with the first eight bars of *NAM 37*. How do both introductions set the mood for the song that is to follow?
2. What is an ostinato? What effect is created by the use of an ostinato in parts of this song?
3. Can you spot any false relations on the first page?
4. How does Schubert illustrate the terror of the poet in bar 35?
5. The climax of the poem occurs when the poet realises that the face he sees is his own (*eig'ne Gestalt*, 'own being' or 'self'). How does Schubert reflect this in his music?
6. How do Schubert's textures reflect the atmosphere of the poem?
7. Listen carefully to the recording. What do you notice about the tempo?

Après un rêve (Fauré)

B *NAM 39* CD3 Track 17
Janet Baker (mezzo-soprano)
Geoffrey Parsons (piano)

There could hardly be a greater contrast between Schubert's lied and Fauré's *mélodie*, *Après un rêve* (After a dream) of 1878:

- Schubert's vocal phrases are fragmentary, Fauré's are long and linked to form continuous vocal melodies
- *Der Doppelgänger* is entirely in the minor mode: *Après un rêve* is in C minor, but modulates decisively to E♭ major and moves fluidly through several other major and minor keys
- Schubert's harmony is either extremely bare or aggressively dissonant: Fauré's chords are rich and sumptuous
- *Der Doppelgänger* is a prophetic nightmare: *Après un rêve* is a remembrance of an ecstatic dream of love.

A *mélodie* is a French song of the romantic period, just as a *Lied* is a German song.

A translation of the text of this song is printed on page 540 of *NAM*.

To give musical expression to the dream-images of Bussine's poetry Fauré is deliberately ambiguous in both key and rhythm. Keys are normally defined by perfect cadences in which the seventh note of the scale rises to the tonic (B♮–C in the case of C minor). Here the vocal melody begins by outlining the tonic chord of C minor but the piano introduces B♭ as early as bar 2, accompanying the singer with richly chromatic harmonies, full of 7ths and 9ths.

The first vocal phrase ends on B♭ in bar 4 and the next phrase (bars 5–8) introduces D♭ and more chromatic chords. Even when we reach a perfect cadence in C minor (V^7–I in bars 7–9) the B♭s of the singer pull against the B♮ in the piano to produce false relations.

But underpinning this complexity is a simple and strong harmonic device – a **circle of 5ths** that begins on C in bar 1 and moves through F, B♭, E♭, A♭, D♮ and G in the left-hand of the piano part before returning to C in bar 9.

Similarly Fauré uses subtlety of rhythm to enhance his dreamy atmosphere. The triplets with which the singer approaches all of the cadences cut across the rhythm of the piano, producing delicate **cross-rhythms** which not only reflect the accents of the French language but which also help to blur the symmetry of the continuous quavers in the accompaniment.

With a return to C minor in bar 17 comes a repeat of the opening melody, but after the first nine bars the music is deflected to the distant key of B♭ minor (bars 31–32) for the 'sad awakening from dreams'. The tonic key of C minor returns once more in bars 37–39, where the voice stretches out the rhythm of the opening five notes for the impassioned plea of 'Return, return' and the radiance of the dream is recalled by the unexpected E♭-major chord at *radieuse* in bar 41. Finally and it seems inevitably, the song slips back permanently into the *nuit mystérieuse* of C minor.

Performing

There are also arrangements of *Après un rêve* available for most instruments.

Although there is a very fine performance of this song from Janet Baker on CD3, there is nothing quite like singing it for yourself, even if you do so in a small group and perhaps with a melody instrument to double the vocal line. This will help you experience the effect of Fauré's long, arching phrases, the elegant drop of a minor 6th in bar 5 and the expressive dissonances in bars 4, 11 and many other places.

?

Private study

1. Briefly list some of the ways in which Fauré establishes a dream-like mood in this song.
2. What is a false relation?
3. What is a circle of 5ths and where is one used in the section from bar 9 to the end?
4. Fauré marks the vocal part *dolce*. What does this mean?
5. The performance on CD3 is sung by a mezzo-soprano. What type of voice is this?
6. How does Fauré darken the piano texture in the last two bars?

A *NAM 40* CD3 Track 18
Yvonne Minton (reciter)
Michael Debost (flute)
Directed by Pierre Boulez

Der kranke Mond (Schoenberg)

In the early years of the 20th century a style that became known as expressionism developed in art, literature and films, particularly in Germany and Austria. The aim was to explore and represent the inner consciousness of the creator. To this end pictorial representation was deliberately distorted until it eventually became unrecognisable. It was at this point (about 1910) that artists such as Schoenberg's friend Kandinsky abandoned representational art altogether. At the same time (and not by coincidence) Schoenberg abandoned the late-romantic style of his early works in favour of a musical language that deliberately avoided any suggestion of triadic melody or harmony, and that used chromaticism and dissonance as self-sufficient means of expression.

A translation of the text of this song is printed on page 540 of *NAM*.

Pierrot Lunaire is perhaps best expressed in English as the moon-struck clown: the sad clown who is obsessed with the moon – although we are never quite clear if he is really a lunatic or merely deluded by its lunar magic.

This is immediately apparent in this **atonal** song from his most famous expressionist work, *Pierrot Lunaire* (the moon-struck clown) of 1912. In the first three bars Schoenberg uses all 12 notes of the chromatic scale. By bar 7 he has used every melodic and harmonic interval from a minor 2nd to a major 7th. (Since there is no tonality it does not matter how a given pitch is notated: the interval G♯–C in the flute part of bar 5 is of the same type as the interval B–D♯ in the same bar because both encompass three semitones.)

The grotesque images of the poem are expressed through:

- enormous melodic leaps (flute, bars 9–10 and reciter, bar 15)
- fragmented melody (bars 14–15)
- extreme range (voice bar 15)
- extreme dynamics (flute, bar 14)
- *Sprechgesang* ('speech-song' – the half-sung, half-spoken notes of the reciter indicated by crosses through note stems).

Equally important is Schoenberg's avoidance of melodic repetition since this could suggest traditional ways of organising musical form. Only at the end do sequential repetitions (flute, bars 22–24) and direct repetitions (reciter, bars 23–26) occur. For the rest the melody mirrors the madness of the moon-struck clown.

Pierrot Lunaire consists of 21 songs in all, written for an ensemble of five players in addition to the reciter. In *Der kranke Mond* (the sick moon) Schoenberg uses only the flute and reciter. In such a thin texture he is able to exploit the flute's very quiet lowest notes without fear of their being masked by other instruments.

Interpretation

There are a number of ways to perform *Sprechgesang*. On CD3 Yvonne Minton tends more to singing than speaking and she slides between slurred notes (a technique known as *portamento*). However her pitches are relative rather than absolute. In bars 23–25 Schoenberg uses the same melody for three highly contrasting lines of text. In bar 24 he instructs the reciter to make *no* difference despite the contrast – 'use the same tone as in the previous bar' – but for the last repetition (bar 25) he writes 'this bar differently, but not tragically'. The final German phrase (*Schluss des I Teils*) simply means 'End of the first part' of this cycle of melodramatic songs.

Composing

The dramatic style of *Pierrot Lunaire* has often led to the work being performed as music theatre. If you are choosing to write something for music theatre in unit 2, Schoenberg's song may provide some useful pointers – not necessarily in the musical style, but perhaps in its heightened form of expression, in techniques such as combining speech with song, and in the use of minimal textures. For example, in *Der kranke Mond* it is possible for the flautist to be on-stage with the reciter, symbolising the moon that so torments Pierrot, and interacting with the clown in a much more immediate way than is possible when the instruments in music theatre are hidden from the audience's view.

Private study

1. What is meant by atonal music?
2. What term is used to describe the half-speaking, half-singing style of the part for reciter?
3. Is this song entirely discordant or are there areas of contrast?
4. Expressionism often seeks to portray psychological states by means of distortion. What musical techniques does Schoenberg use to convey the emotions of the tormented clown, Pierrot?

B *NAM 41* CD3 Track 19
Leona Mitchell (soprano)
Cleveland Orchestra and
Cleveland Orchestra Chorus
Conducted by Lorin Maazel

Summertime (Gershwin)

George Gershwin achieved enormous success as a composer of popular songs, musicals and film scores in America during the 1920s and 1930s. He also wrote several works for the concert hall that combine elements of popular music and jazz with classical genres such as the concerto, most notably in his *Rhapsody in Blue*.

Porgy and Bess, completed in 1935, was another work in which he fused together different traditions. In this case the idea of an opera which sought to portray (albeit through white American eyes) the lifestyle and music of the black American from the south of the USA. The result is something that is often referred to as folk-opera. This musical fusion is evident throughout 'Summertime':

- From the blues comes the clashing E♮ and E♯ in bars 14 and 32. In classical music it would be known as a false relation but in the context of a jazz-influenced work the E♮ is a **blue note**.

- From jazz comes the use of **swing quavers** in the performance. The dotted rhythms of bar 9 are sung approximately as shown *left* (Gershwin could have notated them as even quavers but jazz musicians would still interpret them roughly as shown). Also influenced by jazz is the gentle **syncopation**, which is sometimes improvised ('Fish' in bar 11) and sometimes notated ('Oh' in bar 15). Both swing quavers and syncopation also occur in the accompaniment (the quavers in bars 22–23 are swung and there is written-out syncopation on the accented note in bar 19).
- From black-American folk music such as the spiritual comes the use of the **pentatonic** scale on which the solo melody is based: B–D–E–F♯–A (the C♯ in bar 14, repeated in bar 32, is the only note in the vocal part outside this pattern). From the same source comes the use of portamento (the slides between notes), notated in bar 21 but added by the singer in bar 10. Her ecstatic embellishment of the ending is an effect often heard in gospel music.
- From popular music of the 1930s comes the lush vocabulary of chromatic harmony (bars 20–22), chromatic melody (bars 14–15 in the accompaniment) and chords with added 6ths (bars 8–11), 7ths (bar 12) and 9ths (bar 25). Also from popular and film music comes the added crooning of the women's voices in verse 2.
- From western art music comes the use of an orchestra based on strings, with instruments such as the flute and oboe adding colour.

Composing

The composition topics for Unit 2 include writing a popular song, a piece of fusion music or a song for a piece of music theatre. If you choose any of these options Gershwin will provide an excellent model. The form of 'Summertime' (essentially an eight-bar phrase used four times) is rather repetitive because it is a lullaby. Songs by Gershwin in other forms and styles can be found in any of the following collections: **The Greatest Songs of George Gershwin**, *Hal Leonard* 1989, ISBN: 0-88188-170-8; **The Great Songs of George Gershwin**, *Warner Bros*, 1990 ISBN: 0-94335-141-3; **The Gershwin Collection**, *Hal Leonard*, 1992, ISBN: 0-7935-1337-5.

Private study

1. Is this song strophic or through-composed?
2. How is the music of bar 5 used in bars 6–7? Can you give the correct technical term to describe what happens?
3. Compare the motif sung by Clara in bar 9 with the motif played by the flute in bar 22. How does the flute motif differ in pitch? How do both of these motifs differ in rhythm from what you hear on the recording?
4. Which two motifs heard earlier in the song are used to form the final bass phrase in bars 44–46?
5. Describe as precisely as possible how the singer embellishes her last note.
6. Gershwin describes this song as a lullaby. Which aspects of his music give the song the character of a lullaby?

Sample question 1

(a) Explain what you understand by any **two** of the following:

strophic   atonal   imitation   homophonic

(b) Link each term you have chosen in your answer to question (a) to a context from a specific work. Name the work, the precise location and the instrument or voice parts involved.

Answer the following two questions only if you are taking the exam in 2001 or 2002.

(c) *Ohimè, se tanto amate* (*NAM 35*) was first published only five years after *Sing we at pleasure* (*NAM 34*) and yet the style is very different. Briefly explain what was so new about Monteverdi's madrigal.

(d) How does Schubert's music reflect the meaning of the poem in *Der Doppelgänger* (*NAM 38*)?

Answer the following two questions only if you are taking the exam in 2003 or 2004.

(c) *When I am laid in earth* (*NAM 36*) uses a repeating bass part throughout. How does Purcell avoid the song sounding too repetitious?

(d) What features of *NAM 37* identify *My mother binds my hair* as music of the classical period?

Sample question 2

(a) Explain what you understand by any **two** of the following:

chromatic   ballett   continuo   syncopation

(b) Link each term you have chosen in your answer to question (a) to a context from a specific work. Name the work, the precise location and the instrument or voice parts involved.

Answer the following two questions only if you are taking the exam in 2001 or 2002.

(c) What techniques does Schoenberg use in *NAM 40* to highlight the drama of the text?

(d) Choose some examples to illustrate how dissonance is used as an expressive device in vocal music.

Answer the following two questions only if you are taking the exam in 2003 or 2004.

(c) Name the two types of instruments you would expect to play a continuo part and briefly explain what they might play in *NAM 36*.

(d) What different styles of music are evident in 'Summertime' (*NAM 41*)?

Music for film and television

Music in the early cinema

The moving picture was invented towards the end of the 19th century and it rapidly became one of the most popular forms of public entertainment. By 1912 there were over 4,000 cinemas in Britain. There was no reliable way of synchronising sound and image at this time and so these early black-and-white films had no soundtrack. Instead, spoken dialogue was subtitled on screen and musicians were engaged by each cinema to play accompaniments that would underline the mood of the picture, link scenes, provide entertainment between the short films and serve to mask the noise of the early film projectors.

In a small cinema the music might be provided by only a pianist, but often there would be a group of four or five players or even, in the largest venues, a small orchestra. Such bands had played in the music halls and theatres of Victorian Britain and, as these waned in popularity, the musicians found similar employment in the new cinemas. At first the music played was only loosely related to the picture. The musical director of the cinema would view the film in advance and make a selection of appropriate excerpts from the light classics, café music and favourite marches. These were linked by improvisations from the pianist who sat watching the film and who would, for instance, signal the appearance of the villain with a tremolo diminished-7th chord.

Sometimes there might also be a little specially composed music. The film-music composer William Alwyn recalled helping his flute teacher in a cinema orchestra pit in 1916, when he was only 11:

> In front of me on the music stand was a thick stack of music [and] a piece marked *Theme* which I was told by my mentor to keep separate from the rest and at a given signal from the leader (two raps on the desk?) to abandon whatever piece I was playing and dive abruptly into this special theme.

The cue sheet for the 1910 film *Frankenstein* included:

Girl enters with teapot:
  Andante – *Annie Laurie*
Monster comes from behind curtain:
  Dramatic – *Der Freischütz*
Until wedding guests are leaving:
  Bridal Chorus from *Lohengrin*
Monster appears:
  Dramatic – *Der Freischütz*
Frankenstein enters:
  Agitato

Gradually this chaotic approach was rationalised. As films started to explore more searching topics, producers realised that such an unpredictable mix of different music did little to enhance the aesthetic quality they were trying to develop in this new medium. At first the problem was tackled by publishing 'suggestions for music' that were circulated with the films. These referred in detail to exact points ('cues') in the film where music of a specific type was required. To supplement this, music categorised by mood and supplied in arrangements to suit any size of band, was offered by enterprising music publishers.

However by the 1920s it was clear to many producers that the emotional impact of a film could only be fully realised in music specially composed for the purpose, and thus some of the leading composers of the time, including Milhaud, Honegger and Shostakovich, were engaged to compose film scores.

Live orchestral music in the cinema was an expensive and often unrealistic luxury. Even where it was possible, the problem of synchronising sound with image remained. An alternative solution adopted in the 1920s was the installation of a cinema organ. These instruments adapted traditional pipe organ technology to attempt to sound more like an orchestra and they included special effects (percussion, thunder machines, train whistles, bells and so forth) that could be used to illustrate the visual image. Just like the pianist in the earliest days of cinema the organist could watch the film and improvise. But by then sound film was being developed and the role of these wondrous instruments was more often to provide musical entertainment before and between films, and to fill the not infrequent breaks when the projector broke down.

The sound film

There had been various earlier experiments to synchronise sound on gramophone records with visual images but the first really successful film to use this technique was *The Jazz Singer* of 1927. The producers realised the impact this would have and structured the film around the moment when the lead character cries 'Say, Ma, listen to this' and breaks into the song *Mammy*, which inevitably became an immediate popular hit. However gramophone records could store only a few minutes' worth of music at this time and technically this was not to be a lasting success.

It was a far less well-known film (*The Air Circus*, 1928) which established the film-sound technology to be used for decades to come. This used a technique of recording sound waves as visual images (literally wavy lines) on the film itself, in parallel with the pictures, thus ensuring synchronisation throughout the length of the picture. These waves could be read by optical sensors, amplified and fed to loudspeakers in the cinema.

During the 1930s and 1940s further major composers were attracted to film music, including Prokofiev (*Lieutenant Kijé*, 1933), Walton (*Henry V*, 1944), Britten and Copland. The cinema thus introduced a new audience to contemporary music. The combination of music and picture helped to familiarise listeners with sounds and techniques that sometimes seemed much more perplexing when heard in the concert hall. Sound reproduction in the cinema was not of the quality it is today and the best of these scores were arranged by their composers into 'symphonic suites' so that the music could also be heard in orchestral concerts, as happened with Bernstein's 1954 score for *On The Waterfront*, discussed below.

While some composers only occasionally entered the world of film music, others specialised in it. These include Max Steiner, composer of many scores in a romantic style (such as *Gone with the Wind*, 1939), Erich Korngold and Bernard Herrmann, who wrote the music for Alfred Hitchcock's famous 1960 thriller *Psycho*.

The role of music in the film

The requirements of film often dictate that music cues are short, although the opening title music and any scenes requiring musical illustration (battles, storms, love scenes and so on) provided the opportunity for more extended composing. Composers started to explore ways in which music could be used in more subtle ways. Musical motifs were used to identify particular characters, scenes or events. These motifs could return in the **underscore** (the background music used throughout the film) to remind the audience of previous events without the picture or dialogue necessarily needing to refer to them explicitly. Such a technique is related to the **leitmotif** of late-romantic music, although there was little opportunity for the large-scale development of such motifs as that found in the operas of Wagner.

Similarly, music can involve the audience in the plot in a more intimate way than even the characters themselves. Thus in *Psycho*, when the bank worker Marion innocently takes a shower, Bernard Hermann's spine-chilling music allows the audience to be aware of what she herself does not know, anticipating the fatal stabbing of the knife through the shower curtain and heightening its impact.

The cartoon film, developed most notably by Walt Disney in the 1930s, led to a new type of score in which music was synchronised very precisely with almost every event in the action. For example sliding down a drainpipe might be accompanied by a descending xylophone scale and the dazed bump when the character hits the ground by a 'wah-wah-wah' from muted trumpets. The technique, known as **mickey-mousing** (after Disney's famous animated character), was also widely used in comedy films.

Music can serve a number of different purposes in film and television, many of which we shall see in this chapter, including:

- illustrative music, such as Walton's thrilling depiction of the Battle of Agincourt in *Henry V*
- evocative music to suggest a place, such as the use of the Austrian zither in *The Third Man*, which is set in Vienna
- pastiche (music written in an old style) to evoke a bygone age, as in Eric Idle's television theme music for *One Foot in the Grave*
- dramatic music to enhance tension, as in the capture of the humans by the apes in Jerry Goldsmith's *Planet Of The Apes*
- comic music, as in Auric's scores for the Ealing comedies, such as *Passport to Pimlico*, and in most cartoons
- music to enhance emotional impact as in *Scott of the Antarctic* where the bleak score by Vaughan Williams accompanies the explorers' final doomed attempt to return to base, portraying in music the mens' emotional states in a way that could not easily be expressed by pictures or dialogue in the film
- theme music to identify a product – particularly common in television series, where the 'signature tune' provides a signal that another episode of something familiar is about to start.

B *NAM 42* CD4 Track 1
Royal Ballet Sinfonia
Conducted by Kenneth Alwyn

Passport to Pimlico: The Siege of Burgundy (Auric)

The Ealing comedies were made at Ealing studios in west London. Auric's other scores for these films include *Hue and Cry* (1947), *The Lavender Hill Mob* (1951) and *The Titfield Thunderbolt* (1952).

The French composer Georges Auric may seem a surprising choice as the composer for several of the most famous 'Ealing comedies', in which a distinctly British sense of humour is exploited to the full. However Auric had a reputation as a composer of light, witty music which dated back to the 1920s, when he had been the youngest member of *Les Six*, a group of urbane and satirical French composers which included Milhaud, Poulenc (see *NAM 19*) and Honegger. Auric had also written film scores for the avant-garde film director Jean Cocteau, as well as much theatre and ballet music.

This 1949 comedy is about the residents of Pimlico in central London. An unexploded bomb left over from the war blows up and in the debris they find an old document decreeing that Pimlico is part of the ancient French province of Burgundy. Quickly seizing the opportunity the residents of Pimlico declare the area to be independent of the rest of the country and set about dispelling the gloom of post-war Britain by abolishing licensing laws and the food rationing that was then in place. The music of *NAM 42* ('The Siege of Burgundy') accompanies a scene in which British government officials retaliate by partitioning off 'Burgundy' with a cordon of barbed wire, setting-up customs barriers and cutting off water and electricity. Other Londoners come out in force to throw food over the barricades to the besieged folk of Pimlico.

Auric captures the humour of this busy scene in a musical collage that resembles the circus music so often imitated by French composers of his generation. He does this with

- short, repeated motifs based mainly on scale and tonic triad figures (bar 1–4, bar 5)
- frequent and surprising changes of key (E major in bars 1–8, plunging straight into G major at bar 9)
- rapid changes of texture and instrumentation (bars 13–20)
- witty chromatic writing (bassoon theme, bar 22)
- harmonies that enrich basically simple chords with added notes (such as the perfect cadence at the end of bar 12 in which E is added to the D^7 chord and passing notes decorate the bass)
- mainly quaver and semiquaver rhythms at a fast tempo.

The newspaper headline 'Burgundy is bombarded with buns' is heralded by a bright fanfare in E major. Loud trills on tonic and dominant capture the exhilaration of the moment. The descending horn scale in bar 1 is repeated in 3rds in bar 2 and then, to intensify the excitement, the scales appear in **diminution** in bar 3 and 4.

NAM 42 is printed in a format known as a short score. This gives an indication of the orchestration but does not show all the parts in full.

The motif which enters at bar 5 shows how Auric achieves a bustling, breathless mood. It is based on the tonic chord of E and is immediately repeated in bar 6. Cellos and basses use the same rhythm in bar 7 and the whole package is neatly wrapped up with contrary motion scales and a quick perfect cadence in bar 8. The music then dives straight into G major at bar 9 for a decorated repeat of the previous four bars.

Auric enhances the fun with many witty orchestral effects – the consecutive 5ths between flutes and tinkling glockenspiel in bars 5–6, busy semiquaver scales in 3rds from the accompanying strings, and joyous trills and leaps from clarinets in bars 9–10.

A short link (bars 13–14) features an inverted tonic **pedal** on G spikily offset by a brass entry on F♯. The scale-based motif in bar 15 introduces a new texture (bare octaves) and new keys (B minor, then B major). Strings and wind alternate in **antiphonal** exchanges to illustrate the noisy debates in Hyde Park and Trafalgar Square.

The double strokes through the crotchets in bars 13–14 indicate that the violins are to continue playing semiquavers on these beats.

The music slows as the 'government yields to public pressure' and in bar 20 Auric underlines the point by concluding the political debate with a charmingly old-fashioned but very definitive cadence in B major ('so there!' the music seems to say).

The jolly bassoon motif in bars 21–23 is yet another idea based on the tonic triad of E major – this time decorated with **chromatic** auxiliary notes (marked * in the example *left*). The music drops a semitone at bar 27, the treasury being treated to some suitably luxurious harmonies. Bar 33 sees yet another new key (C major) and a varied repeat of the bassoon motif, which is now transferred to high woodwind.

Presents from other Londoners are seen arriving in bar 39 and so Auric reuses the music from the similar scenes on the first page of the score. There is a clever reversal of sections, though – this time bars 9–12 are heard first (now in E♭ major rather than G) and then the music winches up a semitone so that we can hear bars 5–8 in their original key of E major, but with fuller scoring. A fanfare in bars 49–50 is prematurely interrupted by a 'suspense' motif as the talks suddenly deadlock – cellos and basses play a distorted version of the theme from bar 5 below a mysterious low tremolo on divided violas. But relief comes in the form of an airlift and the harmony of bars 49–50 (based on chord V of C) is resumed in bar 54. In the final section Auric stays entirely in C major (despite the F♯ which naughtily decorates the final cadence in bar 64), hilariously depicting the helicopter with a delicate ballet-like dance for piccolo, celesta and plucked strings.

Private study

1. What is a short score?
2. What is antiphony and where does it occur in this extract?
3. (a) How should the upper strings play bar 23?
   (b) How should the violas play bar 52?
4. Explain how Auric creates a sense of comedy and busy activity in this extract. As a starting point use the list on page 109, but try to find *different* examples of each technique you mention.

On the Waterfront: Symphonic Suite (Bernstein)

A *NAM 43* CD4 Track 2
New York Philharmonic
Conducted by Leonard Bernstein

The 1954 film *On the Waterfront* tells a story, based on reality, of crime and extortion in the New York docks, and of the struggle of a young dock worker (played by Marlon Brando) who fought against the corrupt practices exposed in the film. It was a stark contrast to the romantic comedies and Hollywood epics usually seen in the cinema – its harsh social realism made a great impact.

Bernstein's most famous musical, *West Side Story*, followed just three years later in 1957.

Leonard Bernstein had already achieved considerable success in writing musicals for the theatre before being asked to compose the music for this film. Some of these musicals had been filmed, but *On the Waterfront* was the only actual film score that he ever wrote. The social realism of the film does not entirely extend to its music, which uses the large symphony orchestra that was the norm for big-budget American movies. However the exhilarating percussion rhythms and fearsome brass writing (both characteristics of Bernstein's style) give the music a hard edge which echoes the intensity and violence of the film. Bernstein arranged some of the music from the underscore into a symphonic suite in 1955, and it is from the opening of this version that *NAM 43* is taken.

There could hardly be a stronger contrast between the opening of the suite and Auric's perky music for *Passport to Pimlico*. Instead of lively, one-bar motifs darting around the orchestra in a variety of keys, Bernstein starts with a long, slow **monophonic** melody for solo horn in F (which sounds a 5th lower than written). The minor 3rds, flat 7th (B♭ in bar 4) and flat 5th (G♭ in bar 5) give the music the mournful quality of the blues. Flutes repeat this melody in octaves at bar 7 and a solo muted trombone enters in **canon** – the blues is once again in evidence at the start of bar 11, where C♭ in the flutes clashes against B♭ in the trombone.

Muted trumpets enter at bar 13 – Bernstein indicates that they are to sound distant (*lontano*) – with the music of bar 4 transposed a 4th higher, after which clarinets and bass clarinet end the slow introduction with the opening bars of the main melody, still transposed up a 4th. In bar 19 the ascending minor 3rd of this motif is transformed into a major 3rd in preparation for the next section.

In bar 17 the clarinets are directed to use 'sub-tone' – a very quiet and slightly breathy tone colour.

Presto barbaro means fast and barbaric and the two time signatures indicate that bars of 4/4 and 3/4 alternate. The rising minor 3rd of bar 1 is still evident in the percussive, syncopated theme announced by piano and timpani in bar 20. A second set of timpani enters with this theme a **tritone** higher in bar 26, followed in bar 32 by three drums of different pitches which give an outline of the same theme. The effect is very much like the start of a **fugue** for percussion.

The direction *una corda* in the piano part is an instruction to use the left pedal in order to produce a quieter, muted sound.

The three percussion entries come together in bar 40 to form a **riff** which accompanies a brash, syncopated solo for alto saxophone. The musical style is similar to Bernstein's jazzy *Prelude, Fugue and Riffs* written five years earlier, but it also serves to underline the violent tensions and dramatic contrasts of the film.

In bar 53 the instruction 'S.D. rim shot' indicates that the drummer is to hit the rim and the head of the side drum simultaneously with one stick. This type of accented off-beat ending is another Bernstein fingerprint.

The saxophone melody is repeated at bar 55. How is it varied?

The dynamic level drops in bars 62–63, but the drum pattern continues and almost immediately Bernstein begins another build-up as he develops the saxophone motif from bar 52. This leads to a powerful **tutti** at bar 78 in which the whole orchestra stamps out the percussion theme in dissonant block chords. Notice how Bernstein increases the impact of this section by adding further dissonances above the already dissonant riff.

The rhythm of the percussion theme is maintained by a solitary side drum from bar 88, while high sustained strings (punctuated by upper woodwind) remind us of the falling semitone and falling 4th of the saxophone solo first heard in bar 42. The timpani return and then, in bar 98 the falling semitone is inverted and followed by a piercing major 2nd, sustained by violins, trumpets and high woodwind. More instruments are added as the dynamic builds, with the high E♭ clarinet trilling between C and D and flutes, oboes and trumpets instructed to use **flutter-tonguing** (*flutt.* in bar 105).

The eight-bar **coda** starting in bar 106 begins with a slow and very loud restatement of the motif from bar 52. Beneath this Bernstein reaffirms the importance of the tritone in this music by slowly superimposing two triads a tritone apart (F major and B major – the middle note of the latter is notated as E♭ rather than D♯). This colossal dissonance is hammered out by wind and percussion in bars 108–109. In the rests the strings can be heard very quietly sustaining the same dissonance using the thin, icy tone produced by playing *sul ponticello* (with the bow close to the bridge).

In the last four bars Bernstein uses a similar pattern but a semitone lower – the main triad is now E major (the middle note is again spelled enharmonically as A♭) over which is heard B♭ (the tritone above E) plus a further tritone formed by C and F♯.

?

Private study

1. In which bars does Bernstein use each of the following textures? (i) homophonic, (ii) monophonic, (iii) two-part polyphonic.
2. What does 'con sord.' mean in the trombone part at bar 7?
3. The *Presto barbaro* is based on two main motifs. Where are each of these motifs first heard?
4. The film *On the Waterfront* sometimes depicts an atmosphere of bleak despair, but at other times a mood of anger. Briefly explain how Bernstein's music reflects both of these moods.

Planet of the Apes: The Hunt (Goldsmith)

B *NAM 44* CD4 Track 3
Conducted by Jerry Goldsmith

Bernstein's score for *On the Waterfront* introduced many filmgoers to the dissonant and rhythmically sophisticated techniques of 20th-century music and many other composers followed his lead.

The orchestra on CD4 is not identified. Film soundtracks are often recorded by 'session musicians'. These may include members of one or more well-known orchestras, as well as other professional musicians, who come together specifically for the recording of the soundtrack.

Jerry Goldsmith was born in 1929 and by the age of 21 he was a music director for CBS. He composed music for many television shows and wrote his first film score in 1957 at the age of 28. By the 1960s he had a reputation as one of the first film composers regularly to use **avant-garde** techniques in his film scores. These have included **atonality**, electronic effects and such unusual sound sources as rubbed glass rods and the recorded calls of whales. While his style is often abrasively dissonant he also has an uncanny sense of knowing when to win his audiences over with a traditionally memorable melody (as in the theme to *Star Trek*). This combination of skills has proved very successful in the music for other 'sci-fi' films such as *Alien* (1979) and *Planet of the Apes* (1968).

The plot of the latter centres on a group of American astronauts who become stranded on an unidentified planet. When they eventually stumble on life-supporting vegetation they also come face to face with a population of hunters – gorillas on horseback – who, in this scene of spectacular chase music, succeed in capturing the humans.

The boo bam, or tamboo bamboo, comes from Trinidad. Tamboo is a corruption of tambour (French for a small drum) and the instrument consists of a hollowed-out and tuned bamboo stem, sounding like a small tuned bongo drum. Timbales are cylindrical drums with metal shells; they can produce a powerful sound with a very clear attack to the note. The sound on a friction drum is produced by vibrating the drum skin with a dampened cloth or fingers, or by means of a cord that passes through the drum skin.

Goldsmith's ear for unusual timbres is immediately apparent in the orchestration of *NAM 44*, for which he requires the large symphony orchestra to include boo bams (see *left*) in bar 10, electric harp (bar 23) and electric bass clarinet (bar 52). The second trumpet is required to play the ram's horn (a Jewish religious instrument) in bar 52 while the first trombone has to sound the fearsome Tibetan horn. Timbales and friction drums are required in the percussion at this climactic point. Throughout the score Goldsmith is very specific in the effects he requires – for instance the type of horn mutes in bar 10, the type of conga mallets in bar 16 and the very precise performing directions such as in the violin parts at bar 11.

Although the opening music is highly dissonant, it is given an air of familiarity by a very traditional device – a **pedal** on C is heard in the bass of bars 1–10 and then on G in bars 11–22. The piano motif that intervenes in bar 4 is extended in bars 8–9 and then turned into a driving semiquaver riff from bar 11. Above this the high sustained violins with crescendo and woodwind interjections sound remarkably like the device that Bernstein found so successful in *On the Waterfront* (compare page 390 with page 384).

Having already wound up the tension by moving from quaver rhythms to semiquavers, Goldsmith increases it further with the **cross rhythm** played by the conga drums starting at bar 16. Its two notes per bar cut across the prevailing triple time.

These ideas are then reused with various changes of pitch and scoring. At bar 23 the tonal centre moves to E♭, the piano motif transfers to electric harp and woodwind, and the trombones take over the sustained note (with crescendo to a dissonance) formerly played by the violins.

More complex cross-rhythms add to the climax at bar 42, after which the texture thins out and the piano riff returns, leading to the highly dramatic outburst at bar 52. The terror of the chase is portrayed by the lowest instruments repeatedly rising from E♭ to E♮ against the piano's sustained E♭. The ram's horn bellows out its fearful call, joined by orchestral horns two bars later (the diagonal lines indicate they are to slide up the interval of a 5th). Meanwhile percussion and squeaks from the electric bass clarinet portray the chatter of the excited apes.

The same pattern is used in bars 55–58, with the rest of the orchestra adding scales and cross-rhythms, and increasing the cacophony by decorating the repeated Gs with semitones above and below.

After this central climax the piano riff returns (bar 59) along with the long sustained notes (bar 63). In a change of texture at bar 75 Goldsmith uses mainly strings for the first time (although accompanied by the strange twanging of the vibra-slap). Lower strings sustain G, against which upper strings move up a semitone, echoing the motif used in bar 52. This semitone clash becomes much harsher and more rhythmic from bar 84, where it moves to the high instruments, on which repeated dissonace the extract ends.

A vibra-slap is a percussion device which, when struck in the palm of the hand, produces a chattering sound, like a rattlesnake.

Private study

1. Look at the piano part in bars 8–9. How many of the 12 notes available in a chromatic scale are used in this piano motif?
2. Rising semitones are important in this music. Where are they first heard?
3. The piano part that starts in bar 11 could be described as a riff. What does the term riff mean?
4. Name four features that make bars 42–43 an effective climax.
5. In bar 54 do the orchestral horns sound a 5th higher than the ram's horn or do they play the same notes?
6. What is flutter-tonguing? Which instruments are required to use this technique in bars 55–58?

A *NAM 45*	CD4 Track 4
City of Prague Philharmonic	
Conducted by Paul Bateman	

ET: Flying theme (Williams)

From the 1960s onwards it became increasingly common for films to move away from orchestral soundtracks towards more diverse sources, including rock music, folk, jazz and electronic music. However major film companies continued to have a preference for the wide spectrum of sounds and dramatic effects available from a symphony orchestra, especially for films that had the hope (and budget) of becoming blockbuster hits.

The most successful film composer of the late 20th century to write such orchestral scores is John Williams (born in 1932). After an early career as a jazz musician he was appointed pianist to the studio orchestra of the film company Twentieth-Century Fox. This led to commissions to compose TV music, particularly for science-fiction programmes, and then to write the music for *Jaws* (1975) and *Star Wars* (1977). His music for the latter became a best-seller and was followed by scores for many other box-office successes, including *Close Encounters of the Third Kind* (1977), *Raiders of the Lost Ark* (1981), *Schindler's List* (1993) and *Saving Private Ryan* (1998) – as well as a number of recent works for the concert hall.

ET: The Extra-Terrestrial (1982) is a children's fantasy in which the scary alien of traditional science fiction is transformed into a cute animatronic who is befriended by an American schoolboy. As the sun sets on halloween, the ten year-old takes ET for a ride in the front basket of his bicycle. ET uses his telekinetic powers to take control of the bike which flies through the night sky silhouetted against the moon to the stirring music of *NAM 45*. The film credits indicate that the music was orchestrated by Herbert Spencer, who collaborated with John Williams in many of his film scores.

Bars	*Structure*	
1–8	Introduction	8 bars
9–16	**A** (theme)	8 bars
17–24	**A** (repeated)	8 bars
25–33	**B** (transition)	9 bars
34–41	**A** (in dominant)	8 bars
42–54	**B** (transition)	13 bars
55–62	**A** (in tonic)	8 bars
63–68	**A** (repeated)	6 bars
69–87	Coda	19 bars

Williams has a gift for memorable melodies, often worked out in very traditional ways. This is evident in the regular structure of this extract (shown *left*), with its eight-bar melody appearing in tonic and dominant keys (C major and G major).

The introduction is very minimalist – a repeated staccato quaver motif over tonic and dominant harmonies. If you look at the piano part in bar 1 you will see that the tonic chord of C has an added second (D) while the dominant 7th chord in bar 3 uses a suspended 4th (C instead of B). The notes C, D and G are common to both these chords, so there is very little sense of harmonic movement. The first four bars are repeated with the addition of brass, and a crescendo then leads into the main theme in 3/2 time.

It is worth considering why this theme is so memorable. It consists of a two-bar phrase based on one of the main building blocks of tonal music, the tonic triad. This is decorated with a quaver figure that is essentially the classical ornament known as the turn. If we write it that way (and in 3/4 time, see *left*) the structure is clear.

The motif starts with the confident sound of a rising 5th, tonic to dominant, balanced by a descent to the lower dominant in bar 2. Williams then repeats this two-bar pattern in a free sequence. The rising 5th becomes an octave in bar 11 (and the end of the motif rises instead of falls) and a 7th in bar 13 (where the end of the motif introduces some chromatic colour with an E♭). The repetitions of the basic pattern help fix it in the memory, but the varied sequence prevents it sounding too predictable. For the last two bars of the eight-bar theme Williams avoids a fourth appearance of the motif; bar 15 repeats the E♭–C of the previous bar and bar 16 provides an unusual cadence point with the theme on the leading-note (B) but harmonised by a chord of C.

The long sweep of this eight-bar melody is clarified by a simple texture of melody in octaves (strings and woodwind) with an accompaniment that maintains the chugging quaver rhythm heard in the introduction.

The theme is repeated at bar 17, with a variation in the quaver pattern in that bar and with several changes in the accompaniment. Low strings are now pizzicato and second violins have semiquavers (indicated by the strokes through the stems). Flutes and bells introduce a **countermelody** in bar 18, heard in each alternate bar. It will appear more prominently in the next section.

While the main theme captures the exhilaration of the bicycle flying through the air, the **transition** at bar 25 seems to reflect the magic of the star-lit scene. It develops the countermelody of the previous section, although still with the continuous quaver accompaniment. The range of chords is more varied here (G major and B major in bars 25–28, then E♭ major in bar 29, then down in major 3rds: F♯ minor, D minor and B♭ major). Rolls on timpani and a suspended cymbal, plus a diminished-7th chord in bar 33, herald the return of the main theme in the dominant (G major) at bar 34.

The second transition (bar 42) is similar to the first, but it uses a fuller scoring. Bars 50–54 use the music of bars 29–33 transposed up a 4th, preparing the way for the next return of the main theme to be back in the tonic at bar 55.

The theme is now in double octaves with a mainly thickly-spaced and low accompaniment. For the repeat at bar 63 unison horns enter a bar later in imitation, but this time the theme is interrupted by quavers descending in whole tones (bar 68) that run straight into the **coda**. Ascending scales over a dominant pedal lead to a colossal **false relation** – the C-major chord in bar 74 is underpinned by a loud E♭ anticipated on the previous beat. Upper woodwind refer to the main motif, their F♯ adding to the dissonance still sounding. This pattern is repeated, and then the bass at last moves down to C. Four bars of pure chord I conclude the extract.

Private study

?

1. What word describes the texture of bars 1–8?
2. What in the orchestration makes the main theme sound very warm and romantic?
3. What are the two main differences between bars 34–41 and bars 17–24?
4. What are the *sounding* pitches of the first two horn notes in bar 64? (Remember that they are transposing instruments.)
5. What is the difference between the two types of cymbal in the percussion part of bars 62–63?

A *NAM 46* CD4 Track 5
Conducted by Barrington Pheloung

Inspector Morse: Morse on the Case (Pheloung)

Barrington Pheloung was born in Australia in 1954 and studied at the Royal College of Music in London, after which he settled in Britain. He has composed many ballet scores as well as music for advertising campaigns by companies that include Rover, Andrex and Sainsbury, and music for such multimedia projects as the CD-Rom game *Broken Sword*. He has also written music for films (such as *Hilary and Jackie* and *Nostradamus*) and for a number of television series, including *Boon*, *Dalziel & Pascoe* and the highly successful *Inspector Morse* mysteries.

'In a television cop show, the first thing when he gets in his car and chases after someone, you've got to get the drum machine starting up. Some really up-beat, urgent thing. And I've never believed in car chases, for instance, as particularly glamorous, or murder and death. So I went always the opposite way – don't forget the character hates driving fast and has vertigo. The background music when Morse is ever involved in chases is far more about the horror, in fact ... It has to be said that the people at the network thought that the films wouldn't work in this format, nobody would concentrate on it for two hours. But years later, we had 26 million viewers.'

Many of the Morse episodes require at least an hour's worth of music, with individual cues lasting as long as eight minutes, but unlike the other pieces in this area of study the music is mostly non-intrusive. However it is not just ambient music used to set a mood – it also underlines emotional points and creates particular emphases in the dialogue that it underscores.

Pheloung himself enters into the spirit of the mysteries. The theme music (not part of *NAM 46*) starts with the letters M.O.R.S.E. spelled out in ... what else but Morse code! In a 1993 documentary about the series Pheloung also indicated that he sometimes wrote music that contains Morse-code 'clues' about the identity of the suspect. He was keen to develop a more subtle approach in television music, as he indicates in the quotation *left* from a 1995 interview.

In *NAM 46* Pheloung uses the understated textures and ambient sounds characteristic of much post-modernist music. Unlike the tight, repetitive rhythms of minimalism he frequently uses slow-moving ideas, and avoids creating obvious rhythmic and melodic patterns. Texture, timbre and silence are essential ingredients and these are combined to create a style in which the meditative and sensory experience of the music is the main focus.

For a post-modernist work by John Tavener see *NAM 32*.

The music uses the aeolian mode, which you can find by playing an octave of white notes on the piano, starting from A. The notes A and E are the main pitch centres. Notice the difference between the aeolian mode (no sharps) and A minor (which uses G♯ not G♮).

The long, sustained notes that change in unexpected parts of the bar ensure that there is no obvious sense of pulse and this gives the entire extract a timeless quality. It begins with a thin, two-part texture. The opening intervals played by the piano are echoed in **inversion** by the unison muted strings – the piano rises a 4th, the strings fall a 4th; the piano falls a 3rd, the strings rise a 3rd. The music is entirely **diatonic** for the first 51 bars.

The piano introduces a little more movement from bar 8 and almost imperceptibly the texture thickens as the horns enter and the strings play in two parts from bar 14 and three from bar 29. Notice also how the bass played by the violas very slowly descends over 52 bars, starting on E in bar 1 and eventually arriving on D a 9th lower.

The first two horn notes create a falling major 2nd. The piano and first violins respond with rising major 2nds (bar 18) and the piano adds an extra note to outline a rising 5th (D–E–A). The melodic interval of a 2nd continues to be explored by first violins (bar 19) and piano (bar 24) and it is also used harmonically (piano, bar 22 and low strings, bar 29 onwards). However in the slow organic growth of this texture it is now the three-note motif (D–E–A) which starts to receive more attention, stated in semiquavers by the piano in bar 26, in inversion (A–G–D) by the horns in bars 25–35.

The four-bar version of this motif in the piano (bars 32–35) forms the first (very small-scale) climax of the music, harmonised by an F major triad in the strings but with C and G in the piano left hand. The middle note of the motif is now dispensed with, leaving just the rising 5th, stated in 9ths in bar 37. This first section then dies away to the sound once more of falling 2nds. All the time the focus is on timbre and texture, never on rhythm and melody.

At bar 52 the piano's high F♯, clashing against the oboe G, breaks the mood of gentle diatonic dissonance. The texture reduces to two parts and then becomes **monophonic**, allowing the ear to focus purely on the tone of the oboe. The piano then introduces a new version of the material from bar 8 and the strings return. Pheloung continues merely to hint at ideas rather than to state them directly. For example, chords are suggested by using just their outer notes: G^7 (bar 82), F/A (bar 85) and A minor (bar 87).

It is characteristic of the *Morse* plots that the audience is never quite certain if the lead the inspector is following up is the right one – there is often a note of uncertainty, and this time that note is the A♭ sounded by the piano in bar 92 (and then the oboe) against A♮ and B in the strings. This leads to new investigations or at least, in musical terms, new timbres: four unison horns, harp and (at last) the entry of the low strings. These allow slightly thicker textures as we approach the final bars. *Morse*'s endings are usually enigmatic and so is Pheloung's cadence. Bars 102–112 outline an extended VII^7–I progression in C, but the recurring F♯ adds a note of nagging doubt. The music settles on the none too conclusive sound of a C-major triad in bar 110, but the horn note vaporises, leaving the final chord without its 3rd. Mystery solved … or not?

Private study

1. Why can this style of music be described as post-modern?
2. What does 'con sord.' mean in the string parts of bar 1?
3. Pheloung often restricts motifs to very limited sets of notes. Identify the only four notes used by the piano in bars 8–12.
4. Compared with other pieces in this area of study very little seems to happen in this music. Why is this?
5. How does Pheloung achieve contrasts in this music?

Titanic: 'Take her to sea, Mr Murdoch' (Horner)

B *NAM 47* CD4 Track 6
City of Prague Philharmonic
Conducted by Nic Raine

James Horner was born in Los Angeles in 1953. His family moved to London when he was ten, and he later studied there at the Royal College of Music before returning to America. His first film score to achieve great success was *Star Trek II* (1982) and his many subsequent credits include *Aliens* (1986), *Braveheart* (1995) and *The Mask of Zorro* (1998).

The 1997 film *Titanic* is based on the true and tragic story of the great liner which sank on its maiden voyage in 1912, but it is presented in Hollywood epic style and threaded through with a love story, to give a blockbuster mix of romance and drama. For such a combination Horner uses the traditional medium of a large orchestra, but the instrumentation is given a more contemporary feel by the addition of synthesised vocal sounds that contrast with the **vocalising** of a real choir.

NAM 47 accompanies a scene in which Titanic is about to sail out into the open sea. Horner closely matches his music to the visual images of the film, such as the ship's bells starting at bar 10. In bars 11–14, where we see the enormous engine room, a very low **pedal** on D reverberates at the bottom of the orchestra. As the propellers spin faster and the liner picks up speed the tempo progressively increases (bars 19, 23 and 25) until the film moves outside to a view of the calm, sunlit ocean – greeted by the heroic choral theme at bar 30. Horner not only portrays the visual images but also the mood of this part of the film, the confidence of the maiden voyage of the world's greatest liner being reflected in:

- rising motifs (bar 1)
- sequences of ascending scales (bars 21–27)
- joyful dancing rhythms (bars 4 and 37) and
- driving ostinato figures (bars 8–10).

The harmony is often very static, the same chord being used for a number of bars at a time. When it does change Horner often uses a well-worn device for generating a sense of heroic excitement – a shift to a chord a major 3rd away. Thus bars 1–7 centre on E♭, followed by G at bar 8 and B at bar 15. Notice the progression in bars 78–80 (a chord of C♮–F♮–G moving to D major) where added thrills are provided by the crescendo, harp glissando and suspended cymbal roll. A glance at bars 76–77, though, will show that there is no modulation. We have gone from D major to D major, and the intervening chord is merely exciting chromatic colouring.

So much diversity in a short space of time leads to the music sounding rather episodic – that is, it proceeds in short sections which join but do not always flow. To give shape to the whole cue Horner uses a theme which recurs in a number of different guises. It is first heard in fragmentary form in the **imitative** entries of the choir at the start of *NAM 47*. At bar 30 it appears as a broad, folk-like melody in G major sung by the upper voices. It returns in G major at bar 51 and is then repeated in a varied version by first violins. At bar 86 it moves triumphantly up a major 3rd to B major. Can you spot where it appears in the final bars of the music?

At bar 51 the theme has note values that are twice the length of the version at bar 30. Technically this is known as **augmentation**, but here it is simply a by-product of the change to double speed at bar 37.

Between the appearances of this recurring theme Horner uses a contrasting idea, although based on the same melodic outline. This is much more like a folk-dance, and appears in 5/4 time at bar 37 and in 6/4 time (with much more static harmony) at bar 68. Similar folk-influenced themes often appear in Horner's work, and reflect his deep interest in celtic folk music.

Private study

1. Where is there a cymbal roll? What musical effect does it have?
2. Describe two ways in which the music changes at bar 37.
3. What do you think is represented by the tubular-bell notes?
4. Why do you think Horner's music has proved so popular?
5. How does the music capture the majesty of the Titanic?

Composing

One of the composing options for Unit 2 is Film and television music, for which this Area of Study will provide you with many ideas and models. Try to supplement your study by careful observation of music you hear on film and television – keeps notes on:

- the resources used (full orchestra, small ensemble, etc)
- where and how the composer chooses to reflect the visual image – is it done by using obvious or subtle methods?
- ways in which motifs recall ideas or suggest new developments
- whether the music is unobtrusive and subliminal, or in the foreground, taking a dominant role in the action.

There are many sites on the world wide web that will give you more information about film music. A good starting point is *Film Score Magic*, which has a large number of links to many other sites: http://www.geocities.com/Hollywood/8588/links.html

Sample question 1

(a) Explain what you understand by any **two** of the following:

con sord. cross-rhythm dominant pedal sub-tone

(b) Link each term you have chosen in your answer to question (a) to a context from a specific work. Name the work, the precise location and the instrument or voice parts involved.

Answer the following two questions only if you are taking the exam in 2001 or 2002.

(c) State what is meant by a riff and how Bernstein uses this device in *NAM 43*.

(d) What in *NAM 45* do you think accounts for the popularity of John Williams' film music?

Answer the following two questions only if you are taking the exam in 2003 or 2004.

(c) How is music used for dramatic effect in the excerpt from *Titanic* (*NAM 47*)?

(d) Choose some suitable examples from the music you have studied to show how innovative percussion and electronic effects have been used in film music.

Sample question 2

(a) Explain what you understand by any **two** of the following:

post-modernism flutter-tonguing canon sul ponticello

(b) Link each term you have chosen in your answer to question (a) to a context from a specific work. Name the work, the precise location and the instrument or voice parts involved.

Answer the following two questions only if you are taking the exam in 2001 or 2002.

(c) In what ways is the tritone important in *NAM 43*?

(d) Choose appropriate examples from the music you have studied to show how music can be used for a variety of different purposes in film and/or television.

Answer the following two questions only if you are taking the exam in 2003 or 2004.

(c) Mention four ways in which the music for the hunt is made exciting in *NAM 44*.

(d) How does Auric convey the humour and bustle of the scenes in *NAM 42*?

Popular music and jazz

Popular music: the background

Popular music – music of the people – is often thought of as relatively modern, but it has a long history. It is, though, a poorly documented history before the 19th century for two main reasons. Firstly, in the days when only a small proportion of the population could write, literature and social documentation centred on the interests of those who could read and this rarely included detailed accounts of how the majority of the population lived or were entertained. Secondly, popular music was (until at least 1800) a primarily aural tradition, in which folk songs and folk dances would be learnt, modified and added to by successive generations. There was no need to write down such music, nor would most of its performers have had the skills to do so – and of course there was then no means to record the actual sounds of such music.

We know of the existence of popular music from passing references in contemporary accounts, sometimes to tunes which survived long enough to be notated in modern times. Occasionally composers wrote variations on popular tunes (like Byrd in Elizabethan times) or collected them for the entertainment of the nobility (such as Playford's collection of country dance music in the 17th century and the many popular tunes used in the *Beggar's Opera* of 1728).

As greater prosperity gave rise to a new middle class with members who could read music, or afford to pay for entertainment, we also find evidence of specific types of music being published to fulfil popular demand. Thus Henry Purcell wrote many simple but very lewd songs for businessmen to giggle over in the public houses of 17th-century London at the end of the working day, and Mozart supplied an insatiable demand for the popular 'German Dances' that were all the rage a century later.

Aural traditions and improvisation are central to the nature of popular music and jazz, and therefore music notation has often not always been used in the creation of such pieces. Notation tends to be used if complex arrangements are required, or if the music is intended from the outset to be published for others to perform. The pieces in this Area of Study are all **transcriptions**, made by listening to the recording and notating what is heard. Standard European notation is not well adapted to showing some of the subtleties of rhythm, pitch and timbre in jazz and pop music, and you may come across other notated versions that transcribe the same music in different ways.

A distinct style for popular music began to emerge in the 19th century. As the economy moved from agriculture to industry many people moved from the countryside to the towns, adapting their music to new themes of working in coal pits or on railway building. The more prosperous among the population aspired to be entertained by professional musicians in Victorian music halls and to require music for their own performance in the home. Industrial manufacture of affordable pianos and the invention of cheap music printing made this a realistic prospect. A market that began with simple songs by classical composers (such as *NAM 37*) and short piano pieces by romantic composers, was soon dominated by thousands of short, tuneful waltzes, marches and songs to be played and sung in the parlours of 19th-century Europe and America.

Most commercial popular music was modelled on simple types of European art music in the 19th century, but after 1900 the main influence came increasingly from African-American music. This is first seen in ragtime, a style of popular music related to European dances of the time (such as the military two-step) but featuring a constant **syncopation** of the melody against an accompaniment in march style. Ragtime developed in the midwest of the USA, and its 'ragged time' reflected the rhythmic banjo playing of black Americans in the popular minstrel shows of the late 19th century.

West End Blues (Joe 'King' Oliver)

A *NAM 48* CD4 Track 7
Louis Armstrong (trumpet and voice)
Jimmy Armstrong (clarinet)
Fred Robinson (trombone)
Earl Hines (piano)
Mancy Carr (banjo)
Zutty Singleton (drums)

In the days when international travel was mainly by ship, a rich mix of cultural traditions could be found in major sea ports such as New Orleans in the south of the USA. Here could be heard, in the early years of the 20th century, marching bands, ragtime, European parlour music, black American music such as the blues, visiting dance bands from Mexico, and a combined legacy of west-African and European folk forms. There was also a cheap supply of band instruments that had become available after troops stationed in the area during the American civil war were disbanded.

Louis Armstrong's 1926 recording of *Musk-rat Ramble* can be found in *Aural Matters* (Bowman and Terry), pages 76–77.

This was the city in which jazz first developed and in which Louis Armstrong was born in 1901. By the age of 17 he was already playing cornet in the leading jazz band in the city but by this time work in New Orleans was becoming scarce and, like many of his fellow musicians, Armstrong moved to Chicago in 1922 where he joined a band in which Joe 'King' Oliver (composer of *West End Blues*) played first cornet and Armstrong played second. It was in Chicago that their music was first recorded and thus became internationally famous. Armstrong went on to form his own bands for a series of records made between 1925 and 1928, and it is from one of the 1928 recordings that the music on CD4 is taken.

The instrumentation of *West End Blues* is typical of New Orleans jazz, consisting of a frontline (trumpet, clarinet and trombone) and a rhythm section (piano, banjo and drums). In early jazz there is considerable collective improvisation of the theme by all of the frontline instruments simultaneously, but in the later Chicago style of *West End Blues* there is more emphasis on solo improvisation, allowing the players to establish totally new melodic ideas over the common chord pattern (this is particularly evident in the piano solo, bars 43–54).

Some editions of the *New Anthology* refer to a bass in the score of *NAM 48*, but there is no evidence of this in the recording.

In most jazz the underlying chord sequence, known as the changes, is the most important element, and it forms the foundation for most of the improvised material. Each repetition of the chord pattern is known as a chorus. *West End Blues* uses the best-known of all such chord patterns, the 12-bar blues, which here takes the form:

The precise pattern of chords in a 12-bar blues can vary. For instance the tenth chord is often IV rather than V or V^7.

bars	7	8	9	10	11	12	13	14	15	16	17	18
chord	E♭ I	E♭ I	E♭ I	E♭^{7} I^7	A♭ IV	A♭ IV	E♭ I	E♭ I	B♭^{7} V^7	B♭^{7} V^7	E♭ I	E♭ I

West End Blues is based on five choruses of this pattern, with a solo introduction and short **coda**, in the pattern shown *right*. Listen to it without following the music and see if you can hear the five repetitions of the 12-bar blues.

Form

Intro	
Chorus 1	Theme (trumpet)
Chorus 2	Trombone solo
Chorus 3	Clarinet and vocal duet
Chorus 4	Piano solo
Chorus 5	Theme (trumpet)
Coda	

Did you notice that sometimes the chords are changed? For instance in the sixth bar of the trombone solo the chord is A♭ minor, not A♭ major. This is known as a **substitution chord** and is an important means of giving variety to the changes.

The introduction is one of the most famous moments in early jazz. It combines the cadenza (a **virtuoso** unaccompanied solo) that concluded many light-classical cornet pieces of the time with the

In most types of jazz individual beats are usually divided into uneven pairs of notes in a long–short pattern, known as **swing quavers**. These are not easy to express in conventional notation. The opening of the main theme could be written in any of the following ways (the third of which is perhaps closest to what is actually played):

The 'milk bottle sound' mentioned in bars 18–19 of the score is actually a percussion instrument of the time called a *bock-a-da-bock*. It consists of two metal discs about eight centimetres in diameter, mounted on sprung tongs, which the drummer cups in his hands to play.

type of brilliant high brass playing that Armstrong would have heard from the Mexican bands in New Orleans – and it formed a totally novel way of starting a blues. Notice the rhythmic freedom of the passage, the **blue notes** (F♯/G♭ and D♭) and the way that Armstrong gives little hint of the E♭ tonality of the piece until the final bar, where the rest of the band enters on an augmented version of the dominant chord.

The theme is characterised by the motif F♯–G–B♭ heard at the start (and anticipated by Armstrong in bar 1), but the improvised decoration starts almost immediately. Notice the expressive scoop in pitch in bar 5. The improvisation becomes increasingly elaborate until the top B♭ in bar 18, which is decorated with a fast lip trill up to the C above (made by using the lips, not the valves). The piano and banjo play in a style called comping – the rhythmic playing of chords as a backing to a solo.

The second chorus features a high trombone solo, accompanied by tremolo chords from the piano, and a curious percussion device called a *bock-a-da-bock*. The longer note-lengths of the trombone solo provide an effective contrast with the first chorus and the extensive use of portamento (the slides in pitch, produced with the trombone slide) is a characteristic feature of the New Orleans style.

The third chorus is in the form of a call-and-response duet between the clarinet and vocal solo, sung by Armstrong in a jazz style that he invented, known as scat (singing to nonsense syllables that are chosen to enhance the expressive musical qualities of the solo). The clarinet is entirely in the low (chalumeau) register and is played with the fast vibrato typical of New Orleans clarinettists. Notice how, in bar 32, Armstrong picks up the clarinet figure from back in bar 14. This appears in yet another version in bar 62, adding a further unifying layer to the improvisation.

The fourth chorus provides yet another change in texture, with a brilliant piano solo in salon music style. The right-hand arpeggios are supported by a left hand which leaps between bass and harmony notes in a ragtime technique known as a stride bass.

The full frontline returns for the final chorus, which Armstrong starts with the opening motif an octave higher than before, followed by four bars of top B♭. As the E♭^{7} chord resolves to A♭ he releases the tension with a cascade of notes, the repeated B♭s bouncing off the A♭ chord that supports them. After a final climax in bar 62 a short coda featuring a brief piano solo leads to the last three chords, ending with a highly chromatic version of a **plagal cadence**.

Private study

1. What were the conditions in New Orleans that enabled jazz to develop and flourish?
2. Briefly describe the roles played by the clarinet and trombone in the first chorus of *West End Blues*.
3. Identify **four** substitution chords on page 462 of the score.
4. State what is meant by the following terms and give an example of each from *NAM 48*: portamento, comping, scat, stride bass.

Black and Tan Fantasy (Duke Ellington)

B *NAM 49* CD4 Track 8
Duke Ellington and his orchestra

Duke Ellington is one of the few major figures in jazz whose importance arises more from his compositions than his work as a performer. In 1924 he took over the leadership of a small jazz band in New York which he expanded in size and which in 1927 was awarded a contract to play at the Cotton Club, one of the city's leading nightclubs and a venue for frequent radio broadcasts. Although located in the heart of the black community of Harlem it catered for an entirely white audience, who came to see floorshows based on highly stereotyped ideas of African culture. To accompany these, Ellington developed what is known as his jungle style, featuring heavy drums, dark saxophone textures and rough, growling brass sounds, all evident in the *Black and Tan Fantasy*, first recorded in 1927.

The title refers to 'black and tan' nightclubs – private venues where black and white people could enjoy each other's company, although at considerable risk of humiliation and possible prosecution if mixed couples were seen together in public in that racially intolerant age. The quotation of Chopin's 'funeral march' in the last four bars of *NAM 49* thus forms a rather wry comment on the possible outcome of such 'black and tan' relationships.

Listen to the recording and make sure you can identify the three main sections of the orchestra: reeds (saxophones and clarinet), brass (trumpets and trombone) and a rhythm section of piano, banjo, drums and bass. Collective improvisation is difficult to achieve in a band of ten players and so written arrangements became increasingly common as jazz groups grew larger. Ellington worked closely with his band, adapting his arrangements to the individual talents of its members and leaving space for their individual solos. He often involved members of the band in the arrangement, as in the *Black and Tan Fantasy*, which was a collaboration between Ellington and his lead trumpeter, Bubber Miley.

When you listened to the piece did you notice that it is based on a 12-bar blues sequence? There are six choruses, followed by a four-bar coda, but between the first and second choruses there is a 16-bar section for alto sax, based on an entirely different chord pattern. Ellington became famous for his innovations in the use of musical form in jazz composition. In this piece the very European format of a 16-bar section, with lyrical saxophone melody, contrasts strongly with the gruff sounds of the brass solos in 12-bar units. Ellington may well have used these devices to highlight the 'black and tan' conflict of the title, resolved in the unhappy little coda.

The introductory chorus is a simple blues pattern in B♭ minor – notice the pitch bends in bars 3 and 7, and the use of a full drum kit rather than the very sparse percussion used in *NAM 48*. The change to tonic major (B♭ major) and use of chromatic harmonies for the alto sax solo highlights the contrast mentioned above. The lower reeds accompany with mainly sustained notes (the sort of effect that is these days known as a pad). The use of groups of three quavers that cut across the beat in bars 17–18 is known as cross-phrasing. Bars 21–28 are a varied repeat of the previous eight bars, suggesting that the alto sax solo is predetermined material, not totally improvised. The extensive use of portamento throughout the sax solo is typical of jazz saxophone playing at this time.

Bubber Miley's trumpet solo occupies two choruses and includes two characteristic effects of the jungle style. The plunger mute was originally the rubber suction cup from a plumber's plunger. It can be held close to the bell to suppress the sound, as in bars 29–32, or moved further away for a more open sound, as in bar 33. Listen carefully for the frequent transitions between different positions of the mute. 'Growling' is produced by literally growling with the vocal cords while playing the note. The reference to straight quavers in bar 45 means that these notes are not swung.

Chord substitutions start to appear in these two choruses (for instance bar 37 uses Cm^7 where you would expect F^7) but they become much more prominent in Ellington's piano solo, which concludes with part of a **circle of 5ths** in bars 59–63. Notice the way that he starts with a 'pick-up' in bar 52 to avoid any gap at the end of the trumpet solo.

The last two choruses sound more urgent, with shorter motifs and, in the trumpet solo, fast repeated notes and off-beat drum accents in bars 78 and 80. Finally the coda restores the initial B♭ minor tonality for the brief quotation from Chopin's funeral march.

Private study

1. Name three features of Ellington's 'jungle style'.
2. Which instruments are used prominently in this piece but not at all in Armstrong's *West End Blues*?
3. How does Ellington achieve variety in this work, despite the repetitious nature of the 12-bar blues format?
4. Give three different examples of blue notes in bars 29–52.
5. Where is a circle of 5ths used after bar 64?

A *NAM 50* CD4 Track 9
Miles Davis Quintet

Examples of swing and bebop can be found in *Aural Matters* (Bowman and Terry) pages 78–83.

Four (Miles Davis)

During the 1930s and 1940s many big bands appeared, playing jazz-influenced dance music called swing. But jazz musicians such as Charlie Parker, Dizzy Gillespie and Thelonius Monk found this type of music too predictable and developed a new style of jazz known as bebop. Played by much smaller groups, it was music for listening rather than dancing, and featured driving rhythms and complex, often dissonant harmonies. The trumpeter Miles Davis worked with Charlie Parker between 1945 and 1948 after which he began to lead his own bebop groups. Davis was one of the most innovative jazz musicians in the second half of the 20th century, creating a more lyrical style, known as cool jazz in the 1950s, and experimenting with unusual metres and modal jazz. He went on to use electronic instruments and to popularise jazz-rock in the 1960s and other types of fusion in the 1970s.

Before the invention of the LP (long-playing) vinyl record in 1948, most recordings were limited to just a few minutes of continuous music. The LP, offering some 20 minutes of playing time per side, enabled jazz musicians from the 1950s onwards to record the much longer types of structure they were used to improvising in live performances.

Four was composed by the jazz saxophonist Eddie Vinson and was first recorded by Miles Davis in 1954. The transcription in *NAM 50* is the first two minutes of a recording from a live concert given in New York on 12 February 1964, at which the complete performance lasted over six minutes. On other occasions Davis extended the work to as long as 15 minutes. *Four* is a head arrangement (see *left*), the most common structure used in jazz. After the drum introduction the theme is announced by the trumpet. The harmonies of the theme (the changes) are then repeated in each 32-bar chorus, above which the soloist improvises new material to fit the chord pattern. The head is usually repeated near the end, to form an out-chorus.

Head arrangement

Intro
Head (establishes chord pattern)
Solos (based on chord pattern)
Head (or 'out chorus')
Coda

Eddie Vinson loosely based the changes of *Four* on a popular song of the 1940s called *How High The Moon*, one of a number of songs known as jazz standards whose harmonies have provided the basis for much creative improvisation. A comparison with the chords used in *NAM 48* and *49* will show *Four* has a much more complex harmonic vocabulary – almost all chords have 7ths and many have 9ths, 11ths, 13ths and chromatic alterations. The melody line makes little use of the variation techniques seen in earlier works – instead there is a process of thematic substitution, in which a short motif is briefly developed, and then substituted with a new idea that fits over the same pattern.

Charlie Parker's *Ornithology* is one of the best-known jazz works based on this set of changes.

Very few of the chords in the head are on down-beats, giving an impression of furious activity but an elusive sense of pulse. It is only when the **walking bass** commences in the first chorus that the pulse really becomes clear. Notice how, in the fourth bar of the chorus for example, the bass is often not playing harmony notes, just as the trumpet often plays away from the basic chord progression, creating a richly dissonant counterpoint with the comping of the piano. Subtle inflections of pitch are an important feature – not only in the pitch bends but in places such as bar 31 of the second chorus, where the unusual accidental indicates a pitch between A♮ and B♭. Some of the trumpet techniques employed are listed *right*. The tenor saxophone has no independent material in *NAM 50*. This reflects the origin of *Four* in 1954 as a work for quartet. It is, in effect, an extended and often **virtuoso** solo for trumpet, accompanied by rhythm section.

The wavy line in bar 1.15 indicates a fall-off – a short downward slide. The bracketed note in bar 2.1 is a ghost note – a deliberately weak, almost inaudible note. The diamond-headed notes in bar 32 are marked '½v.', referring to the use of half-valving – the partial opening of a valve to give a note of thin tone and uncertain pitch, and in this case having the effect of ornamenting the main note.

The rhythm section players on CD4 (Herbie Hancock on piano, Tony Williams on drums and Ron Carter on bass) all went on to work with jazz trumpeter Wynton Marsalis in the 1980s.

Private study

1. What are the main stylistic features of bebop?
2. How do the changes in *Four* differ from the changes used in *NAM 48* and *NAM 49*?
3. What is meant by a head arrangement?
4. Which notes are blue notes in the first eight bars of the trumpet solo?

I'm Leavin' You (Chester Burnett)

Much popular music in the first half of the 20th century was influenced by the techniques of jazz, although not by its essentially improvised nature. Swing quavers, blue notes and a rich harmonic vocabulary of chromatically altered chords are found in the music of such American song writers as Irving Berlin, Cole Porter, Jerome Kern and George Gershwin (see *NAM 41*), and big bands adopted the idioms of swing in the dance music of the age.

A *NAM 51* CD4 Track 10
Howlin' Wolf (vocal, harmonica)
Hosea Lee Kennard (piano)
L. D. McGhee (guitar)
Hubert Sumlin (guitar)
S. P. Leary (drums)

The invention of recording, radio and the musical film helped the rapid dissemination of this new style of popular music, but such technology also accelerated a change that had begun many years before. No longer was popular music created primarily for the people to perform, but for them to consume – as listeners and dancers. Microphones allowed vocalists such as Bing Crosby and Frank Sinatra to use a soft, light singing tone (known as crooning) and still be heard over the sound of a big band.

Popular music in America was more diverse than in Britain, partly because the many different radio networks focused on developing regional tastes. Thus country music, blues and gospel music continued to develop alongside the mainstream popular styles of more commercial music. As black singers from the south of the USA moved to industrial cities such as Chicago in search of work, the blues changed from a rural type of music to a harder urban style. Rhythm and blues, which emerged in the 1940s, later became one of the key influences on rock music. It invested the traditional blues format with the rhythms of jazz and, to fulfil a role as dance music in the large dance halls of the time, much louder sounds – the drum kit, saxophones and amplified voices and guitars.

The term 'shuffle rhythm' indicates swing quavers at a moderate speed and in a legato style.

The G minor pentatonic scale on which the pianist improvises at the start consists of the notes G–B♭–C–D–F.

A 'stop chorus' is a section featuring stop-time, in which attention is focused on the soloist by confining the accompaniment to mainly isolated beats.

The term 'fill' in bars 17–18 simply indicates a short improvisation.

Chester Burnett (1910–76) was an black American blues singer, guitarist and harmonica ('mouth organ') player who worked under the name Howlin' Wolf and was famous for keeping alive the impassioned vocal delivery of the Chicago rhythm-and-blues style. *I'm Leaving You* was recorded in September 1958 as one of a dozen songs on an LP entitled *Moanin' in the Moonlight*. The format is entirely typical of rhythm-and-blues songs of the 1950s – six repetitions of a 12-bar blues pattern, without modulation, and with the singer replaced by an instrumental solo in the fourth chorus. There is a two-bar introduction, a two-bar link before the instrumental, and the piece finishes with a coda in which the fade-out indicates that the song was conceived more for recording than for live performance (it also rather nicely illustrates the final words).

The blues influence is apparent not only in the structure but also the blue notes – see how many you can identify in the vocal part on the first page. The jazz influences are in the shuffle rhythm, the improvised guitar lines and (although not very prominent on CD4) the emphasis of the backbeats (beats 2 and 4) by the drummer. Howlin' Wolf was extremely influential in shaping British rock 'n' roll in the 1960s and 1970s, the bands that recorded his songs including the Rolling Stones, the Yardbirds, the Grateful Dead, Cream, Little Feet, the Doors, and Led Zeppelin.

Private study

1. Write out the basic chord pattern of the 12-bar blues in G.
2. How is the end of this chord pattern varied?
3. Compare bars 13–14 with bars 1–2.
4. Why is the notation of the singer's part in bars 15–17 not an accurate representation of what Howlin' Wolf sings?

B *NAM 52* CD4 Track 11
Carl Perkins (vocal, guitar)
James 'Buck' Perkins (rhythm guitar)
Lloyd 'Clayton' Perkins (upright bass)
W. S. Holland (drums)

Honey Don't was released on 1 January 1956 as the B side to Carl Perkins' *Blue Suede Shoes*. An extract from the latter can be found in *Aural Matters* (Bowman and Terry) pages 87–88.

Honey Don't (Carl Perkins)

Rock 'n' roll began when white people started playing rhythm and blues in about 1954, and became instantly popular when Bill Haley's *Rock Around the Clock* was included in the 1955 film, *The Blackboard Jungle*. It combines elements of rhythm and blues with an American country-music style known as rockabilly. This tends to be much more tightly rhythmic than the laid-back jazz-like style of *NAM 51*, as can be heard in the walking bass and the regular strumming of the acoustic guitar part in *NAM 52*.

The instrumentation of rockabilly music rarely varied:

- lead guitar – an electric guitar played with a plectrum ('pick guitar') and a good deal of echo effect
- acoustic rhythm guitar
- plucked double bass ('upright bass')
- drums, playing predominantly the pattern seen in bar 4, with a firm backbeat on the snare drum.

The distinctive echo effect of the lead guitar was produced at this time by a device with a loop of magnetic tape. The signal was recorded and then immediately picked up by a number of adjacent playback heads to give a series of closely-spaced echoes.

A distinctive technique used by most bass players in rockabilly (and which comes from jazz bass playing) is the slap – so commonly used that the instrument was sometimes called the slap bass. The string is pulled hard away from the fingerboard and then allowed to snap back, producing the percussive slap represented by the x-headed notes in the score.

After a five-bar introduction the song is based on the following modification of the by now familiar 12-bar blues progression:

Bars 6–17:	E	E	C	C	E	E	C	C	B	B	E	E
Bars 18–29:	E	E	E	E	A	A	E	E	B	B	E	E

The second set of 12 bars is totally standard, but the use of the unrelated chord of C major in the first set gives the harmonies a taste of country music. Can you work out how the complete 24-bar pattern is reduced to 20 bars in the first instrumental (bars 30–49) and cut down still further in the second (bars 74–83)?

Although the harmony is based on two 12-bar patterns, the way the complete 24-bar unit is divided is much more European than blues in style, since it is split into an eight-bar verse in stop-time (bars 6–15) contrasting with a 16-bar refrain featuring clipped vocal phrases over a continuous accompaniment. The style of this backing is one of the most identifiable features of rockabilly and early rock 'n' roll. The walking bass outlines each chord, adding passing notes (marked * in the example *right*) and a 7th at the top of the pattern, while the lead guitar decorates the same pattern an octave higher. The simultaneous performance of two different versions of the same melodic material is known as **heterophony**.

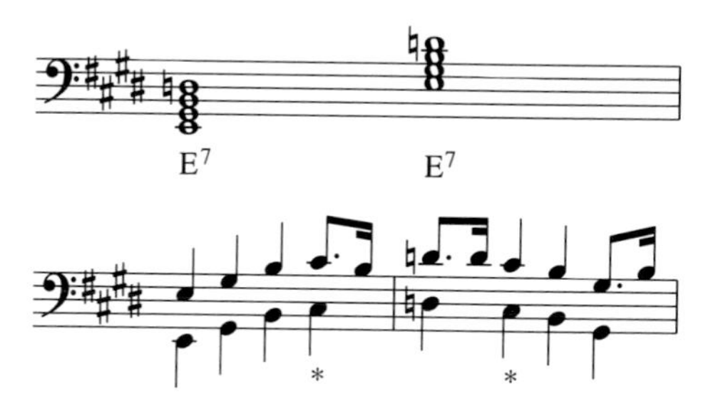

The two instrumental solos feature a characteristic lead guitar technique – the parallel 4ths in bars 30–33 and 74–80. These are produced by **double-stopping** the top two strings (which are a 4th apart) with one finger.

Just as rhythm and blues was a key influence for the Rolling Stones in the creation of 1960s British rock music, so rockabilly was an important influence on the Beatles, who included this Carl Perkins song on their 1964 LP, *Beatles For Sale*.

Elvis Presley, who never wrote any music himself, recorded a number of rockabilly songs, including Carl Perkins' *Blue Suede Shoes*.

Private study

1. What is meant by (a) stop-time, (b) walking bass, (c) slap bass?
2. Which drum-kit instruments are represented by the three different levels of notes on the drum stave?
3. Which are the blue notes in the first verse of the vocal part?
4. How is the 12-bar blues format given variety in this song?

A *NAM 53* CD4 Track 11
The Kinks

Waterloo Sunset (Ray Davies)

With just the substitution of bass guitar for upright double bass, the instrumentation of rockabilly formed the basis of most 1960s rock music, including that of The Kinks. Like most British groups of the time they had begun by playing blues-influenced music, but under the direction of singer, guitarist and song-writer Ray Davies they were soon one of the few groups to resist copying everything American. Davies drew on very ordinary aspects of British culture such as afternoon tea, London sunsets, commuters and the taxman, as themes for a series of wry miniatures which were still very influential 30 years later in the Britpop of the 1990s, especially in works such as Blur's album *The Great Escape*.

Waterloo is home to one of London's busiest railway stations for commuters. It is close to the Thames, which was still a very dirty river when this song was written.

Listen to *Waterloo Sunset* and see if you can detect any sign of the 12-bar blues or the blue notes that have so far featured in most of the pieces in this area of study. Did you spot that the song is written in mainly four-bar phrases? Here are the main chords in each of these patterns during the 16-bar verses:

Bars 9–24: E–B^7–A–A E–B^7–A–A F♯m–C♯–F♯m^7–B^7 E–B^7–A–A

The first five notes of the vocal part form a hook (a memorable figure) that is repeated at different pitches in all of the A patterns. When it is set to the words 'Waterloo sunset' in bars 21–22 it is known as the title hook. The B pattern in AABA song form is often called the bridge, but note that in pop music and jazz this term is also used to refer to any contrasting transition section (see the description of *NAM 54* below).

The verses thus use a very traditional popular song form: AABA. The A pattern (E–B^7–A–A) was set up in the introduction, following the descending bass scale and V^7 harmony bars 1–4. The B pattern (or bridge) occurs in bars 17–20. Equally traditional is the 'middle eight' between the verses (bars 25–32). Its first four-bar pattern modulates to the dominant (B major). When the pattern is repeated the chord of B major becomes B^7 and this chord is extended to form a two-bar 'turnaround' (bars 33–34) that takes the music back back to E major for the next verse. The last verse finishes at bar 50 and is followed by a coda, fading out on another extended B^7 chord.

Double-tracking (bar 8) refers to an effect possible with the multi-track recording that came into use in the 1960s. After the vocal solo was recorded it was sung again and recorded on a new track which was then mixed with the original recording to create a thickening of the sound.

The backing vocals are inherited from 1950s pop music, in which a separate backing group of singers was often used. In the 1960s a similar role was usually taken by the other members of the group who sang these parts as they played their instruments. Notice how guitar licks (short solos, as in bars 11 and 15) frequently decorate the ends of the vocal phrases.

Private study

1. In what ways does the bridge differ from the verses?
2. What is meant by (a) a lick, and (b) a turnaround?
3. How does the bass part differ from the bass part of *NAM 52*?
4. Compare *NAM 53* with *NAM 51*.

B *NAM 54*
This song is not included on the CDs that accompany the New Anthology.

A Day in the Life (Lennon and McCartney)

On page 121 we mentioned how the cosmopolitan life of a busy sea port brought together a rich mix of musical influences in New Orleans, and the same is true of Liverpool where all four of the Beatles and many other pop musicians of their generation grew up. John Lennon said 'It's where the sailors would come home with blues records from America ... I heard country and western music in Liverpool before I heard rock 'n' roll'.

A Day in the Life is the concluding song from the Beatles' 1967 album *Sergeant Pepper's Lonely Hearts Club Band*. This was what is now called a 'concept album' – a collection of related songs, in this case linked by a theme of loneliness. As in many of the Beatles' later songs the lyrics are subtle and the music sophisticated. John Lennon wrote the verses, Paul McCartney contributed the bridge, and the Beatles' producer (the classical oboist George Martin) directed the orchestra and effects.

Form

1–4	Intro	4 bars
5–14	Verse 1	10 bars
15–23	Verse 2	9 bars
24–34	Verse 3	11 bars
35–46	Transition	12 bars
47–57	Bridge	11 bars
58–67	Transition	10 bars
68–78	Verse 4	11 bars
79–89	Outro	11 bars

The key is often ambiguous. The verses each start with the same chord progression in G major, but chord V (D major) is avoided and they each end differently (but inconclusively) in the area of E minor. The bridge is more clearly in E major, but the orchestral sections are virtually **atonal** – only the final colossal chord of E major resolves the conflict. The verses are also of different lengths, with many subtle changes in their endings. For instance compare bars 13–14 with 21–23 and 30–34. The first ends plainly on a low G. The second adds a semiquaver figure before launching to a high G. The third goes straight to the high G and *then* uses the semiquaver figure in **inversion** (the semitones now rise instead of fall), which is extended and then taken up by the orchestra, rising higher and higher as it becomes more dissonant. Can you work out how the similar passage in the fourth verse (bars 74–78) is yet again different and yet still related to the previous three verses?

When comparing the verses be aware that some editions of the *New Anthology* have the first chord symbol of bar 24 incorrectly printed as C – it should be G, as at the start of the other verses.

Much of the material is deceptively simple. The bass in the verses is formed from simple descending scales; the vocal motifs are rhythmically free but short and of limited range – most begin and end on the same pitch in the first verse (Lennon gradually broadens their range in later verses). The accompaniment in the verses is very restrained – the drum part is very sparse at the start but builds throughout the song, providing a firm contrast in the bridge. The 40-piece orchestra is used sparingly but with colossal effect. Its dissonant crescendo in the first transition removes the sense of key and the cymbal fill at its end (bar 44) removes the sense of pulse – only to be replaced by the clock-like ticking of the E-major piano chords in bar 45. In the second transition the orchestra's role is more subtle, underpinning the bass of the root-position harmony that illustrates the dream. The reappearance of the crescendo in bar 79 acts as a structural device, linking the coda (or 'outro') with the first transition. But this time it leads to a dramatic silence followed by an E-major chord on three pianos, overdubbed four times and supported by George Martin playing a harmonium.

The songs on the *Sergeant Pepper* album are linked musically as well as by the theme of loneliness in their lyrics. One of these links is a bass line built on descending scale patterns, which occurs in four of the songs on the album.

After the final chord of the song has died away, the *Sergeant Pepper* album finishes with a 'locked groove' (a device that causes a tiny part of the record to play incessantly) consisting of noise from the post-recording party, recorded twice, chopped into pieces, reassembled in a different order and then played backwards – a return to reality that is as strange and innovative as the songs that preceded it.

Private study

1. How does the introduction relate to the first verse?
2. How does the bass-guitar part relate to the left-hand part of the piano in bars 5–8? Can you think of the term to describe this relationship?
3. Almost all of the phrases in the verses begin after a quaver rest on the strong beat. What do you notice about the starts of most of the phrases in the bridge?
4. How else does the bridge contrast with the verses?

B *NAM 55* CD4 Track 13
Desmond Dekker and the Aces

You can get it if you really want (Jimmy Cliff)

See *NAM 60* for an earlier example of music from the Caribbean.

Many people in the west are oblivious of the vibrant pop music traditions of other cultures – the rai music of north Africa, Israeli rock, Nigerian highlife or south-east Asian dangdut. Only rarely do such styles slip through the barriers of western commercialism, but in 1969 the Jamaican singer Desmond Dekker had a number one hit in the UK with his song *Israelites*. The style, like that of his 1970 hit *You can get it if you really want* (written by Jamaican singer-songwriter Jimmy Cliff), is an early version of reggae known as rock steady. Like reggae, there is a clear backbeat (see the drum part from bar 5 onwards) and a concentration on short repeated patterns based on a limited number of chords. Also like much reggae, the lyrics allude to a struggle against poverty and oppression, although set in the context of irresistibly tuneful dance music.

Form

Bars	Section	Length
1–3	Intro	3 bars
4–13	Refrain	10 bars
14–25	Verse 1	12 bars
26–13	Refrain (repeat)	10 bars
14–25	Verse 2 (repeat)	12 bars
26–35	Refrain	10 bars
36–43	Instrumental	8 bars
44–53	Refrain	10 bars
54–57	Outro (repeat to fade)	

Play the recording, listening particularly to the bass and chords. Unlike reggae there is very little syncopation in the bass part of rock steady. Did you notice that the song is built in mainly two-bar units on the progression I–IV (D♭–G♭)? This supports the main melodic motif, a **stepwise** descent from F to D♭, heard three times in bars 4–9, followed by I–V–IV–V^7 to end the refrain. The motif is repeated throughout much of the song, acting as a unifying **riff**.

For most of the song the lead vocal melody is based on the major pentatonic scale (D♭–E♭–A♭–G♭–B♭) although the other parts use the full scale of D♭ major.

The verses are very similar to the refrain: four repetitions of the I–IV pattern, but this time ending iii–IV–V–V^7. The melodic material is also essentially the same, but notice Desmond Dekker's use of falsetto in bar 25 to produce a climax at the end of the verses. Refrain and verses alternate as shown *above left*. The instrumental introduces a surprising chord of E major, but it is used merely for colour and not for modulation – the entire song remains in D♭ major.

The accompaniment reflects the rich mix of influences in Jamaican music. The busy drum rhythms are Latin American in style (with no hint of swing), the close-harmony backing vocals are a legacy from 1950s doo-wop, and the perky trumpet lines come from Mexican bands such as the Tijuana Brass popular in the 1960s.

?

Private study

1. In which bar(s) is the bass syncopated?
2. Describe how the motif in bars 1–2 is varied in bars 4–9.
3. Where does Dekker sing a pitch outside the pentatonic scale?
4. What do you notice about the rhythm of the part played by the organ and second guitar throughout the song?

B *NAM 56* CD4 Track 14
Van Morrison

Tupelo Honey (Van Morrison)

Van Morrison grew up in Belfast, although he has lived most of his life in America where he developed a unique style of nostalgic music that combines elements of rhythm and blues (which he played in Ireland), rock, jazz, soul and Irish folk music. Tupelo Honey is from Van Morrison's 1971 album of the same name. Its mellow style and free vocal delivery are typical of the slow rock ballads that had become popular ever since the release of Procul Harum's *A Whiter Shade of Pale* four years earlier.

Tupelo honey is a famous type of honey produced in Florida, in the south of the USA.

An excerpt from *A Whiter Shade of Pale* can be found in *Aural Matters* (Bowman and Terry) page 91.

The rhythmic freedom of the vocal part comes from soul, a highly influential style of black music that developed in the 1960s from a combination of gospel music and rhythm and blues. Look at bars 5–12 to see the extent to which the melody of verse 1 is displaced and adapted in verse 2. The vocal line uses a major pentatonic scale (B♭–C–D–F–G) revealing the influence of Irish folk music in Van Morrison's work. Remove the complex rhythms and the basic melodic outline of bars 13–16 is shown in the simple pattern *right*.

Do you feel that the music has a hypnotic quality? One reason is that the entire song is constructed from repetitions of the chord pattern heard in its first two bars (I–iii–IV–I). This is repeated to form a four-bar unit in which the last chord is alternately V or I. Otherwise there is no significant change (and no modulation) for almost seven minutes. The hypnotic effect is reinforced by the similarity of the vocal phrases, which mostly have a descending shape and end on notes of the tonic chord. Variety is provided by Van Morrison's almost jazz-like ability to improvise on this basic material, forever adapting it to new contexts. For instance the climax of the first coda is highlighted by starting on the highest note of the song (top B♭, bar 37) while the climax in the second coda is marked out by constant returns to a high G. Further variety comes from the variations in the bass part and in the guitar counter-melody, while the instrumental (with saxophone solo played by Van Morrison) adopts a contrasting texture of dense **counterpoint**.

Private study

1. Compare the bass part in bars 13–16 with that in bars 5–6.
2. In which bar is there a texture of four-part counterpoint?
3. Name three ways in which the two codas differ.
4. How is the fade-out (bars 53–56) related to the introduction?

Don't look back in anger (Noel Gallagher)

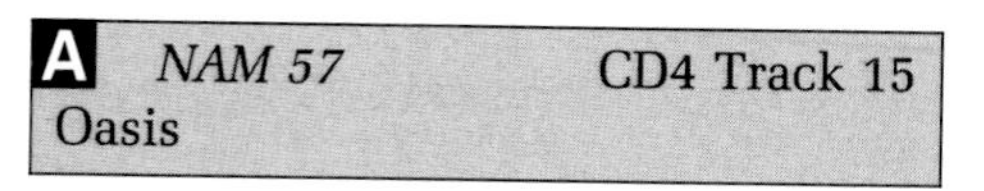

Noel Gallagher has made no secret of his admiration for the work of the Beatles, and *Don't look back in anger* is clearly a tribute to John Lennon who was killed in 1980. The opening bars are based on the start of Lennon's song *Imagine*, and the lyrics of bars 13–16 are a quotation of Lennon's own words.

The song is based on four-bar phrases. The verses are constructed from two ideas. Firstly, the chord pattern established in bars 5–8, which is repeated in bars 9–12. Secondly, a contrasting 12-bar pattern starting at bar 13 and formed from three four-bar units.

The opening pattern returns at bar 25 where it supports the new melodic material of the refrain, giving an ABA form to the entire verse. The predictability of this scheme is offset by cutting the main pattern down to three bars in bars 29–31 (for verse one only). The instrumental (bars 33–44) is a lead-guitar improvisation over the B-section chord pattern and is followed by two performances of the refrain (A), the second of which is interrupted at bar 58 to form the quiet, reflective coda. The arrangement consists mainly of repeated chords in simple rhythms, particularly evident in the piano and string parts. Guitar distortion and the very low bass-guitar part (mostly played on the lowest string) thicken the texture of the music, but the main centre of interest is the solo vocal line, lightly decorated by guitar licks in the verses

Private study

1. The opening melody is mainly pentatonic. Where is the first non-pentatonic note in the vocal part?
2. What is the correct description of this non-pentatonic note?
3. Compare bars 25–28 with bars 5–8. How is the refrain differentiated in terms of melodic material and accompaniment?
4. Does the song ever use chords in inversion, or do all of the harmonies consist of root position triads?

Sample question 1

(a) Explain what you understand by any **two** of the following:

walking bass   comping   blue note   stop chorus

(b) Link each term you have chosen in your answer to question (a) to a context from a specific work. Name the work, the precise location and the instrument or voice parts involved.

Answer the following two questions only if you are taking the exam in 2001 or 2002.

(c) Describe four techniques used by Louis Armstrong in *NAM 48* to enhance the expressive qualities of his solos.

(d) How successful is *Don't look back in anger* in recreating the style of earlier pop music? Compare the song with *NAM 53* and mention any points which identify *NAM 57* as a much more recent song.

Answer the following two questions only if you are taking the exam in 2003 or 2004.

(c) Name four ways in which technical advances in recording have had an impact on jazz and popular music.

(d) In what ways do *NAM 51* and *NAM 49* illustrate two very different approaches to the 12-bar blues?

Sample question 2

(a) Explain what you understand by any **two** of the following:

circle of 5ths   backing vocals   pentatonic   plunger mute

(b) Link each term you have chosen in your answer to question (a) to a context from a specific work. Name the work, the precise location and the instrument or voice parts involved.

Answer the following two questions only if you are taking the exam in 2001 or 2002.

(c) Name four features of *NAM 53* that you feel contributed to its success for the Kinks.

(d) Choose appropriate examples to show how the role of the drummer has changed over the years in the music you have studied.

Answer the following two questions only if you are taking the exam in 2003 or 2004.

(c) Describe four examples of specific types of music notation that are helpful in the notation of pop music and jazz, but that are rarely used in other types of music.

(d) To what extent was *NAM 54* (*A Day in the Life*) a revolutionary new approach to pop music?

World music

World music is a widely used but very vague term. In one sense all music is world music, but the expression is normally used to refer to traditions that have developed independently of western music. However a clear definition is impossible for a number of reasons:

✦ It depends on your perspective. To many western Europeans, Chinese music is a type of world music – but to most Chinese people it is not.

✦ The music of many cultures includes styles that have arisen from a blend of local traditions with western idioms, such as the highlife music of west Africa or the fusion of Punjabi music with western pop in bhangra. These cross-over styles are usually classified as world music. However some types of western music that are strongly influenced by other cultures, such as jazz, are not normally regarded as world music.

✦ World music is not necessarily non-western. Styles such as the flamenco music of Spain or the two pieces of Irish folk music in *NAM 61* (one newly-composed and the other traditional) are widely regarded as types of world music.

Perhaps the best we can do is adopt the words of the anonymous wit who remarked that world music is local music – but not local to here.

It will also be apparent that world music encompasses a huge and diverse range of styles. Many countries have different types of music for different purposes including ceremonial occasions, dancing, religion, entertainment, expressions of grief or rejoicing, and work songs to lighten the load of repetitive manual tasks. Some have separate classical and popular traditions (as in the west) and in many larger countries the styles of music vary between regions.

These different types of music often share an important social purpose in binding a community by reliving the history, politics and customs of its people, and thus reinforcing their cultural identity. At the same time it is important to remember that in the modern world, music is seldom exclusive – Indonesian gamelan players are just as likely to enjoy the latest American or Indian pop tunes as anyone else.

Most countries have traditions of instrumental music, and singing is universal. However the frequently heard statement that music is a 'universal language' is highly questionable. As we shall see, some types of music will probably seem familiar because they draw on European traditions (we deal with these first in this chapter). But there are others in which the language of non-western scales, complex rhythms, unexpected approaches to harmony and unusual timbres will require more effort before the experience starts to become as meaningful and enjoyable as it is to its creators.

Few people encounter more than just a little of this rich diversity. Even experts in world music (ethnomusicologists) who spend long periods living in the cultures they study and learning to play its music, rarely become familiar with more than just two or three

Further reading

Music Worldwide by Elizabeth Sharma. *Cambridge University Press*, 1998. ISBN: 0-521-37622-X (book); 0-521-37481-2 (CD). This book in the *Cambridge assignments in music* series provides short and practical introductions to seven world-music topics, including four of those in this Area of Study.

World Sound Matters by Jonathan Stock. *Schott and Co Ltd*, 1996. ISBN: 0-946535-79-5 (teacher's book with pupils' questions); 0-946535-81-7 (music transcriptions); two-CD set available separately. This is a more detailed study that includes 58 pieces from 35 different countries. It too provides more information on four of the topics in this Area of Study.

musical traditions. However even a limited study of world music will expand the amount of music we can enjoy, widen our understanding of the hopes and values of other cultures, and increase our awareness of different methods of expressive communication. All this can, in turn, enhance our own composing and performing.

A *NAM 60* CD4 Track 18
Red Stripe Ebony Steelband

An aural test based on this piece can be found in *Aural Matters* (Bowman and Terry) page 71.

Yellow Bird (traditional)

The rich musical traditions of the tiny Caribbean island of Trinidad arise from its diverse mix of people – it was occupied first by the Spanish, then the British, and it has been home to immigrants (many unwilling) from France, west Africa and the East Indies.

Yellow bird, up high in banana tree.
Yellow bird, you sit all alone like me.
Did your lady friend leave the nest again?
That is very bad, makes me feel so sad.
You can fly away, in the sky away
You more lucky than me.

Yellow Bird is a calypso, a type of music that reflects something of this range of influences. The calypso was traditionally sung at carnival time in the island's capital, Port of Spain. The repertoire was based on about 50 tunes to which new words were constantly improvised – sometimes mocking and satirical, and often topical. Although *NAM 60* is a purely instrumental arrangement, the opening words associated with the original tune are printed *left*, and refer to the unfaithful wife or girlfriend.

Listen to the music and answer the following questions:

1. How many different chords are used?
2. What instrument do you hear that is not in the score?
3. How are the long notes sustained by the melody instruments?

Steel-pan playing was originally an aural tradition in which the players would work out their parts, or be shown what to play by the leader, and would then memorise it. *NAM 60* is a **transcription** of the recording and does not reflect all the detail of the performance.

The melody probably derives from a French folksong (called *Chou-coune*) from nearby French-speaking Haiti. The rhythm (steady dotted notes in the bass and **syncopation** in the upper parts) derives from the samba, a Latin-American dance from Spanish-speaking South America. The harmony is distinctly European – you probably noticed that is uses mainly just three chords (G, C and D) with the sort of **chromatic** decoration (such as the C♯ in the first bar of the tune and the F♮s in bar 8) that is associated with western music. The instrumentation sounds characteristically Trinidadian, even though steel pans have spread from there to other Caribbean countries, Britain and many other parts of the world.

Instrumental music at carnival time was once provided by African drums, but these were banned in 1884 after which the resourceful Trinidadians developed the tamboo-bamboo band – instruments made of hollowed-out bamboo that could be tuned to different notes. The word tamboo is a local dialect version of the French *tambour* (a small drum) but these 'drums' were relatively quiet and in the 1930s they were supplemented (and soon replaced) by the sound of metallic percussion – in the form of homemade instruments fashioned from anything to hand that would make a noise, such as dustbin lids and car brake-drums.

One of these, called the ping pong, was made from a large paint tin and struck with wooden sticks. The beaters left indentations and it was discovered that if these were pushed out to form small bumps, they could be tuned to notes of different pitch. During the second world war the Americans used Trinidad as an army base, leaving behind vast quantities of big empty oildrums. The principle of the ping pong was extended to these much larger containers, which quickly proved to be very versatile instruments.

The oildrum is turned upside down and its base hammered into a concave curve. Individual notes are then grooved with a steel punch. There may be only three or four separate notes on bass instruments but as many as 29 on a soprano pan. The steel is tempered by heating and then cooled rapidly in water to give a better tone. The height of the drum is reduced as needed to give the optimum resonance for its range and its notes are then fine-tuned. Smaller steel pans are suspended by wire from a stand, but bass pans usually consist of entire oildrums that stand on the ground. They are played with sticks made of bamboo or other wood that have bands of rubber wound around the ends (or sponge rubber balls for bass pans).

The layout of notes on a pan, and the names given to the various sizes of pan vary between ensembles and regions, but their musical functions are usually similar:

Name	Musical function
Soprano, Tenor, First tenor, Ping pong	Melody-line pans, usually with a chromatic range of about two octaves
Double alto, Double second, Double tenor	A pair of pans that can play an alto melody line or chords
Cello, Guitar, Triple cello, Four-pan cello	Half the height of bass pans, these can play a tenor part or chords
Bass, Boom	Bass line (usually a set of five or six pans, each with three or four notes)

Modern steel bands often include a drum kit, and perhaps bongos and conga drums. Some also use other metallic percussion instruments such as the vibraphone. The size of bands can vary from just a quartet to large ensembles of 100 or more players.

Yellow Bird is typical of traditional steel-band music in its use of simple harmonies, and clearly defined structures. Modern steel-band playing has widened this repertoire considerably, with many innovative arrangements of different types of music.

Private study

1. What is meant by syncopation?
2. Give the number of the first bar in which there is no syncopation in any printed part.
3. What do you notice about the part played by the four-pan cello?
4. In bars 1–8 the melody is mainly constructed from **stepwise movement**. On what is the melody of the next six bars based?
5. Why can this be described as tonal music? (If you are not sure read the entry on **tonality** in the glossary).
6. This piece has six sections (including repeats). Using letter A to identify the first 16 bars and other letters to identify different sections, express the form as six letters (eg AABBCA).

B *NAM 61* CD4 Track 19
Niall Keegan (Irish flute)

Further examples of folk music from the British Isles can be found in *Aural Matters* (Bowman and Terry), pages 54–64.

Tom McElvogue's (jig) and New Irish Barndance (reel)

The fact that this pair of folk dances seem so well matched, and yet the reel is traditional and the jig newly composed, is a reminder that folk music is a living tradition, enjoyed daily in pubs and folk clubs. It is also a tradition with a very long heritage.

Of the two dances represented, the jig has as long and continuous a tradition as any of the pieces in the *New Anthology*. It has been known as a dance since at least the 15th century and by the 17th century the basic character of the first piece in *NAM 61*, with its fast compound-time metre, was already established. Indeed, the style was so well known throughout Europe (where it was called a *Gigue* in French and a *Giga* in Italian) that it was frequently transformed into art music, usually to form a rollicking finale to a multi-movement piece by composers such as Bach (*NAM 21*) and Corelli (*NAM 15*) – the latter clearly a jig in style, if not in name.

The reel may be equally ancient – the word derives from the Anglo-Saxon verb *rulla*, meaning to whirl (which rather nicely describes the character of the reel in *NAM 61*). It was known as a dance on the Scottish borders by the late 16th century, later migrating from Scotland to Ireland.

The Irish traditional flute

The two dances are played on the Irish traditional flute, a wooden instrument based on the design of the flute as it was in the early 19th century, before the more complex keywork of the modern flute was invented. Indeed it is thought that the flute became popular in Irish folk music at the time when these older instruments were in cheap and plentiful supply because flautists were moving to the new style of flute and selling off their old instruments. Some players of Irish folk music use flutes with no keys at all, others prefer instruments with a small number of keys (usually not more than six) to facilitate the production of notes such as F, G♯, B♭ and E♭.

For more information on the Irish flute see the website of the flute maker, Terry McGee: http://www2.dynamite.com.au/t.mcgee/

The Irish flute has a conical bore (unlike the cylindrical bore of the modern flute) and large fingerholes. The latter help to give it a fuller tone, but since it was, in the 19th century, played mainly in the home there was no need for a loud sound, and the shrill notes of the flute's third octave were never normally used.

If you play the flute or recorder, you will know of the importance of tonguing to articulate the notes in classical music. In folk music tonguing is often very light and is sometimes reserved to mark the starts of phrases. As you can hear on CD4 the music is articulated primarily through ornamentation, a characteristic that comes from the piping tradition of bagpipe playing. A number of these ornaments are printed in *NAM 61*, including the slide (bar 9), mordent (bar 34), **acciaccatura** (bar 60) and trill (bar 81), but as indicated in the score there are many others that have not been notated.

Other characteristics of Irish flute playing include the absence of breath vibrato (finger vibrato is sometimes used as an ornament), strong attack on lower notes, little dynamic variation and avoidance of hard staccato. The styles and repertoire of Irish flute music vary around the country. The Sligo style is rhythmic and highly ornamented, the Leitrim style is breathy and uses less decoration, while the Galway style is famous for its smooth, silky tone.

Niall Keegan said of the CD from which this recording is taken that 'the arrangements are simple ... but the music is not'. This can be seen in the structures of both dances, in which a basic musical idea is repeated with ever more exciting elaboration. The texture of the entire piece is **monophonic** – that is, it consists of an unaccompanied melody. Notice the foot-tapping, which is particularly effective in establishing the slower tempo at the start of the reel, and the shouts of encouragement from the audience as the reel whirls to its close. These are just as important a part of the performance tradition of folk music as the practice of audiences sitting silently in classical concerts until the time comes to show their appreciation through a round of applause.

The jig

The 64 bars of the jig are formed from eight repetitions of an eight-bar phrase. None are identical and many start in different ways, disguising the repetitive nature of the dance. Compare the third bars of the pattern (bars 3, 11, 19, 27, 35, 43, 51 and 59) to see how the degree of variation is often less in the middle of the phrases.

The music stays in G major throughout. When F♮ occasionally appears it is never followed by a broken chord of C, so there is no sense of a modulation to C major. Instead it gives the music a slightly **modal** character, characteristic of folk music.

The reel

The last note of the jig (the G at the start of bar 65) is also the first note of the reel, thus allowing the two dances to overlap without a break. The reel is also a fast dance, but differs from the jig in being in simple time (either 2/4 or 4/4).

- ✦ Compare bars 67–68 with the first two bars of the reel.
- ✦ Now compare bars 69–72 with the whole of the first four bars (bars 65–68).
- ✦ Finally compare bars 73–76 with the first four bars.

You will probably have spotted that bar 67 is a varied repeat of bar 65 and that while bar 68 doesn't repeat bar 66 exactly, it also starts on C, ends on D and uses similar rhythmic figures.

These four bars are then repeated with increasing amounts of elaboration, like a decorated **riff**, until bar 96. Notice how the shapes of the motifs start to mutate. For instance bar 73 starts with a high G and then falls to E, instead of rising a 6th as it did originally. From bar 97 the excitement is built up by still more virtuoso decoration, a gradual increase in speed and the effect of compressing the repetitions into smaller units

Private study

1. Name two characteristic features of a jig.
2. How does the Irish traditional flute differ from the modern flute in (a) construction, and (b) style of playing.
3. How does the **texture** of *NAM 61* differ from that of *NAM 60*?
4. Is there any modulation in *NAM 61*?
5. Why does the reel create such a hypnotically exciting effect?

A *NAM 62* CD4 Track 20
Mustapha Tettey Addy

Agbekor dance (traditional Ewe)

In west Africa, societies such as the Ewe people of Ghana possess a type of music that is rich in rhythmic complexity. European music, for all its harmonic sophistication, often seems rhythmically dull to the African musician, who strives for the interaction of several markedly different rhythms played at the same time. This simultaneous use of layers of opposing rhythms is known as polyrhythm and gives the music its sense of vitality. The exciting rhythmic style of African music spread via the slave trade to the Caribbean and the southern states of America, from where it had a direct influence on many of the jazz and pop music styles of today.

In many parts of Africa drums have special significance as symbols of political or religious power, and are often associated with tribal chiefs and royal families. African musicians do not refer to playing their instruments, but to teaching them to speak – they do not like playing drums from other regions because these 'don't speak the same language'. This link between language and music is important. The relative pitch of spoken words affects their meaning in most African languages and these inflexions can be imitated by the 'talking drum' to communicate messages, as explained below.

The dance

The *agbekor* is a ritual war dance which was originally performed as a preparation for battle, although nowadays it is performed for entertainment at social gatherings and at cultural presentations. The dance is presented in platoon formation and features stylised movements to represent reconnaisance, surprise attack and hand to hand combat. The main part of the dance is, of course, fast paced, as illustrated by the music of *NAM 62*.

The instruments

The *gangkogui* is a double bell (two bells joined to one handle) made of iron and struck with a beater: the two pitches are shown in the score. Its main function is to provide an **ostinato** pattern that keeps time and forms a reference point for everyone in the group. The rhythm it plays in *NAM 62* is common in drumming throughout much of Africa.

The *atsimevu* is the master drum. It is a tall narrow drum (about 1.3 metres high) that is leant against a wooden frame. The head is about 28cm in diameter and the drum is open at the bottom. The *atsimevu* can be played with one stick, two sticks or with the hand, and a variety of muting effects are possible, as explained at the head of the score. The variety of pitches possible through the use of different drum strokes can emulate the tonal and rhythmic inflections of speech (the 'talking drum') and this property can be used to communicate directions to the other players and dancers, or to incorporate statements of praise to the tribal chief on ceremonial occasions. The master drummer will also sometimes indicate cues by playing the *gankogui* pattern on the side of the drum. Can you see where this happens in *NAM 62*?

The *sogo* is a barrel-shaped drum about 75cm high with a closed bottom. It is played in a sitting position, with the drum resting on the ground between the player's knees. It plays its own rhythm against the basic pattern, and sometimes adds variations and improvisations.

The dance is started by the *gankogui* and this introduces the first aspect of rhythmic complexity to western ears (although it would sound astonishingly basic to the drummers). The ostinato part is syncopated, but there is no regular beat at the start of the pattern and so this is not obvious. Thus it is the *atsimevu* part that initially appear to be syncopated when it first enters. Before we have time to adjust to this, the *sogo* enters with a device found in much African music. It plays patterns that are the same length of the other parts, but they are staggered so that they enter one quaver after the metrical pattern of the bell. At the end of bar 13 the master drummer uses this device in the opposite direction – the *atsimevu* patterns enter one quaver before the bell. As the piece proceeds the interactions of the three instruments become increasingly complex. In bar 35, for instance, dotted quavers cut across the *sogo* quavers, and triplet rhythms are added in bars 41 and 42.

It would form an excellent exercise to perform this dance on whatever percussion instruments you have available – despite its outward simplicity it will require the utmost concentration.

If you get stuck you could try sequencing it – but it is much more fun to attempt a live performance.

Private study

1. What type of dance is the agbekor dance?
2. What is an ostinato and which instrument plays an ostinato?
3. What is the function of the master drummer?
4. What do you think is the meaning of the unusual key signatures in the score of *NAM 62*?

Se quema la chumbambá (Familia Valera Miranda)

B *NAM 63* CD4 Track 21
Familia Valera Miranda

We have already seen that the slave trade, which forcibly took so many Africans to the Carribean and America, resulted in many new musical styles as African and European cultures interacted. In Cuba, settled by the Spanish, Afro-Cuban music developed from a combination of minor-key Spanish melodies and harmonies with African rhythms. The instrumentation, too, is a mix of instruments introduced by the Spanish (the guitar and double bass) with percussion of African origin. This produced dances such as the rumba in the 1930s and the mambo two decades later. Another 20 years on the salsa became the new dance craze of the age.

A translation of the words is given on page 540 of the *New Anthology*.

Other music from Latin America can be found in *Aural Matters* (Bowman and Terry) pages 71–72.

The salsa developed from a type of Cuban music called the *son*, whose main features are:

- call-and-response patterns between singer and chorus
- simple and short texts about everyday life
- a strongly rhythmic, off-beat bass
- a five-note syncopated rhythm pattern played on the claves (polished hard-wood sticks that are clicked together).

All of these features are evident in *NAM 63*, in which *Córo* refers to the chorus and *Pregón* is the lead singer. The *córo* is generally a fixed part, but the *pregón*, like the accompanying parts, is largely improvised around the basic chord pattern. Listen to the music and identify the pattern of two chords on which it is based.

The part played by the claves is fundamental to Afro-Cuban music. It provides the metronome-like pulse that identifies the style of the music and provides the timing for both the improvisations of the other players and the dancers. The particular clave rhythm used in *NAM 63* is the most common of all salsa rhythms and is known as the 'son clave'.

The guitar-like *cuatro* that introduces the music is an instrument from nearby Puerto Rico, another country closely identified with salsa. The diminished-7th chord it outlines in bar 2 hints at dominant harmony, but it is only in bar 9 that the complete chord pattern is fully revealed. As you probably noticed, it uses only tonic and dominant-based chords, in a hypnotically repeating pattern, a very European influence and typical of salsa.

The vocal melody has a rest on the first beat of every phrase which, in combination with the off-beat bass and syncopated claves, avoids the feeling of a strong down-beat at the start of each bar. The resulting web of interacting syncopated rhythm hints at a little of the complexity of African music, but the constant repetitions make for easy and irresistible dancing – try it!

The song is **strophic**, but improvised variations are introduced by the *pregón* from verse 2 onwards. See if you can identify some of the detail in these. Further variety is provided when the call-and-response format is interrupted for the instrumental improvisations described and notated on the last page of the piece.

Private study

1. What is meant by (a) strophic, and (b) call-and-response?
2. Why can this style of word-setting be described as **syllabic**?
3. How is variety achieved in this song?
4. What makes this style of music so popular for dancing?

Rag Bhairav (North Indian)

A *NAM 58* CD4 Track 16
Ram Narayan (sarangi)
Charanjit Lal Biyavat (tabla)

The classical music of northern India is based on a series of pitches called a *rãg* (known as a *raga* in the south) and a rhythmic system called a *tãl*.

Further examples of music from both the north and south of India are given in *Aural Matters* (Bowman and Terry) page 67.

The *rãg* is both a scale and a melody, while the *tãl* is a rhythmic pattern with a particular number of beats grouped in a specific way. The music is improvised within the limits of the *rãg* and *tãl*, and according to the conventions of the style. Like the other pieces in this Area of Study, Indian music is not normally written down.

There are hundreds of *rãgs* – each expresses a particular mood and is associated with a particular time of day or season of the year. *Rãg Bhairav* has a tender and melancholy mood, and is played during the first quarter of the day, after sunrise.

The pitches for *Rãg Bhairav* are printed at the head of the music. The names resemble western *sol-fa* ('*doh–re–mi*') but the pitches are governed by certain conventions. *Sa* and *pa* (rather like tonic and dominant) are not allowed to be sharpened or flattened. *Ma* may be sharpened but not flattened, while the remaining notes may be flattened but not sharpened.

The *tintal* rhythm cycle used in this piece one of the most common to be found in north-Indian music and it consists of 16 beats arranged in four groups of four. These groups, which are rather like bars, are called *vibhags* and are not necessarily of equal length, although they are here. The improvising musicians must arrive together on the first beat of the *tãl* (marked X in the score, and known as *sam*). Each *tãl* must have at least one contrasting *vibhag* known as *khali* (meaning empty and marked 0). During the *khali* the *tabla* (drum) player lightens the texture by using just the smaller of the two drums.

Notice that in *NAM 58* only the *sam* and *khali* sections are marked, at the start of each line (beginning at line 19).

The performance of *Rãg Bhairav* on CD4 is relatively short (some improvisations can last for hours) but it reflects the conventional pattern in which an opening section (called *alap*) features the main performer, who sets the mood by exploring the main characteristics of the rag with considerable rhythmic freedom. This is followed by a section called *Jhor* in which there is a greater sense of pulse (starting at line 14) and is concluded by a section known as *Jhala* in which the tabla player enters and often exchanges rhythmic phrases with the soloist.

Instruments

The *sarangi* is a bowed string instrument. The player sits cross-legged and the instrument is held against the chest its base resting on the player's feet. The sympathetic strings are adjusted to the notes of the *rãg* and resonate of their own accord when the same (or a related) note is fingered on one of the three main strings. Notice how the player often slides between notes for expressive effect (a technique known in western string playing as *portamento*).

The *tampura* is a large stringed instrument that is plucked to provide a drone in the background. The *tabla* is a pair of small drums that can be played with various combinations of finger and hand strokes known as *bols* (meaning words). Different pressure can vary the tone, and the drum heads are mounted with a patch made from a paste of iron filings and rice flour which gives further opportunity to vary the sound.

The pitches played by the *tampura* are G and C – early editions of the *New Anthology* have the G misprinted as a B at the head of the score.

Private study

1. What is (a) a *rãg*, and (b) a *tãl*?
2. What is the importance of the beats marked X in the score?
3. How is the *tabla* part varied during the piece?
4. How does the music become more exciting after line 13?
5. To what does the term *Jhala* refer?

Baris Melampahan (traditional Balinese)

B *NAM 59* CD4 Track 17
Gong Kebyar de Sebatu

Gamelan is an ensemble of instruments consisting mainly of tuned gongs and metallophones. There are a number of different gamelan traditions in Indonesia, classical and modern. *NAM 59* is from Bali, in the east of the region, and is an example of *gong kebyar* style, in which traditional techniques are still being enthusiastically developed by Balinese musicians. *Kebyar* refers to the explosive unison attack with which such pieces often begin (*NAM 59* is an excerpt taken from after the start of the piece).

There are examples of both Javanese and Balinese gamelan music in *Aural Matters* (Bowman and Terry) pages 67–68.

The pitches of *pelog* can only be expressed very approximately in western notation – notes 1 and 5 are flatter than indicated, the other slightly sharper by varying amounts.

The instruments of the gamelan are made, tuned and kept together as a set – they are not owned and brought in by the individual musicians as happens in most western ensembles. The players do not regard themselves as individual musicians, but as performers on one common instrument. Every gamelan is tuned in a slightly different way, using one of two possible scales, neither directly related to western scales. *Slendro* is a five-note (or pentatonic) scale that divides an octave into roughly equal steps. *Pelog* is a seven-note scale of uneven steps. This piece uses just five pitches taken from the *pelog* and these are shown at the head of the score.

The basis of the music is a 'nuclear' melody – a basic melodic outline from which the entire piece develops, often using a technique called **heterophony** in which the instruments simultaneously perform different versions of the same melody.

The piece is punctuated by gong strokes to mark its main divisions. Between these the music is organised into four-beat groups, each called a *keteg* (rather like a bar). The whole rhythm cycle is known as a *gongan*.

The basic structure of contrasting sections is outlined at the head of the score. Notation is not normally used in gamelan playing and you may find it easier to follow the music by listening and following the main gong strokes.

The instruments are explained in the score, but it can be helpful to think of them as four groups, each with its own function:

- *Balungan* instruments play the main theme; they include the one-octave metallophones and the *suling* (a quiet bamboo flute).
- Gongs divide the *gongan* into sections. The largest, which hangs from a frame and is called the *gong ageng*, marks the end of the *gongan*. Smaller gongs mark the fourth or eighth *keteg*, and the smallest ones, mounted horizontally over resonator boxes, outline the pulse.
- *Panususan* instruments (larger metallophones that have bamboo resonators) decorate and embellish the theme.
- Drums and cymbals, which add contrast, particularly in the loud *angsel* sections.

Private study

1. What is meant by a metallophone?
2. Why do the notes of *pelog* sound so different to western scales?
3. What is heterophony? Where do you first hear a heterophonic texture?
4. Explain how the function of the gongs differs from the function of *panususan* instruments such as the small metallophones.
5. Both *NAM 59* and *NAM 60* are based on the sound of metallic instruments. Why do the two pieces sound so different?

Sample question 1

(a) Explain what you understand by any **two** of the following:

tremolo   ostinato   syllabic word-setting   tabla

(b) Link each term you have chosen in your answer to question (a) to a context from a specific work. Name the work, the precise location and the instrument or voice parts involved.

Answer the following two questions only if you are taking the exam in 2001 or 2002.

(c) (i) Briefly describe the role of each of the three instruments in *NAM 62*.

(ii) What is the difference between the way the instruments relate to each other in *NAM 62* and the way the instruments in *NAM 60* relate to each other?

(d) How does *NAM 58* create the tender and tranquil mood associated with its *rãg*?

Answer the following two questions only if you are taking the exam in 2003 or 2004.

(c) Explain the difference between a monophonic texture and a heterophonic texture, and give an example of each.

(d) What are the main characteristics of the Irish traditional flute, and its method of performance, as used in *NAM 61*?

Sample question 2

(a) Explain what you understand by any **two** of the following:

strophic   tintal   son clave   calypso

(b) Link each term you have chosen in your answer to question (a) to a context from a specific work. Name the work, the precise location and the instrument or voice parts involved.

Answer the following two questions only if you are taking the exam in 2001 or 2002.

(c) What makes *Yellow Bird* (*NAM 60*) such a happy piece?

(d) Describe some of the important characteristics of northern Indian music found in *NAM 58*.

Answer the following two questions only if you are taking the exam in 2003 or 2004.

(c) Mention some of the types of ornamentation used in *NAM 61* and state why ornamentation is such an important part of the style of this music.

(d) In what ways does *NAM 63* reflect a combination of different musical traditions?

Glossary

Acciaccatura. An ornament (or grace note) above or below a main melodic note, printed as a small note with a slash through the stem and flag. It is either played as fast as possible, or is played with the main melodic note and immediately released. It often forms a discord with a harmony note, as is the case with the acciaccaturas in the second half of bar 15 in *NAM 37*.

Air. English or French for a song. The second part of *NAM 36* is an air. See also **Aria**.

Alberti bass. An accompaniment pattern in which the notes of a chord are sounded in the order low, high, middle and high again. It is named after an obscure Italian composer who was rather addicted to the device. See *NAM 22*, bars 71–80 (left hand).

Antiphony. The alternation of two or more contrasting groups of instruments and/or singers, as found in *NAM 14*.

Appoggiatura. A melodic decoration that produces a dissonance before resolving on a note of the chord. It is like a **suspension** but without the preparation. Appoggiaturas are sometimes written as small notes, like ornaments, as in bar 12 of *NAM 37*, where the C♯ in the vocal part clashes with B in the accompaniment before resolving on the same note.

Aria. Italian for a song or air. The fourth movement of *NAM 28* is an aria. See also **Air**.

Atonal. Music that avoids using scales in which one note (the tonic) acts as a home note to which all other notes are related. This means, in particular, that atonal music avoids using major and minor keys, modes, and so forth. *NAM 8* is atonal.

Augmentation. A proportionate increase in the note-lengths of a melody. The last bar of *NAM 32* is an augmented version of the previous bar. The opposite of augmentation is **diminution**.

Avant-garde. A French expression meaning 'ahead of the front'. It is used to refer to composers and other artists who use techniques which are perceived to be breaking new ground.

Balanced phrasing. *See* periodic phrasing.

Binary form. A two-part musical structure, usually with each section repeated, as in the first piece of *NAM 23*. In longer binary form movements the first section often ends in a related key and the second section modulates back (perhaps by way of other related keys) to the tonic. This can be seen in the two D-major dances of *NAM 21* where the first section of each ends in the dominant (A major) and the second in the tonic.

Blue note. A term used in jazz for a note (usually the third, fifth or seventh of the scale) that is made more expressive by slightly lowering its pitch. On fixed-pitch instruments such as the piano a similar effect can be achieved by playing two notes together (or in close proximity) – for example, by playing a minor 3rd against a major chord (as in *NAM 41*, bar 14, beat 3).

Cadence. The last notes of a phrase, suggesting a point of repose. When harmonised the chosen chords can define the degree of completion more exactly. See **Perfect cadence**, **Imperfect cadence**, **Interrupted cadence**, **Plagal cadence** and **Phrygian cadence**.

Cadential 6–4. A triad in second inversion, so called because its upper notes form intervals of a 6th and a 4th above its bass note. The cadential 6–4 is a progression that starts with the second inversion of the tonic (Ic or I^6_4) to lead into either a perfect cadence (Ic–V–I) or to form an imperfect cadence (Ic–V). It is one of the most characteristic chord progressions of the classical style and can be found in *NAM 22*, bar 57 (I^6_4), 58 (V^7) and 59 (I): a perfect cadence in F major.

Canon. A device (sometimes an entire piece) in which a melody in one part fits with the same melody in another part even though the latter starts a few beats later. The device occurs in the type of song known as a round. There is a canon between the trumpet and oboe parts of *NAM 28*.

Chamber music. Ensemble music intended for only one performer per part, such as *NAM 16*. The term originally referred to music that was suitable to be played in a room (or chamber) of a house.

Chromatic. An adjective describing notes outside the current key or mode that are added for colour (the word chromatic meaning 'coloured') and that do not cause a change of key. Accidentals are not necessarily chromatic. In bars 1–8 of *NAM 15* the music is in D major; the G♯ in bar 4 is chromatic because it does not belong to the scale of D major and is contradicted by G♮ in the next bar. However in bar 9 G♯ has different purpose. It effects a modulation to A major because, unlike the previous example, it is followed up with a cadence in this new key. The music from here until bar 19 is in A major and the G♯s used in this section are not chromatic – they are diatonic notes in the new key of A major. See also **Tonality**.

Circle of 5ths. A series of bass notes each a 5th lower than the previous note. In real life this would be impossible because the series would soon drop below the lowest note available on most instruments. Instead the bass more commonly falls a 5th and then rises a 4th, producing the same sequence of pitches. *NAM 39* starts with such a progression in the bass of bars 1–9.

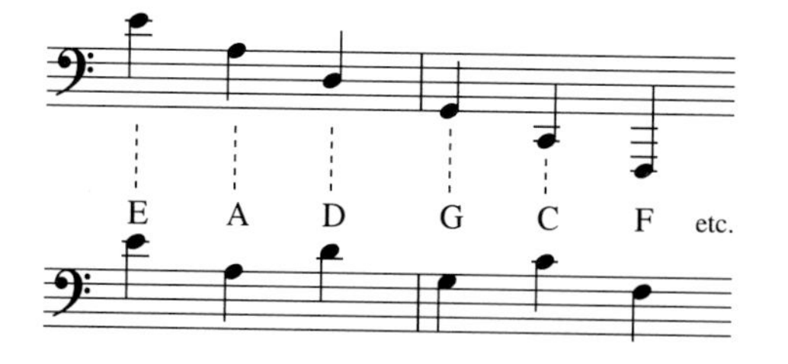

Coda. The final section of a movement. In tonal music the coda will often consist of material to confirm the tonic key. For example the coda of *NAM 2* (bars 122–133) contains four perfect cadences in the tonic key of D major.

Codetta. A little coda. The final section of part of a movement.

Consonant. Harmonious, not discordant.

Continuo. Abbreviation of *basso continuo*. A continuous bass part of the baroque period from which one or more bass instruments played. Chordal instruments (harpsichord, organ, lute, etc) also used this part to improvise harmonies in accordance with the conventions of the time and guided by any **figured bass** that was given in the part. The term is also used to to mean the instrumental group that plays the continuo part. See *NAM 15* or *NAM 36*.

Contrapuntal. A texture that uses **counterpoint**.

Countermelody. A melody of secondary importance heard at the same time as (and therefore in counterpoint with) a more important melody. In *NAM 9* the first violin melody at bar 55 is accompanied by a countermelody in the second violin.

Counterpoint. The simultaneous use of two or more melodies with independent rhythms. There may be some **imitation** between the parts but counterpoint can also be non-imitative. Whole movements may be contrapuntal, such as the fugue in *NAM 25*, or the music may alternate between contrapuntal and other textures, such as *NAM 29*, where a section of fugal counterpoint begins at bar 22. The term is now often used interchangeably with polyphony.

Cross-rhythm. A passage in which the rhythmic patterns of one or more parts runs counter to the normal accentuation or grouping of notes in the prevailing metre. The effect of 'two-against-three' in bar 3 of *NAM 39* is an example.

Diatonic. An adjective describing music which uses only the notes of the prevailing key. The first two bars of *NAM 37* are purely diatonic. Bars 3 and 6 are not diatonic as they contain chromatic notes which colour the harmony although they do not establish a new key.

Diminution. A proportionate reduction in the note-lengths of a melody. In *NAM 42* the music of bar 1 occurs twice in diminution in bar 3. The opposite of diminution is **augmentation**.

Dissonance. Two or more sounds that clash, producing a discord. The concept of which intervals sound discordant has varied over time. Before the 20th century it was normal for the tension produced by a discord to be 'resolved' by means of the dissonant note moving to a concord. In *NAM 36* there is, in bars 47–54, a dissonance between the uppermost part and the bass on the first beat of each bar. In every case this resolves down to a consonance on the second beat. Since about 1900 dissonance has often been used as an effect in its own right.

Double-stopping. The performance of a two-note chord on a string instrument, as occurs in violin 1 of *NAM 16* at bar 41.

False relation. The simultaneous or adjacent occurrence *in different parts* of a note in its normal form and in a chromatically altered form. In *NAM 35* a false relation occurs between the B♮ in bar 38 and the B♭ in bar 39. In *NAM 41* an example of a simultaneous false relation between E♮ and E♯ occurs on the third beat of bar 14.

Figure. A clearly-defined melodic fragment such as the six notes heard in the ripieno violin 1 part in bars 14–15 of *NAM 1*. This is repeated in sequence in the next six bars. When a figure such as this is repeated exactly, varied, or in sequence the result is called figuration, as also occurs in the solo violin part in bars 18–22 of this same piece. See also **Motif**.

Figured bass. Numbers and other symbols below a basso **continuo** part to indicate the harmonies to be improvised by chordal instruments. See *NAM 36*.

Flutter-tonguing. On wind instruments the rolling of an 'r' with the tongue to produce rapid repetitions of the same note. For example, *NAM 43* bar 105 in flute, oboe and trumpet parts.

Fugal. In the style of a **fugue**. As in *NAM 15*.

Fugue. A type of composition based on a melody that initially enters in succession in each of several parts. This is called the subject (or the answer if it is transposed). While each subsequent part introduces the subject, the previous part continues with a new idea called the countersubject that fits in counterpoint with the subject. After each part has introduced the subject these ideas are manipulated in a variety of ways, often including **stretto** (particularly close entries of the subject). *NAM 25* is a fugue.

Galant. A light-textured, elegant style of the early classical period, characterised by ornamented, regularly-phrased melodies, simple diatonic harmonies and clear-cut modulations to closely related keys. *NAM 37* is a late but nonetheless typical example of the style.

Genre. A category or group, such as the piano sonata or the madrigal.

Ground bass. A variation technique in which a repeating bass part supports an evolving melody in an upper part together with a variety of harmonic progressions. For example the second part of *NAM 36* (the 3/2 time section).

Hemiola. A rhythmic device in which two groups of three beats are articulated as three groups of two beats. An example from bars 42–43 of the first movement of *NAM 28* is printed on page 82. The same effect occurs when a bar of 6/8 time is articulated as a bar of 3/4 time. This occurs in bar 27 of *NAM 15*, where the hemiola can be most clearly seen in the second violin part.

Heterophony. A texture in which a melody and a decorated version of the same melody occur simultaneously. For example in bars 9–15 of *NAM 29* the orchestra play a heterophonic version of the choral melody that occurs in these same bars.

Homophonic. A texture in which one part (usually the uppermost) has all the melodic interest to which the other parts provide an accompaniment (as opposed to a polyphonic or contrapuntal texture, in which all the parts are melodically interesting). The last five bars of *NAM 30* are homophonic; they use a purely chordal texture. You could also describe this texture as one of 'block chords'. The opening of *NAM 39* illustrates a different type of homophony, sometimes referred to as 'melody and accompaniment'.

Imitation. If a motif in one part is immediately taken up by another part while the first part continues with other music, the motif is said to be treated in imitation. The imitation is usually not exact – some intervals may be modified, but the basic melodic shape and rhythm of the opening should be audible. Often the imitative entry may start at a different pitch from the original. *NAM 15* begins with imitation in all three parts. If the parts continue in exact imitation for a number of bars, they will form a **canon**.

Imitative point. A motif that is used as the subject for imitation.

Imperfect cadence. Two chords at the end of a phrase, the second of which is the dominant. As in *NAM 37*, bars 3–4.

Interrupted cadence. Two chords at the end of a phrase, the first of which is the dominant and the second being any other chord than the tonic (most often chord VI, as in bars 16–17 of *NAM 4*).

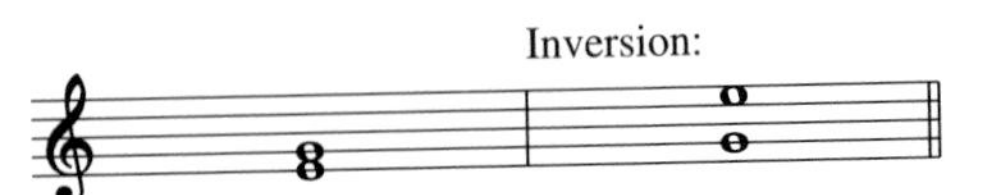

Inversion (1). An interval is inverted when its lower note is transposed up an octave while the other note remains the same (or vice-versa).

Inversion (2). A chord is inverted when a note other than the root of the chord is sounding in the bass. In *NAM 27* an A-major chord in root position is sounded at the start of bar 1. On beat 4 the chord is inverted by having its third (C♯) sounded in the bass.

Inversion (3). A melody is inverted when every interval is kept the same but now moves in the opposite direction (eg a rising 3rd becomes a falling 3rd). The alto part in bars 5–6 of *NAM 32* is an exact inversion of the soprano part above it.

Leitmotif. A musical idea associated with a particular character, setting or situation. It is most commonly used by the composer to suggest a recollection, anticipation or sometimes a development, of the circumstance with which the music was originally associated. See the examples from *NAM 4* on page 34 of this guide.

Melisma. Several notes sung to one syllable, as in bar 2 of *NAM 36*.

Mickey-mousing. The process of adding music to synchronise exactly with the visual action in a film. It is commonly used in comedy films and cartoons (such as for the footsteps of the cat in *Tom and Jerry*), hence the name. See *NAM 42*.

Modes. These are usually taken to mean seven-note scales other than the modern major and minor, although some people also refer to these as the major mode and minor mode respectively. The aeolian mode consists of the notes A–B–C–D–E–F–G–A. Although it begins and ends on the note A (like A minor) it differs from A minor in that is uses G♮ as its seventh note, not G♯. All of the notes in the last four bars of *NAM 32* belong to the aeolian mode, which is transposed down a 4th to start on E (E–F♯–G–A–B–C–D–E).

Monophonic. A texture that consists of a single unaccompanied melody, as in the first six bars of *NAM 43*.

Monothematic. A movement constructed from material that derives from a single theme, such as *NAM 16*.

Motif. A short but memorable melodic fragment which is subject to manipulation through techniques such as sequence, inversion, extension and so forth. For example the motif in bar 4 of *NAM 44* is repeated and extended in bars 8–9 and is transposed in bar 11, where it then forms a repeating bass part in the left hand of the piano part. See also **Figure** and **Leitmotif**.

Ostinato. A repeating melodic or rhythmic pattern heard throughout a substantial passage of music. For example the percussion parts in bars 40–49 of *NAM 43*. In popular music and jazz a melodic ostinato is known as a riff. A **ground bass** is a type of ostinato.

Passing note. A decorative melody note filling the gap between two harmony notes a 3rd apart. In the third bar of *NAM 1* the second quaver in both recorder parts is a passing note between harmony notes belonging to the chord of G major.

Pedal (or 'pedal point'). A sustained or repeated note against which changing harmonies are heard. A pedal on the dominant (*NAM 16*, bars 16–28) creates excitement and the feeling that the tension must be resolved by moving to the tonic. A pedal on the tonic anchors the music to its key note (*NAM 29*, bars 15–21). A pedal on both tonic and dominant (a double pedal) is used at the start of *NAM 3*. If a pedal occurs in an upper part, rather than the bass, it is called an inverted pedal.

Pentatonic. Music based on a scale of five pitches. You can find one such scale by playing the five black notes on a music keyboard. *NAM 43* begins with a minor pentatonic scale based on C.

Perfect cadence. Chords V and I at the end of a phrase, as in the last two chords of *NAM 15*.

Periodic phrasing. Balanced phrases of regular lengths (usually two, four or eight bars). A technique particularly associated with music of the classical period. The introduction to *NAM 37* consists of a four-bar statement ending on the dominant (an antecedent) followed by a four-bar answer ending on the tonic (a consequent).

Phrygian cadence. A type of **imperfect cadence** used in minor keys. It consists of the chords IVb–V, as in bars 8–9 of *NAM 36*.

Plagal cadence. Chords IV and I at the end of a phrase. For example the last two bars of *NAM 14*.

Polyphony. The simultaneous use of two or more melodies. The opening of *NAM 26* is polyphonic. The term is now used interchangeably with **counterpoint**, although it is more common to use polyphony when referring to renaissance music.

Recitative. A vocal solo that follows the rhythms and inflexions of speech, supported by a subservient accompaniment. In operas, oratorios and cantatas recitative is most frequently used for dialogue and narrative. The second movement of *NAM 28* is accompanied by strings and continuo and is known as accompanied recitative. A different type of recitative is seen in the first eight bars of *NAM 36*, where the accompaniment is provided only by **continuo**. This is known as secco ('dry') recitative.

Riff. A short repeating melodic pattern heard throughout a passage of music, as in the percussion parts in bars 40–49 of *NAM 43*. A riff is a type of **ostinato**.

Ritornello form. A form used for large-scale movements in the late-baroque period, including arias, choruses and the fast movements of concertos. An opening instrumental section (called the ritornello) introduces the main musical ideas. This is followed by a contrasting texture, featuring the singer(s) or soloist(s), during which material from the ritornello returns, sometimes in different keys and often only in part. It is the fragmentary nature of these repetitions that gives the form its name – ritornello means 'a little return'. *NAM 1* and the fourth movement of *NAM 28* both use ritornello form.

Rondo. A musical form in which a refrain alternates with different episodes, creating a structure such as ABACA or ABACABA. *NAM 16* is a rondo.

Seconda prattica. The 'second practice' of Italian vocal music of the early 17th century in which music was governed by the text, as in Monterverdi's text-orientated setting of the verses in *NAM 35*. The prima prattica ('first practice') is typified by 16th-century polyphony such as *NAM 26*.

Sequence. The *immediate* repetition at a different pitch of a phrase or motif in a continuous melodic line. A series of such repetitions is frequently used in the spinning-out of baroque melodic lines, as in bars 69–76 of *NAM 1* (where recorders perform an ascending sequence based on the initial three-note figure).

Sonata form. The most common form for the first movement (and often other movements) of sonatas, symphonies, concertos and chamber works in the classical period and later. The essence of sonata form is the use of two contrasting tonal centres (tonic and either dominant or another closely related key such as the relative major) in a first section called the exposition; the use of a wider range of keys to create tension and excitement in a central section called the development; and a recapitulation in which music from the exposition is repeated in the tonic key. *See NAM 22*.

Stepwise movement. Movement to an adjacent note (a tone or a semitone away) in a melody. The semiquavers in bars 23–31 of *NAM 20* move mainly by step.

Stretto. The telescoping of imitative parts so that entries come closer to each other than they originally did. In bars 22–29 of *NAM 29* the subject introduced by the basses is imitated at two-bar intervals by the other voice parts. In the stretto of bars 46–48 entries of this subject are telescoped so that the sopranos come in only one bar after the altos, and tenors enter only one bar after sopranos.

Strophic. A song that uses the same music for every verse (such as *NAM 37*) rather than one which is **through-composed** (such as *NAM 38*).

Substitution chord. A term used in jazz for the replacement of a chord by one with a similar harmonic function (eg as a tonic, dominant or subdominant). For example instead of chord IV a jazz musician might use II^7 or a minor version of chord IV or perhaps a complex chromatic chord that has only a single note in common with chord IV. In bar 24 of *NAM 48* a minor version of chord IV is substituted for the major version previously heard in bar 12.

Suspension. A harmonic device in which a note is first sounded in a consonant context (the preparation) and is then repeated (or held) over a change of chord so that it becomes a dissonance (the suspension itself). Finally, there is a resolution when the suspended note moves by step (usually downwards) to a consonant note. These three stages can be seen in the violin 2 part of *NAM 15*: the note A is prepared in bar 17 (it is part of both chords in that bar), it then sounds against B in violin 1 at the start of bar 18 (this is the actual suspension) and it resolves by falling to G♯ (thus forming part of the prevailing chord of E major) in the second half of that bar.

Swing quavers. Also known as swung quavers. In jazz the division of the beat into a pair of notes in which the first is longer than the second. In music notation this approximates to crotchet–quaver pattern in compound time (see *right*). Swung quavers can be heard in *NAM 41* (see the music example on page 104). If even quavers are required in jazz they are described as straight quavers.

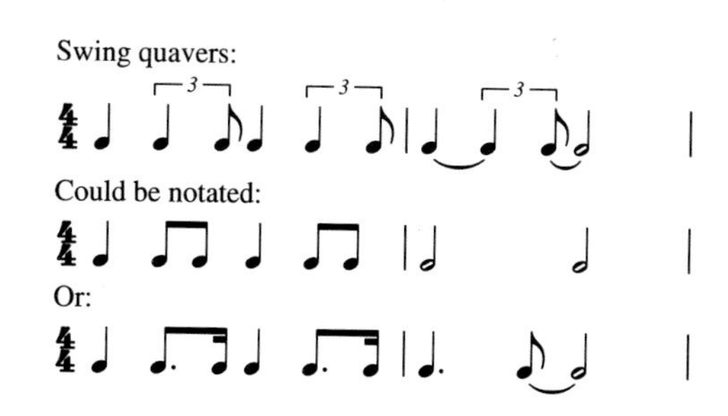

Syllabic word setting. One note per syllable, as in NAM 34.

Syncopation. Off-beat accents or accents on weak beats. In *NAM 60* the middle part is syncopated in bars 1–7 because the first beat of each of these bars is *delayed* by a quaver. The top part is syncopated in bars 3 and 7 because the second crotchet beat is *anticipated* by a quaver. The entire piece is characterised by almost constant syncopation.

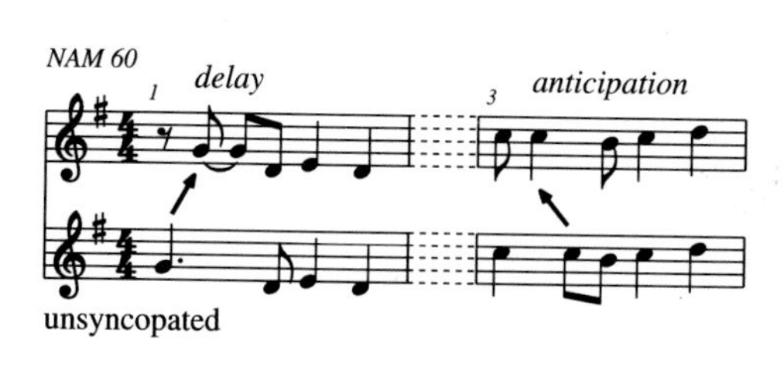

Ternary form. A three-part musical structure in which a middle section is flanked by two identical or very similar passages, as in the scherzo–trio–scherzo format of *NAM 18*.

Tessitura. That part of the pitch range in which the music mainly lies. For example in bars 242–261 of *NAM 18* all the instruments use a low tessitura.

Texture. The total effect produced by the inter-relationship of elements such as rhythm, melody and **timbre**, particularly the effects determined by the number of parts sounding at the same time and the way they relate to each other. Textures can range from a single **monophonic** line (such as the unaccompanied horn melody with which *NAM 43* begins) to a complex **contrapuntal** combination of simultaneous melodies, as seen in *NAM 13*. **Homophonic** textures can range from just a succession of chords (such as the last five bars of *NAM 30*) to a complex melody with broken-chord accompaniment (eg bars 71–81 of *NAM 22*). Density of texture can range from the simple octaves of bars 20–22 in *NAM 24*, through two-part textures (bars 5–6 of *NAM 32*) to the dense chords that conclude *NAM 27*.

Through-composed. A song that uses mainly different music for each verse (such as *NAM 38*) rather than one which is **strophic** (such as *NAM 37*).

Tierce de Picardie. A major 3rd in the final tonic chord of a minor-key passage. For example *NAM 33* is in A minor, but the C# in bar 24 makes the last chord A major.

Timbre (pronounced tam-bruh). Tone colour. The clarinet has a different timbre to the trumpet, but the clarinet also has different timbres in various parts of its range. The timbre of an instrument can also be affected by the way it is played, for example by using a mute or plucking a string instead of using the bow.

Tonality. In most western music the relationships between seven pitches that can be arranged to form a diatonic scale or mode, particularly the relationships between six of these pitches and a pre-eminent pitch (or 'home note') called the tonic. The first two bars of *NAM 29* include all seven notes of the D-major scale (D–E–F#–G–A–B–C#). The composer's use of these pitches ensures the pre-eminence of D and this is supported by the use of the three main chords of the key (I, IV and V). The phrase ends on chord V and when the full ensemble enters in bar 3 (with a complete scale of D major in the bass) it is totally clear that D major is the tonic. This sense of a D major tonality is not disrupted by the colourful D♯ that appears in bar 4. This is a **chromatic** note outside the key, and it is immediately cancelled by D♮. It does not cause the key to change because there is no cadence in a new key. In bar 21 Haydn uses G♯. This *does* cause a brief modulation to A major at the start of bar 22 because it is underpinned by a perfect cadence in the new key of A major (V^7c–I). The progression V^7–I totally defines a key because it consists of a combination of notes that are not found in any other key. The pre-eminence of D-major tonality is firmly established at the end of *NAM 29* with the use of a tonic pedal beneath V^7–I progressions from bar 71 onwards, a two-octave D-major scale in bar 80 and conclusive perfect cadences.

Transcription. An adaptation of a piece of music for different or more elaborate performing resources. Parts of *NAM 20* are a free transcription of *NAM 33*. The term is also used to describe the notation of music that was previously unnotated or that existed in some other type of music notation. *NAM 48* is a transcription of the performance on the original recording.

Tritone. An interval of three tones, such as from B up to F, as occurs between the outer parts on the last beat of bar 16 in *NAM 34*. Other examples occur at the ends of bars 10 and 13 in this piece.

Tutti. 'All' – the full ensemble, or a passage of music intended for the full ensemble. For example bar 78 of *NAM 43*.

Underscore. The complete collection of background or incidental music written to accompany a film or video. *NAM 46* is just part of the underscore for a television programme.

Virtuoso. A performer of great technical skill. The term is also used to describe music which requires a high level of technical skill.

Vocalising. Singing to vowel sounds rather than real words, as at the start of *NAM 47* (choir) or in bars 31–42 of *NAM 48*.

Walking bass. A bass part that maintains the same note-lengths throughout a substantial passage or an entire movement. The bass part of the fourth movement of *NAM 28* uses nothing but quavers apart from the crotchet in bar 79 and at the end.

Word painting. The musical illustration of the meaning or emotion associated with particular words or phrases, such as the use of a falling dissonance (a tritone) on the word 'trouble' in bar 12 of *NAM 36*.

Remember that if you need help with any of the music terminology you encounter the *Rhinegold Dictionary of Music in Sound* by David Bowman provides detailed explanations of a wide range of musical concepts and illustrates them using a large number of specially recorded examples on its set of accompanying compact discs. The *Rhinegold Dictionary of Music in Sound* is published by Rhinegold Publishing Ltd, ISBN: 0-946890-87-0.